Child Sexual Abuse

Impact and Aftershocks

A comprehensive foundation
for understanding and dealing with
child sexual abuse, the people affected,
and the systems involved

by *Susan Freese*
Project IMPACT

Project IMPACT • Government Training Service • St. Paul, Minnesota

*Know you what it is to be a child?...
It is to believe in love,
to believe in loveliness,
to believe in belief.*
—Percy Bysshe Shelley

Copyright (c) 1989 by Government Training Service
480 Cedar Street, Suite 401
St. Paul, MN 55101

All rights reserved. No part of the material protected by this copyright notice may be reproduced or utilized in any form or by any means, electronic or mechanical, including photocopying, recording, or by any information storage and retrieval system, without the written permission of the copyright owner.

This project was supported by 85-SF-CX-0027 grant award by the Bureau of Justice Assistance. The content of this book does not necessarily reflect the view and policies of this grantor agency.

Project Administrator: Barbara Peterson
Program Planner: Diane Campbell
Executive Director, GTS: Helene Johnson
Copyeditor: Sally Stickney
Text Design/Composition: Alternative Graphics

The cover art is an original illustration by Ursina Amsler, age 19, of Marblehead, Massachusetts.

Library of Congress Cataloging-in-Publication Data

Freese, Susan, 1958-
　　Child sexual abuse: Impact and aftershocks.
　　"A comprehensive foundation for understanding and dealing with child sexual abuse, the people affected, and the systems involved."
　　Includes bibliographical references.
　　1. Child molesting—Minnesota.　I. Title.
HQ72.U53F74　1989　　　　　362.7'6　　　　　　89-17117
ISBN 0-9622478-0-4

Printed in the United States of America
10 9 8 7 6 5 4 3 2 1　93 92 91 90 89

Contents

Foreword   vii

Preface   ix

Part I The Problem   1

Chapter 1 Introduction   3

Defining Child Sexual Abuse   3
    Definition by Researchers   4
    Definition by Law   6
    A Working Definition   8
Public Knowledge about Child Sexual Abuse   9
    Myths and Stereotypes   9
    Finkelhor's Boston Survey   10
Research on Child Sexual Abuse   15
    Validity Problems   15
    Reporting Problems   22
Summary   25

Part II The People   27

Chapter 2 Adult Sexual Offenders   29

Characteristics of Adult Offenders   29
    Abel's Findings   30
    Additional Psychological Characteristics   33
Theories of Adult Offenders   36
    Dichotomous Classifications   36
    Alternative Theories   38
    Special Offender Groups   40

A Model of Child Sexual Abuse   50
   The Four-Factor Framework   51
   The Four Preconditions for Child Sexual Abuse   52
   Operation of the Model   56
   Application of the Model   57
Summary   57

Chapter 3 Adolescent Sexual Offenders   61

Characteristics of Adolescent Offenders   61
   Early Research   62
   Demographics   63
   Personal and Family Variables   68
Adolescent Offender Typologies   72
   The PHASE Typology   72
   The Female Adolescent Offender Typology   77
Summary   79

Chapter 4 Victims of Child Sexual Abuse   81

Description of Victims: Risk Factors for Child Sexual Abuse   82
   The Victim   82
   The Nature of the Abuse   88
   Boy Victims   89
Risk Factors for Trauma   94
The Effects of Child Sexual Abuse   102
   Initial Effects   103
   Long-Term Effects   108
A Model of Child Sexual Abuse   113
   The Four Traumagenic Dynamics   113
   Review of the Model   116
   Application of the Model   117
Summary   120

Chapter 5 Incest and Family Dynamics   123

The Study of Incest   124
   Definitions   124
   Prevalence   126
   Incestuous Partnerships   126

Theoretical Orientations   130
　　The Circumplex Model of Families   132
The Incestuous Family   136
　　Family Characteristics   136
　　Individuals within the Family   138
Five Phases of Sexual Abuse   144
Treatment Recommendations   145
　　Assessment   146
　　Treatment Issues   147
　　Multicultural Concerns   150
　　Prognosis for Success   151
Summary   152

Part III   The System   155

Chapter 6   Reporting Child Sexual Abuse   157

Mandated Reporting   158
　　General Provisions of the Minnesota Reporting Law   158
Proactive Reporting   163
　　Who Reports?   164
　　Identification   164
　　Documentation   168
　　Credibility   172
　　Packaging Your Report   175
Disclosure   177
　　Suppression   178
Summary   179

Chapter 7   Introduction to Systems Theory   183

Defining the System   183
　　Resources   184
　　Structure   184
System Dynamics   185
　　Closed versus Open Systems   185
　　Organizational Incest and Closure   188
Identifying Problems   189
What Works Best?   190
Summary   190

Chapter 8 The System at Large 193

Overview 193
Working through the System 195
    Reporting 195
    Intervention 195
    Legal Proceedings 202
    Corrections 207
    Health Care Professionals 214
    Educators 214
    Support Services 214
Summary 217

Chapter 9 Making the System Work 221

A Survey of Professionals 222
    Experience with Child Sexual Abuse 223
    Survey Topics 223
Characterizing the System 227
Policy Issues 228
    Professional Limits 228
    Legal Ambiguity 232
Resolving the Problems 235
Conclusion 238
Summary 239

Epilogue Divergent Issues 241

The Rights of the State: Over- and Underintervention 241
The Veracity of Children 242
Treatment versus Punishment 243
Ritualistic Abuse 244
The Importance of Conflict 245

Readings and References 247

Index 253

Foreword

We are all affected by the actions and abilities of other professionals with whom we must interact. Therefore, we cannot underestimate the value of interdisciplinary cooperation and communication to achievement by both individuals and the groups to which they belong.

In November 1984, the Criminal Justice Policy Task Force identified interdisciplinary training as a way for society to increase the protection of children who are victims of sexual abuse. The Minnesota Interagency Team on Child Abuse and Neglect was given the responsibility to implement this recommendation. In 1985, the Team secured funding toward this purpose through the Federal Justice Assistance Act, and Project IMPACT was initiated.

In Minnesota, as well as in other states, the problem of child sexual abuse has long been considered a critical issue. As the number of reports of abuse increased, many professionals became frustrated by the difficulty of working within the complex system that addresses child sexual abuse. In short, roles and responsibilities were unclear. What *was* clear, however, was the need for improvement in how different professionals and agencies within the system at large worked together cooperatively to respond to the problem of child sexual abuse.

Child Abuse: Impact and Aftershocks was written to provide a broad base of information—in one source—for the many professionals working with child sexual abuse cases. To be sure, however, this is not a training manual. Rather, it is an overview of the current state of knowledge about child sexual abuse from various perspectives. Although portions of this book will be less relevant to some professionals than others, we urge readers to become familiar with all the material presented. Informed professionals who understand the nature of their role and how it fits into the larger system will be better able to meet the ultimate goal: increased protection of children.

The experience of building a working team comprised of professionals with varying opinions and concerns provided a valuable lesson for everyone involved in Project IMPACT. Assessing the needs of many diverse groups and building appropriate skills-training and systems change models proved to be both challenging and rewarding. This experience has been shared by professionals everywhere who continue to work together toward the best interests of children. Moreover, this process could be successfully applied to areas other than child abuse, namely, to those in which an interdisciplinary approach is essential.

Minnesota Interagency Team on Child Abuse and Neglect

Attorney General's Office
  Norman Coleman
* William Klumpp

County Attorneys Association
  Jean Gerval

Department of Corrections
  Dottie Bellinger
  Jay Lindgren
* Barbara Raye
  Barbara Sanderson
  Peggy Specktor

Department of Education
* Marykay Haas
  Ruth Ellen Luehr
  Robert Wandberg
* Barbara Yates

Department of Health
* Jean Cronje
* LaVohn Josten
  Anne Kane
  Nancy Okinow

Department of Human Services
  Jean Swanson Broberg
  Becky Montgomery
* Erin Sullivan Sutton
* Janet Wiig

Department of Public Safety
* Maureen Cannon
  Paul Gerber
  Harry Halden
  David Knefelkamp
* Rina McManus
* Joy Rikala
* Fern Sepler

State Planning Agency
* Ann Jaede

State Public Defender's Office
  Susan Maki
* Scott Swanson

State Supreme Court
  Michael Moriarity

University of Minnesota
* Carolyn Levitt, M. D.

* Current members (at time of publication)

Preface

Child sexual abuse—Many of us think it's something that happens to other people. It happens to specific types of children from specific types of families. And these families fall into certain socioeconomic groups and maybe even live in certain parts of the country.

The fact is, child sexual abuse happens to all kinds of children from all kinds of families. They're not necessarily rich or poor; black, Hispanic, Native American, or white; and they live all over the country—in cities, suburbs, small towns, and rural areas.

The latest statistics from the National Center on Child Abuse and Neglect show that nearly 140,000 children are abused each year. When cases of endangerment are added to cases of demonstrable harm, the number rises to nearly 156,000. Put differently, 25 of 10,000 children will be sexually abused or in danger of being sexually abused during a single year (NCCAN, 1988).

The media have focused enormous attention on the subject of child abuse. To their credit, they have brought a once taboo topic into the open, illustrating the prevalence and severity of a problem that many were unaware existed. Unfortunately, in some cases, coverage has been exploitive and inflammatory and may have resulted in spreading misinformation and even hysteria.

Even so, 93% of the general public report that they have been exposed to information about child sexual abuse during the last year, through TV, newspapers, magazines, or school- or civic-sponsored programs. And over half report that they have had some personal experience with an incident of child sexual abuse: their own child or that of family or friends was abused (Finkelhor, 1984).

Even though people know and hear about child sexual abuse, there remains some misunderstanding about who is likely to be abused under what circumstances and by whom. It seems that although people know abuse happens, they are reluctant to admit that it strikes so close to home. This is literally the problem in cases of intrafamilial abuse, where denial is strong enough to prevent abuse from being reported and maybe even discovered.

This misunderstanding and denial is rooted in the difference between reason and emotion: Although people may have an objective, intellectual understanding of child sexual abuse, the issue is so emotionally charged that it produces strong and subjective reactions of all kinds. Even the most informed, reasonable, and open-minded individuals would be likely to respond with dramatic emotion if a child close to them were sexually abused.

Those who work with children are well aware of the emotions behind the issue of child sexual abuse. Depending on their level of experience with the problem, they are likely to have their own strong feelings and opinions. As professionals, however, they must be able to sort out these personal values and address the problem from a controlled and educated perspective. Those who are mandated reporters, in particular, must understand what constitutes sexual abuse, how to recognize it, and what to do about it once it's discovered. This is not only an ethical, professional responsibility but a legal one, as well—certainly one that must be taken seriously.

Project IMPACT

Confirming that responsibility was perhaps the overall purpose behind Project IMPACT. Project IMPACT was established in 1986 by the Minnesota Interagency Team on Child Abuse and Neglect and the State Planning Agency, who were awarded a grant from the Bureau of Justice Assistance. Those monies, matched with equal monies from state and local funds, were designated for use in a project to train workers in the area of child sexual abuse. As such, the State Planning Agency contracted with Government Training Service to implement Project IMPACT.

The credo of Project IMPACT was to provide "training and cooperative action on the criminal justice system's response to child sexual abuse." The specific goals of the Project, as outlined by the Interagency Team, were threefold:

1. to build communication and cooperation among professionals;
2. to improve the skills of individuals involved in the detection, intervention, adjudication, and treatment of child sexual abuse cases; and
3. to develop statewide consistency through recommended guidelines that enhance the ability of the criminal justice system to respond effectively to sexual abuse of children.

Project IMPACT sought to achieve these goals during its $3\frac{1}{2}$-year course by offering forums and workshops and producing newsletters, proceedings, and other publications dealing with a number of topics related to child sexual abuse. On the whole, the Project was highly successful; in fact, it was extended six months in order to provide additional services. Over 3,500 people from all over the state participated in Project-sponsored activities. Project IMPACT hopes to leave a legacy of skilled professionals, increased acceptance of working in multidiscipline teams, acknowledgment of the unique roles each professional brings to the issue, and an established curriculum that can be enhanced as knowledge and experience on child sexual abuse evolve.

About this Book

Child Sexual Abuse: Impact and Aftershocks is intended to be a significant part of that legacy. The information presented will provide those individuals who work with children with a foundation of knowledge on which to base an informed, responsible perspective. And hopefully, if a common foundation can be established among workers in various disciplines, cooperative efforts at intervention in child sexual abuse can be made more efficient and effective.

The book is divided into three parts: The Problem, The People, and The System. In Part I, child sexual abuse is defined in several contexts, including legal definition according to Minnesota statutes. Common research methods and their implications for theory and analysis are discussed, as well.

Part II looks at the people involved in child sexual abuse. Chapters 2 and 3 profile adult and adolescent offenders, respectively, identifying typical characteristics and proposing several models of offenders. Chapter 4 follows a similar pattern but considers victims, again, identifying common characteristics and looking at a model of the abuse scenario. Chapter 5 addresses family dynamics and incest, analyzing patterns of communication and authority and how they contribute to family dysfunction and incest.

Part III considers the system that responds to child sexual abuse. Chapter 6 outlines the responsibilities of mandated reporters, discussing legal requirements and also recommending practices for effective reporting. Chapter 7 serves as a preview to 8 and 9, providing an overview of systems or organizational theory. Chapter 8 examines the system at large, considering the roles played by various agencies such as child protective services, law enforcement, the courts, corrections, and support services. Chapter 9, "Making the System Work," summarizes some of the controversy about how well the system functions, presenting several viewpoints and offering the multidisciplinary approach as a model. The Epilogue offers remarks on issues facing workers in the system today and in the near future.

Acknowledgments

Many individuals, most of them members of the Minnesota Interagency Team on Child Abuse and Neglect, have assisted in writing this manual. Special thanks are extended to the following people who were kind enough to offer advice, comments, or information:

- Dottie Bellinger, Assistant Director, Minnesota Program for Victims of Sexual Assault, Minnesota Department of Corrections, St. Paul;
- Janis Bremer, Director, Juvenile Sexual Offender Program, Hennepin County Home School, Minnetonka;
- Jean Swanson Broberg, Acting Supervisor, Child Protective Services Section, Minnesota Department of Human Services, St. Paul;
- S. Margretta Dwyer, Licensed Psychologist, Coordinator, Sex Offender Treatment Program, Program in Human Sexuality, Department of Family Practice and Community Health, Medical School, University of Minnesota, Minneapolis;
- Paul Gerber, Coordinator, Male Victims Program, PHASE, Maplewood;
- Robin Goldman, Corrections Behavior Therapy Specialist, Minnesota Correctional Facility, Oak Park Heights;
- Ann Jaede, Director, Criminal Justice Program, Minnesota State Planning Agency, St. Paul;
- William Klumpp, Assistant Attorney General, Attorney General's Office, St. Paul;
- Faye Honey Knopp, Director, Safer Society Programs and Press, Orwell, Vermont;
- Jay Lindgren, Deputy Executive Director, Texas Youth Commission, Austin, Texas;
- Jane McNaught, Licensed Child Psychologist, Private Practice, Minneapolis;
- Mindy Mitnick, Licensed Psychologist, Uptown Mental Health Center, Minneapolis;
- Michael O'Brien, Director, PHASE, Maplewood;
- Robert Prentky, Director of Research, Massachusetts Treatment Center; Assistant Professor, Department of Psychiatry, Boston University School of Medicine; Research Associate, Department of Psychology, Brandeis University; partner, New England Forensic Associates;
- Gail Ryan, Facilitator, National Adolescent Perpetrator Network, C. H. Kempe National Center, University of Colorado Health Sciences Center, Denver, Colorado;
- Fern Sepler, Executive Director, Minnesota Crime Victim and Witness Advisory Council; and
- Gary Stern, Senior Consultant and Project Director, Non-Profit Communications Center, Management Support Services, Amherst H. Wilder Foundation, St. Paul.

Special acknowledgment is made to Deborah Fisher for her early work on this publication.

Part One

The Problem

Chapter One

Introduction

The readers using this handbook are a diverse group, composed of individuals from many different fields, with many different interests and opinions. The purpose of this chapter is to provide some common ground, ensuring that readers begin with the same essential information. To establish that foundation, we will first examine various definitions of child sexual abuse that have been suggested by researchers, outlining several factors that must be included to explain the term specifically and completely. We will also consider what national and state laws mandate in terms of prevention, treatment, and criminality.

Next, we will look at what the general public knows about child sexual abuse. Researchers often assume that people hold a number of myths and stereotypes about sexual offenders and how they have access to children. While it is true that certain misconceptions are common, lack of knowledge about child abuse may not be the reason behind them.

Finally, we will review some of the problems with reporting and validity that affect the nature and quality of the data available about offenders and their victims. It's important to acknowledge the limitations of data before evaluating any theory they are used to support.

Defining Child Sexual Abuse

One of the most pervasive problems affecting the prevention and treatment of child sexual abuse is the lack of a specific, complete, and universal definition of the phenomenon. Researchers do not agree about what constitutes sexual abuse, which affects not only how the topic is studied but how and what information is shared. Perhaps even more serious is the legal ambiguity in defining child sexual abuse; confusion about statutes and inconsistency in creating and defining them are responsible for problems in reporting, intervention, and prosecution.

Definition by Researchers

Although no two researchers define child sexual abuse in exactly the same way, there is some consensus about the factors that must be addressed to produce an adequate definition. Namely, three factors must be considered: (1) the age of the victim; (2) the type of behavior enacted; and (3) the specific criteria that indicate abuse (Peters, Wyatt, & Finkelhor, 1986).

The age of the victim is obviously basic to defining child sexual abuse, but the issue is not as clearcut as you might think. There is some disagreement about the upper age limit that should be set to define childhood. Most researchers set that limit at 17, since 18 is the legal onset of adulthood. Others set 15 or 16 as the age, arguing that an older adolescent has the ability and authority to consent or not consent to sex.

Defining the type of behavior that should be considered abusive is similarly complicated. In general, sexual activity can be categorized as either contact or noncontact. *Contact* activity includes fondling, intercourse, and oral or anal sex. *Noncontact* activity includes exhibitionism and various types of propositioning, including making obscene or harassing phone calls.

Some researchers feel that noncontact sex should be excluded when defining abuse, arguing that this type of activity is certainly a nuisance or an annoyance but not seriously harmful. Others argue that noncontact sex must be included, for it can be damaging to the victim and is therefore abusive. What's more, they say, noncontact activities are against the law, which should warrant their inclusion.

Whether or not noncontact activity is included in a definition of child sexual abuse has a significant impact on prevalence statistics. When noncontact activity is included, prevalence rates for sexual abuse go up considerably, as much as 10% to 15% (Peters, Wyatt, & Finkelhor, 1986, based on data from Russell, 1983).[1]

The third factor—what criteria specify abuse—is clearly the most complicated, for it is essentially based on opinion. For instance, most people agree that the use of force or coercion qualifies activity as being abusive. But what about factors such as the motivation for the sex? Is filming children to make pornographic movies any more or less abusive than fondling them or propositioning them for sexual fulfillment? More difficult yet, what about the respective ages of the individuals involved? Can a consensual sexual relationship between a 17-year-old female and 19-year-old male be described as abusive, regardless of whether or not it is illegal (i.e., statutory rape)? Can peers sexually abuse peers (Peters, Wyatt, & Finkelhor, 1986)?

Psychosocial Perspectives

These questions about the nature of abuse all relate to issues of power and authority. In this regard, child sexual abuse is similar to rape. Both have been described as acts of power, not sex, by those who look at the psychosocial dynamics involved. This opinion is especially compelling in the case of child sexual abuse because the victim is a child. Suzanne Sgroi and associates assert that the misuse of power is basic to all child sexual abuse.

> *Child sexual abuse is a sexual act imposed on a child who lacks emotional, maturational, and cognitive development. The ability to lure a child into a sexual relationship is based upon the all-powerful and dominant position of the adult or older adolescent perpetrator, which is in sharp contrast to the child's age, dependency, and subordinate position. Authority and power enable the perpetrator, implicitly and directly, to coerce the child into sexual compliance. (Sgroi, Blick, & Porter, 1982, p. 9)*

David Finkelhor has addressed the issues of power and authority from another perspective, that of consent. He points out that, in order to give consent, you must know enough about what you're contemplating to make a rational decision. In addition, you must be free to make the decision on your own. Clearly, given these terms, children are not capable of consenting to sex with adults. As Finkelhor says,

> *Concern about sexual abuse of children is not part of a Victorian resurgence. It is compatible with the most progressive attitude toward sexuality being voiced, a position which urges that consent be the only standard by which the legitimacy of*

sexual acts is evaluated. Ethical clarity in this issue can help society move toward some more coherent outlook on sexual matters and by doing so, combat at least one source of the problem of abuse. (1984, p. 22)

Clinical Perspectives

From a clinical viewpoint, child sexual abuse is a psychosexual problem. As such, those individuals who sexually abuse children are diagnosed as having some type of psychosexual disorder. In simple terms, they have abnormal, or deviant, sexual interests and practices.

The *Diagnostic and Statistical Manual of Mental Disorders* (third edition-revised, 1987) (*DSM-III-R*) labels abnormal sexual behavior as *paraphilia,* which literally means "deviation (*para*) in what the individual finds attractive (*philia*)." Paraphilia is characterized by "recurrent intense sexual urges and sexually arousing fantasies" that involve (1) the use of a nonhuman object for sexual arousal; (2) sexual activity with humans involving real or simulated suffering or humiliation; and (3) sexual activity with children or other nonconsenting partners (*DSM-III-R*, 1987, p. 279).

Note that behavior of these types can be termed paraphilia only when it constitutes the individual's exclusive or preferred sexual activity. The behavior must be consistent, at least over a given time period, but not necessarily permanent. (See Chapters 2 and 3 on offenders.)

The specific use of children to achieve sexual gratification is *pedophilia (pedo* meaning "child"). Pedophilia is "the act or fantasy of having sexual activity with prepubertal children" (again, as one's exclusive or preferred sexual activity). One who commits such activity is a *pedophiliac.*

Definition by Law

Federal Law

The federal Child Abuse Prevention and Treatment Act was enacted in 1974 and amended and reauthorized in 1984 (P.L. 98-457). The purpose of this statute is to coordinate the distribution of federal funds to state governments for the prevention and treatment of child abuse. It is not a federal criminal statute outlawing child abuse; criminal enforcement is the jurisdiction of the state.

Federal law defines child abuse, both physical and sexual, within the context of authority over a child, citing the injury, maltreatment, or exploitation of a child "by a person who is responsible for the child's welfare." Sexual abuse, specifically, includes "the obscene or pornographic photographing, filming or depiction of children for commercial purposes, or the rape, molestation, incest, prostitution or other such forms of sexual exploitation of children under circumstances which indicate the child's health or welfare is harmed or threatened" (P.L. 98-457).

State Statutes

As mentioned above, each individual state has established its own criminal statutes for child sexual abuse. Because states must conform to national policy in order to receive federal funding for child sexual abuse programs, there is some basic consistency in what constitutes child sexual abuse from state to state. Nonetheless, specific legal definitions of abuse and types of offenses vary considerably from one state to another. It is imperative that mandated reporters know how child sexual abuse is defined by their state codes.

Minnesota statutes, sections 609.342 through 609.3451, specify five degrees of criminal sexual conduct involving children; in essence, abuse is defined by penetration and contact.[2]

First- and third-degree criminal sexual conduct involve penetration or intrusion, however slight, into the genital or anal openings. The presence of semen is not necessary for validation, nor does sexual intent have to be proven. Consent of the child involved is irrelevant; it does not establish a defense.

Second-, fourth-, and fifth-degree criminal sexual conduct involve contact, or touching the intimate parts of the body (genitals, breasts, buttocks, groin, or inner thighs), clothed or not. The issue is not really who touched whom; such intimate contact is illegal whether the offender touched the child or had the child touch him or her or someone else. Instead, the issue is specific sexual or aggressive intent. Successful prosecution of the offender depends on proving that he or she committed the act for a sexual or aggressive purpose. Once again, the child's consent is not a defense.

Several factors affect how these laws are applied.

1. *Child's age*—Sixteen is the usual age of consent in Minnesota, but when the situation involves an adult in a significant relationship with a child, the age of consent is raised to 18. According to

Minnesota law, penetration or contact is criminal sexual conduct if the child is less than 13 and the offender is more than 36 months (3 years) older than the child. Penetration or contact is criminal if the child is between 13 and 16 and the offender is more than 24 to 48 months (2 to 4 years) older and/or in a position of authority that he or she used to initiate the sex.

2. *Use of coercion or force*—The criterion applied is whether the victim had reason to fear great bodily harm or imminent death. Use of a weapon, for instance, increases the severity of the offense.

3. *Relationship between victim and offender*—The offense is considered more severe if it involved multiple acts and/or if the offender abused a child with whom he or she had a significant relationship, as established by blood, marriage, or adoption (i.e., a relationship between a child and parent, stepparent, or guardian; sibling or stepsibling; first cousin, aunt, uncle; grandparent, great aunt, great uncle, etc.). Similarly, the law is applied more harshly to offenders who have abused children with whom they live on a regular or intermittent basis (i.e., live-in acquaintances who have no legal relationship to the child). In cases in which there is a significant relationship, the victim/offender age difference and the offender's position of authority need not be proven.

We will return to legal issues in Chapter 6 on reporting and Chapters 7, 8, and 9 on the system.

A Working Definition

Given all this information, we will adopt the definition proposed by the National Center on Child Abuse and Neglect (NCCAN), which defines *child sexual abuse* as "contacts or interactions between a child and an adult when the child is being used for the sexual stimulation of that adult or other person." According to the NCCAN, an adult is 18 years or older. However, someone less than 18 may commit sexual abuse "when that person is either significantly older than the victim or . . . in a position of power or control over the child."

We will use the term *child sexual abuse* almost exclusively. Be aware, however, that others use the terms *child molestation, child sexual assault,* and *pedophilia*. In addition, we will use the term *offender* consistently, although others prefer *perpetrator, molester,* and *pedophiliac*. Nearly everyone agrees on the term *victim,* although some legal descriptions use the term *complainant*. We will not argue whether these terms are truly synonymous but will use them interchangeably.

Finally, keep in mind that, although we will examine child sexual abuse from a number of perspectives throughout this book, mandated reporters must follow the policies established by the state. Again, we stress that mandated reporters must be familiar with state codes regarding child sexual abuse.

Public Knowledge about Child Sexual Abuse

Myths and Stereotypes

Stereotypes portray the child molester as a stranger lurking about schoolyards and parks and drawing children into the bushes with candy or money. The stereotypic molester is an old man, and he is either retarded, deranged, alcoholic, or otherwise out of control. Or worse yet, he is a homosexual who is recruiting young boys to fulfill his needs. His deviant sexual preference for children has grown out of his own seduction as a child, perhaps by his mother or even by other seductive children.

Myths such as these have proliferated throughout generations and contributed to the problem of sexual abuse; they have obscured the facts and made it difficult to discern what is known from what is unknown. While increased reporting and media attention have brought the issue of sexual abuse out into the open, the information that is provided is not always communicated accurately. In fact, some myths are actually perpetuated by the media and public officials, causing even more misunderstanding and fear. For instance, a 1971 article in *PTA Magazine* about preventing sexual abuse warned to look out for the mysterious stranger who loiters around the schoolyard, thus reinforcing several stereotypes about who offends and where offenses are committed (Finkelhor, 1984). This is not to say that children should not be warned about dealing with strangers. Rather, their instruction in self-protection should be complete, including the real possibility of abuse by family and acquaintances.

We cannot be sure about how many people hold onto these myths or about the degree of misinformation that has been spread.

Finkelhor took issue with this presumption of ignorance, pointing out that no survey had ever been done to find out what the general public knows and believes about child sexual abuse. Finkelhor asserted that to begin a study with a review of the so-called mythology has become a handy pedagogical device that researchers have employed for years—a sort of "straw man" to knock down, something easy to disprove (1984).

In 1981, Finkelhor conducted a study to find out what people really know about the facts and issues surrounding child sexual abuse. We will examine the results of this study in some detail.

Finkelhor's Boston Survey

Funded by a grant from the National Center for the Prevention and Control of Rape, Finkelhor surveyed the general public, interviewing Boston-area parents (1984). Parents were selected because of the vital role they play in the lives of their children. Their knowledge and attitudes about sexual abuse determine how they address the issue with their children, both in terms of education and handling an incident of abuse.

The Boston sample included 4,344 households. After screening to locate families with children aged 6 to 14, 700 households were selected. The 521 parents who responded (a 74% response rate) each participated in a one-hour interview. Generally, the sample can be characterized as follows:

- The 521 parents included 187 men and 334 women, reflecting a large number of single-parent, female-headed households (20% of the total).
- The 521 parents had a total of 1,428 children between the ages of 6 and 14.
- The median age of the parents was 38. Only 8% were under 30, and 7% were over 50.
- Eighty-nine percent of the sample were white, 6% were black, and 3% were Hispanic. (This is representative of the area, since Boston does not have a large minority population.)
- Fifty-six percent of the sample were Catholic, 26% were Protestant, 9% were Jewish, and 7% were of another or no professed religion.

- Sixteen percent of the households earned less than $10,000 per year, 59% earned between $10,000 and $35,000, and 25% earned over $35,000.
- The majority of the group, 72%, were employed. Only 3% considered themselves to be unemployed; the remainder (25%) were retired or worked as homemakers.
- Fifteen percent of the sample had completed graduate school, 33% had at least some college education, 33% had completed only high school, and 12% had not even completed high school (Finkelhor, 1984, pp. 70-71).

Finkelhor's survey asked parents a series of questions about their own experiences and those of their children, about their awareness of sexual abuse, and about their general level of knowledge about the topic. In response to questions about what they knew about child sexual abuse, parents provided the following information.

Availability of Information

Nearly all the parents (93%) had been exposed to a discussion of child sexual abuse during the previous year. Ninety percent had seen something about it on TV, and 85% had read about it in the newspaper. Over half had some personal experience with child abuse (i.e., their own children or children of friends or relatives had been abused).

Seriousness of the Problem

Parents consistently rated sexual abuse as the most harmful event when asked to rank a list of potentially traumatic events, including the death of a friend or the divorce of the parents.

Prevalence of the Problem

Parents did not believe that child sexual abuse was a rare occurrence. In fact, their estimates were fairly accurate: Over half estimated that 1 in 10 girls had been abused, and 40% estimated that 1 in 10 boys had been abused.

About the Offender

Here, parents were not very accurate; in fact, they contradicted their own experiences, which they had reported earlier in the survey. Half said they thought that the most likely abusers were strangers; only 28% cited acquaintances, and 22% cited relatives. In the "relatives" category, both parents and stepparents were mentioned as likely offenders. Parents with low income levels and little education were more likely to believe the stranger myth, perhaps because of less access to information and resources.

Parents were more accurate in describing the offender's age and sex. Most felt the typical offender was 30 to 40 years old. Eighty percent of the parents felt men were more likely offenders. Twenty percent felt women were more likely to abuse, an estimate that is higher than the actual reported incidence.

While parents gave a number of reasons as to why they thought people sexually abused children, 62% agreed that sexual abuse is a mental health problem. Only 22% attributed the problem to alcoholism, and 2% felt senility was a factor. Only 5% of the parents blamed the abuse on something the child had done.

About the Victim

Parents did have an accurate perception of the typical child victim of sexual abuse. Fifty percent estimated that the child was under 11 years old; 25% estimated that the child was less than 8. Thus, parents were aware that a child does not have to be sexually mature to be a target. Parents were less aware of the significant risk of abuse for children under 5 years.

About the Offenses Committed

Sixty-three percent of the parents cited an act other than intercourse, although most did mention intercourse in relation to sexual abuse. Forty-one percent of the parents estimated that force was used in committing the offense.

About Children Reporting

Most parents guessed that children would not report being sexually abused. Specifically, parents estimated that 33% of the boys and 39% of the girls would report.

About Parents Reporting

Given a hypothetical situation regarding their exclusive knowledge of an abusive incestuous relationship outside their own family, 93% said they would report the incident. (This is unrealistically high, given actual reporting statistics. See the discussion of reporting problems later in this chapter.) The nonreporters said that it was none of their business, that they didn't know who to report to, that they'd try to handle it themselves, and that they feared retaliation. The nonreporters did not mention uncertainty about the situation as a reason, which is often cited in real cases.

Most parents' first thought about where to report was to the police. But when they were given the information that the state had a child abuse hotline and a child protective agency, most people cited those agencies as the most appropriate for reporting.

About Offender Treatment

When forced to make a choice in the survey, most parents chose providing psychological help for rather than prosecuting the offender (88% versus 12%, respectively). Fifty-two percent felt jailing the offender was inappropriate; 32% recommended probation. Parents with higher income and education levels tended to be more lenient.

About Victim Treatment

Parents were given the same hypothetical incest situation and then queried about public policy regarding the use of protective custody for abused children: 15% favored removing the child from the home, and 51% favored removing the offender (i.e., father) from the home. The remaining 35% felt that keeping the family together was the most important factor.

Conclusion

Based on these findings, Finkelhor concluded that the general public is "relatively knowledgeable" about the sexual abuse of children. Most people realize that the myths about sexual offenders are untrue, which demonstrates the increase in public awareness and knowledge over recent years. However, there are three topics about which some common misunderstandings still exist:

1. *The stranger myth*—The truth is that strangers make up a small proportion of the total number of sexual offenders; parents and other relatives are much more common offenders. Finkelhor concludes that this problem is "not entirely one of misinformation. . . . This truth is a very difficult one to accept" (1984, p. 99). It seems as if the image of a friend or relative sexually abusing one's child is just too disconcerting.

2. *Where to report*—The police are just one of many agencies to which child sexual abuse may be reported. A number of special agencies deal with children, the family, and even child sexual abuse, specifically. (We will address reporting in Chapter 6.)

3. *Offenders being mentally ill*—Whether or not you believe offenders are mentally ill depends upon your definition of mental illness. Few offenders are schizophrenic or psychotic; in fact, many are described psychologically as being normal. In this sense, then, child sexual offenders are not mentally ill. However, in most people's minds, mental illness also includes social deviance and other behavioral problems that can't otherwise be explained. Child sexual abuse is certainly one such problem.

In the Finkelhor sample, most people preferred treating rather than punishing offenders, which seemed to convey their feeling that these individuals were mentally ill. On the other hand, this preference for treatment may be an attempt to resolve conflicting feelings about reporting family members, who are common offenders. Given two hypothetical situations about a particular offense committed by (1) a stranger and (2) a father, most people would punish the stranger but not the father. Thus, it seems that few people want to criminalize acts that take place between family members. The importance of the family is often placed above that of the individual members. (Also see Chapter 5 on family dynamics.)

Finkelhor concludes that the problem is not one of knowledge but of accepting reality. Child sexual abuse is an emotional issue. Some people won't talk about it; others are afraid even to think about it. Until these people are willing to deal with the realities of sexual abuse, the myths will be sustained. To quote Finkelhor, "If any vestige of [the myth] remains, it is because the truth is more unpalatable than the myth" (1979, p. 73).

Research on Child Sexual Abuse

Researchers have examined child sexual abuse from many angles and offered just as many theories about why it happens. However, few of these studies can be characterized as "comprehensive reviews of the problem that have looked at these theories in the light of empirical research" (Araji & Finkelhor, 1986, p. 89).

Finkelhor cautions us to look at the *methodology*—how the research is done—before accepting or rejecting any of the conclusions the research offers. That is our final goal in this chapter: to identify the problems with validity and reporting that affect the nature and quality of the data produced. Our purpose is not to discredit existing research or to suggest that accurate data collection and analysis are impossible feats. Rather, our purpose is to point out the limitations of these data and the need for careful evaluation and interpretation.

Validity Problems

The study of child sexual abuse began in the late 1950s and early 1960s, but it was not until the 1970s that the topic seized the attention of professionals in the health and child-care fields. With the passage of state legislation and improved public awareness came large increases in the number of cases of abuse reported. Since then, researchers have been somewhat obsessed with documenting these increases and producing statistics about how widespread child sexual abuse is. Although statistics are often enticing, we must be careful in interpreting these figures without understanding how they have been produced and what they really mean.

For instance, some studies examine the *incidence* of abuse— how many new cases are reported in a year (given as a number)— while others examine the *prevalence* of abuse—what proportion of the population are victims (given as a percentage). A look at national incidence statistics from 1980 to 1986, prepared by the National Center on Child Abuse and Neglect (NCCAN, 1988), reveals a considerable increase in child sexual abuse over six years, from 42,900 cases in 1980 to 138,000 in 1986. When cases of endangerment are added to cases of demonstrable harm, the 1986 total goes up to 155,900.[3]

Now, consider prevalence estimates prepared from the same NCCAN data. The 42,900 cases for 1980 can be converted to a prevalence estimate of 7 cases per 10,000 children, or .0007%. The 138,000 cases for 1986 can be converted to a prevalence estimate of 22 cases per 10,000 children, or .0022% (.0025% for the revised data) (NCCAN, 1988).

What do these findings mean? Actually, because they are based on the same data, the statistics say the same thing: The number of cases of child sexual abuse reported from 1980 to 1986 increased threefold. Certainly, though, the incidence statistics sound much more alarming than the prevalence statistics.

Incidence statistics are of limited value for two reasons. First of all, knowing how many cases of abuse are reported per year is of little real value unless we know how many children are involved and what proportion of the population they make up. Prevalence statistics give us that information. Second, trends in incidence statistics, such as the large increases over short periods reported above, do not necessarily reflect actual levels of abuse. Increased reporting, due to improved public awareness, may be largely responsible for the rising figures. The NCCAN drew that conclusion about the increased incidence of all types of child abuse and child sexual abuse in particular (1988). And regardless of what the statistics say, we know that child sexual abuse is still grossly underreported (Peters, Wyatt, & Finkelhor, 1986).

Data about Offenders

Many of the validity problems that confound the data about sexual offenders are related to the nature of the sample studied. Many such samples are very small, including as few as four or five offenders, which makes extrapolation to a larger population questionable. But because of participation and anonymity problems, it is difficult to find large samples without resorting to incarcerated offender populations.

This is not a unique problem; the data used to study most types of criminal behavior are based on interviews with individuals who have been arrested and/or convicted of the given crime (e.g., rapists and child molesters form the sexual offender sample). Typical survey samples include inmates in various correctional facilities and psychiatric institutions (Burgess, 1985). Data will also vary depending on whether they were collected by a social agency or some component of the criminal justice system.

Such surveys obviously exclude offenders who have not been reported, adjudicated, and/or incarcerated (Finkelhor, 1986a). Rather, they focus on those offenders who are "the failures of the world of deviant behavior" (Finkelhor, 1979, p. 34). These individuals are either so blatant, so compulsive, or so incompetent that they get caught—some of them a number of times. Clearly, this is not a representative sample, given the reporting problems with child sexual abuse (see "Reporting Problems," later in this chapter).

These individuals may also give questionable reports when interviewed. They may not be "enthusiastic or cooperative subjects, and the matters of most interest to the researcher are often the exact ones the subjects are least interested in divulging" (Finkelhor, 1986a, p. 142). Self-reports are the most common source of data about both offenders and victims, yet their credibility must be weighed.

The credibility of self-reports is especially questionable when adult offenders report on their experiences as youths. Much of the early information on adolescent sexual offenders was based on self-reports of adult offenders looking back. Clearly, the accuracy and detail provided by such accounts may be dubious, at best. Moreover, since the data describe past events, it is impossible to draw any conclusions about contemporary trends or patterns. The use of self-reports, however, continues to be one of the most common means of gathering data about both victims and offenders, despite the fact that we know the sample is limited.

A final problem with data gathered from incarcerated sexual offenders is that they typically overrepresent individuals from low socioeconomic levels, even though we know that the problem of child sexual abuse cuts across all levels of society. For instance, cases of incest are more easily exposed in families that are generally dysfunctional and require aid with other problems (i.e., welfare, unemployment, alcoholism) than in families in which no other problems have been identified or at least reported (Finkelhor, 1979). Moreover, families in upper socioeconomic levels have the resources to handle family problems through private means rather than seek public assistance and risk exposing the problem. This is another problem that is aggravated when examining adolescent offenders; affluent parents frequently have sufficient money and influence to prevent public exposure and intervention. The data about reported adolescent offenders therefore portray youths from a disadvantaged background, which is misleading.

Research validity is also affected by numerous definitional problems. The field of child sexual abuse is so new and underdeveloped that researchers even disagree over what to call the phenomenon. For instance, victim-oriented research prefers the term *sexual abuse*, while offender-oriented research uses the terms *child molesting* and *pedophilia*. The different orientations of the various disciplines and ideologies that study child sexual abuse—from psychoanalysts to sociologists to feminists to law enforcement personnel—further complicate definitional problems (Araji & Finkelhor, 1986).

Definitional inconsistencies in how sexual offenses are reported and described under the law also confound data from arrest and conviction records. At the beginning of this chapter, we pointed out that individual states define sexual abuse according to their own statutes. Thus, on a national level, the general category of *sexual offense* may include everything from indecent exposure to assault and battery to lewd and lascivious conduct to contributing to the delinquency of a minor to sodomy to incest to rape (Groth, 1978).

Although some of these differences may be semantic, they do affect what is reported and how it is described. Consider, for example, that, in early studies, homosexuality was defined as a crime and accounted for as much as 20% to 25% of all sexual offenses reported (Burgess, 1985). In addition, specific data on recidivism are often unavailable because crimes committed by repeating offenders are not distinguished from other sexual offenses (Finkelhor, 1986a). Finally, these reporting differences make it difficult to provide a reliable estimate of the incidence of sexual abuse, particularly on a national scale (Groth, 1978).

The legal handling of sexual offenses only compounds the problem. Vagueness in defining legal charges often misrepresents the true nature of the offense. For instance, a rape in which the victim was killed may be charged as a homicide, or a break-in in which underclothes were taken may be called a burglary (Department of the Youth Authority, 1986). Decisions to plea bargain (e.g., reducing a rape charge to simple assault) or dismiss cases (perhaps due to lack of evidence or reluctant witnesses) distort the picture further (Burgess, 1985).

Perhaps the most significant problem with existing theories of adult offenders is that most are single factor in design. That is, they identify one or possibly two mechanisms to explain why the offender has a sexual interest in children. Such an approach is just too simplistic, much too inadequate to explain the complex range of behaviors involved with sexual abuse.

> *This behavior ranges from the man who spends a lifetime masturbating over children's underwear ads in Sears catalogs but never touches a single child, to a man who after many years of respectable heterosexual fidelity to his wife is possessed by a strong sudden impulse to caress his granddaughter's genitals, to a man who persuades his girlfriend to help him bring a child into their bed after reading about such activities in an X-rated novel. (Araji & Finkelhor, 1986, p. 92)*

We will discuss several multifactor models of child sexual abuse in Chapters 2 and 3 on adult and adolescent offenders, respectively.

Data about Victims

First of all, it's important to point out that almost all the research on child sexual abuse is about female victims. It is true that the overwhelming majority of reported cases of abuse involve girls, and it is accepted that girls are more often victimized than boys. But this does not mean that boys are not sexually abused. Unique reporting and definitional problems limit the study of abused boys and thus perpetuate the stereotype of the girl victim. (We will discuss boy victims specifically in Chapter 4 on victims.)

Another important fact is that it is difficult to find large numbers of individuals who are willing and able to describe their abuse. What's more, the so-called conspiracy of silence that surrounds the issue because of the social stigma of being sexually abused ensures that an unknown proportion of victims will never be heard from (Chandler, 1982).

Researchers therefore find subjects are of limited availability. The individuals most often used as samples in victim research are typically from one of three groups: (1) children who have been sexually abused and are involved in some type of treatment program; (2) adults (usually women) who are receiving counseling or medical treatment for psychological problems; and (3) adults who are participating in some type of community or college survey.

The basic problem with the first victim group is obvious: It includes only those children whose abuse has been reported and who are being treated in some type of program. Right away, this means a large group of child victims is being missed. Also, since these cases were reported and the children are in treatment, it is likely that this child-victim group has been severely abused and highly traumatized. This alone may distort the findings in a negative way, perhaps portraying more victim trauma than is representative.

There are similar problems with the second group, the adults in treatment, in that it, too, is a very self-selecting sample. These individuals are not necessarily in treatment because of their abuse as children; in fact, this history of abuse is often discovered during the diagnosis of other psychological problems. Nonetheless, the fact that these people are receiving treatment may prevent them from being representative, especially if they were severely traumatized by being sexually abused (Browne & Finkelhor, 1986).

The community or college-student survey samples are considered to be better than the victim samples, for several reasons. They are more representative of the general public than any group that has been referred through law enforcement, social services, or treatment programs.[4] In addition, such samples have built-in comparison groups, which means that victims and nonvictims from the same general background may be studied (Finkelhor & Baron, 1986).

The importance of a legitimate comparison group cannot be underestimated, since data are fairly meaningless unless they can be measured against some type of norm. Some studies of clinical populations (children and adults) do not have comparison groups, and some use other clinical populations for comparison, most likely introducing complicating factors. For instance, patients in a psychiatric hospital may share a number of basic problems (e.g., depression), which will produce high scores for these variables. But this may have nothing to do with whether these individuals were sexually abused as children.

Similarly, it is difficult for research to establish whether a certain factor *contributes* to a child's victimization or *results* from it. Studies that address long-term effects of abuse, such as promiscuity and sexual adjustment, tend to conclude that the abuse is responsible for the later behavior. To draw such a clearcut conclusion is unrealistic, though, because what happened in someone's past does not necessarily explain his or her current behavior (Browne & Finkelhor, 1986).

Other validity issues are related to the ages of the individuals surveyed. The problem that must be addressed with any adult sample is that of memory. First of all, how accurate is an adult's memory of childhood going to be, particularly when questions about nonfactual, interpretive issues like family relationships are asked? And second, how much of what the adult supposedly remembers is actually an interpretation of events and circumstances? Unfortunately, when an adult sample is used, the child's view is lost (Finkelhor & Baron, 1986).

Research on effects of abuse run into similar age-related problems. For instance, children or college students will not yet display certain long-term effects of abuse, such as problems with sexual adjustment and partner relationships. And the immediate effects of sexual abuse that are critical to children's functioning and development will be lost or obscured in adult samples (Browne & Finkelhor, 1986).

This relates to what Finkelhor has termed the "adultocentric" bias of the study of child sexual abuse. Researchers are engrossed in the study of long-term effects of abuse, hoping to establish that being abused as a child sets the pattern for subsequent problems in adulthood. This implies, however unintentionally, that the initial effects of abuse are less significant simply because they don't last as long. After all, "it is only 'childhood,' a stage which . . . everyone outgrows" (Finkelhor, 1984, p. 198).

A final bias that characterizes some studies in which victims are examined separately from offenders is that the victims seem to be blamed for what has happened, even though that is clearly not the intent of the study.[5] What happens is that the data present all the things that make the victim vulnerable—in short, what is supposedly wrong with him or her (Finkelhor & Baron, 1986).

Also, even when a correlation between a given factor and abuse can be clearly established, the real question of *why* has usually not been answered. For instance, exactly what about a poor parental relationship creates risk: lack of love and attention? lack of supervision? lack of sex education? other types of abuse? Certainly, knowing the danger signs is important, but understanding why they mean danger is more important (Finkelhor & Baron, 1986).

We discussed a similar problem with theories about offenders that offer simplistic, single-factor theories of abuse, ignoring other important variables. To truly explain the phenomenon, the entire abuse scenario must be examined. We will present more realistic, multifactor theories in Chapters 4 and 5 on victims and family dynamics, respectively.

Reporting Problems

In an ideal research world, we would know how much child sexual abuse is not reported, and we would be able to distinguish between reported cases and unreported cases. For until we know the exact proportion of children who are abused and who is likely to abuse them, we cannot generalize with any certainty. Even the most thorough research and scrutinized data must be interpreted with the caveat that a large proportion of both victims and offenders remains unknown.

In Finkelhor's Boston survey, respondents were asked about their own experiences with sexual abuse.[6] Although most people *said* they would report an offender in response to a hypothetical situation, only about half had actually reported an offender in a real abuse situation. Most of the offenses reported were noncontact incidents committed by strangers. Parents were unlikely to report incidents that involved intercourse or were committed by relatives (Finkelhor, 1984).

Parents in Finkelhor's survey were also accurate in estimating that less than half of the children would tell them if they had been sexually abused. Based on actual reports, 63% of the female and 73% of the male victims never told anyone that they were abused, let alone officially reported the incident (Finkelhor, 1979). Others estimate that only 10% of all victims report their abuse (Chandler, 1982).

Why don't children tell? Reasons often given include fear, confusion, and ignorance: about what happened, about why it happened to them, about who they could turn to for help, and about what would happen after they'd told. What's more, children normally try to hide their sexuality from their parents and other adults, so it should be expected that they would hide having been sexually abused (Chandler, 1982).

Even when children do tell, parents are often reluctant to report. Sometimes, parents don't believe the child or are afraid that, if they do report, others will not believe the child. Even if parents do believe that abuse occurred, they may feel embarrassed or ashamed and want to avoid public exposure. Some parents dismiss or minimize the incident, refusing to admit that anything serious took place and believing that the child had a "close call" (Finkelhor, 1984). Denial continues even after the abuse has been discovered. Many parents respond angrily during treatment and legal proceedings with questions like "Why can't you just leave her alone?" or "Why can't you let him forget?" Unfortunately, parents with this naive "everything-will-be-all-right" attitude will also be unable to see the effects that being abused has had on their children (Porter, Blick, & Sgroi, 1982).

Whether the abuse will be discovered and how the family will react are directly related to how severely this experience has affected the victim. For instance, in cases of incest, a father abusing a daughter (or a stepfather abusing a stepdaughter) is the most often reported type, accounting for as many as three-quarters of all reported cases (Kempe & Kempe, 1984). This offense is usually reported because of the traumatic impact it has on the family and because it so violates social values. Most families are torn apart by such an incident, which requires the involvement of social and legal agencies and thus results in a report.

Brother/sister incest, on the other hand, is believed to be the most common type of incest—perhaps as much as five times more common than parent/child incest—but it is the least reported. According to some views, it is less traumatic for the victim and may therefore go undetected for quite some time (Finkelhor, 1979). It may also be less traumatic for the family than parent/child incest, since the breakup of the marriage is usually not involved and outside intervention may be avoided. Other research has found that brother/sister incest may be incredibly traumatic but remains undetected because of the dysfunctional nature of the family.

The issue of victim trauma must also be considered from another perspective. It is possible that there are children who are not affected by being abused and that they have not reported the experience because it hasn't traumatized them. Some believe that reporting itself may create the most significant trauma, an idea that warrants consideration and research (Sgroi, Blick, & Porter, 1982).

There is a particular problem with boys reporting abuse. Boys are more reluctant than girls to admit to being abused. Although feelings of powerlessness are experienced by all victims, for boys, victimization brings feelings of being unmasculine or weak. And since most offenders are male, there is also the issue of homosexuality—that somehow, being abused by a man means the boy must be homosexual (Finkelhor & Baron, 1986).

The stereotype of the girl abuse victim contributes to this reporting problem. Because more girls are victimized than boys, adults are more prone to worry about girls. They may thus not suspect the abuse of a boy child as readily and may even ignore common identification signs. From a research viewpoint, this means that many more data are available about girls than about boys, which, in fact, may enhance the stereotype and other similar misconceptions about victims (Finkelhor & Baron, 1986).

There is a similar problem with reporting adolescent offenders, for several reasons. Historically, adolescent offenders have not been taken very seriously. Myths about sexual play and experimentation, along with stereotypes about supposedly normal male aggression (i.e., "boys will be boys"), have been used to rationalize all but the most abusive and aggressive sexual offenses. People have also been afraid of stigmatizing a young offender and perhaps jeopardizing his or her future.

Another reason for underreporting is that children are less likely to report other children, even for a personal violation as serious as sexual abuse. In fact, a study of incest found that, when children did report being molested by a sibling, their motive for doing so was usually retaliation for something else the sibling had done (de Young, 1982).

Part of this unwillingness to report is based on a sort of childhood code of honor, which prohibits "telling on" one's peers. This unspoken pact is often used by abusers to coerce their victims into secrecy and compliance (O'Brien, 1988). Another explanation offered by some is that sexual abuse by an age peer is less traumatic than abuse by an adult. If this is true, it may explain why many cases of adolescents abusing children go unnoticed, even within families (Finkelhor, 1979).

The conclusion to be drawn about reporting problems is somewhat ironic. We know that child sexual abuse is grossly underreported, which means that we have only limited knowledge of how it happens and who does it to whom. But increased reporting per se will not solve the problem, because it seems that only certain types of abuse are discovered and only certain types of people report. It's the unreported abuse that we don't know about—that we may never know about—that makes up the bulk of the problem.

Summary

Child sexual abuse has been defined in a number of ways by professionals from various disciplines. Although researchers do not always agree on a specific definition, there is some consensus about what it should include. To be complete and useful, a definition of child sexual abuse must include the age of the victim, the type of activity that took place, and what specific element denotes abuse. The misuse of power and authority, rather than the expression of sexuality, is basic to determining what is abusive.

Child sexual abuse has also been defined in legal terms. National legislation provides for distributing funds for the prevention and treatment of abuse, but it does not establish criminal codes. Individual states have criminal jurisdiction. In Minnesota, criminal sexual conduct is categorized into five degrees. First- and third-degree criminal sexual conduct involve penetration, and second-, fourth-, and fifth-degree criminal sexual conduct involve contact. The severity with which offenses are judged also depends on factors such as the child's and victim's respective ages, whether or not coercion or force were used during the abuse, and the nature of the victim/offender relationship.

In this book, we will adopt the definition established by the NCCAN. *Child sexual abuse* is "contacts or interactions between a child and an adult when the child is being used for the sexual stimulation of that adult or other person." An adult is 18 years or older; however, someone less than 18 may commit sexual abuse when he or she is significantly older than or has authority over the child.

According to Finkelhor's Boston survey (1984), the general public is "relatively knowledgeable" about child sexual abuse. There is some misunderstanding about the frequency with which strangers commit abuse, about where abuse can be reported, and about whether offenders are mentally ill. These misconceptions are likely tied to myths and stereotypes. It seems that, even if people have the knowledge, emotions may prevent them from accepting the realities of child sexual abuse.

It is important to review the research methodology—namely, the effects of validity and reporting problems—before evaluating what the research has to say. Most research is based on studies of incarcerated offenders and reported victims undergoing treatment, which means there are severe problems with representation. Unless or until researchers are able to survey large samples of unreported offenders and victims—which means that these individuals must come forward on a voluntary basis and be offered some anonymity and/or protection—the data on child sexual abuse will be of questionable quality.

Even though we must be realistic and accept that we will never know about every case of abuse, we must use what information we have to learn how to prevent abuse and to know how to treat it when it happens. We can do this if we scrutinize research before accepting or rejecting any of the conclusions it offers.

Notes

1. In the Russell study (1983), the prevalence of child sexual abuse was 38% when only contact acts were included and 54% when both contact and noncontact acts were included.
2. Other Minnesota statutes that address child sexual abuse include 609.321, prostitution; 609.322, solicitation of children to engage in sexual conduct; 609.365, incest; 617.241, child pornography; 626.556, reporting of maltreatment of minors; and 260.133, domestic child abuse.
3. This reflects a change in how the NCCAN defined abuse in accordance with 1984 revisions to federal child protective legislation.
4. One could argue whether college students are representative, since they typically reflect individuals from the middle and upper socioeconomic levels. Regional demographics would have to be considered, as well.
5. Feminists see sexism at work here, since sexual abuse is considered by some to be a women's issue because of the preponderance of female victims and the advocacy of the women's rights movement for abuse victims (Chandler, 1982).
6. Data about respondents' own experiences were not presented earlier in this chapter. The complete survey is reported in Finkelhor (1979).

Part Two

The People

Chapter Two

Adult Sexual Offenders

Certainly, the overwhelming question in the study of the sexual abuse of children—one that everyone would like answered—is, Why would anyone do something so terrible to a child? So far, no one has been able to answer this question with any surety; in fact, it may not be totally answerable, given the complexity of the issue. But researchers are able to give us more and more information about the types of people who molest children and what their motivations may be.

The bulk of this chapter will address characteristics of adult offenders, along with various theoretical typologies that have been suggested. We will end with the work of David Finkelhor, reviewing his four-factor typology and his model of sexual abuse.

Characteristics of Adult Offenders

A number of studies have documented general characteristics of adult sexual offenders, examining individual and sociological factors. One of the most revealing of such studies was done in March 1987 by Gene Abel, Judith Becker, and colleagues (Abel, Becker, Mittelman, Cunningham-Rather, Rouleau, & Murphy, 1987). This group interviewed 561 nonincarcerated offenders in Memphis, Tennessee, and New York City; the interviewees were recruited through contacts with health care professionals, announcements during meetings and presentations, and ads in the local media.[1]

An elaborate system was established to protect the identities of self-reporting offenders:

- Only voluntary subjects were accepted.
- Each signed a detailed consent form that outlined the importance of full disclosure.
- Each was assigned a confidential identification number.
- Codes matching the patient's name and number were held outside the United States to prevent possible subpoenas of the material.

Abel also secured a Certificate of Confidentiality from the Secretary of Health, Education, and Welfare. Finally, interviewers stressed the importance of obtaining complete and accurate information.

Before proceeding to the findings, a few cautions are in order. Abel himself warns,

> *Even though the data presented here are sufficiently numerous to be representative of each of the categories of paraphiliacs [i.e., types of sexual offenders], they do not represent, because of pre-selection, the normal distribution of categories of paraphiliacs in the general population. Therefore, the fact that child molesters were more numerous in this study does not imply that this category of paraphilia, relative to other categories, is more numerous in the general population.* (Abel et al., 1987, p. 8)

Some researchers hesitate to generalize Abel's findings because of the self-selecting nature of his subjects. While Abel and others believe that self-reporting offenders may tend to downplay the number of acts they've committed because of feelings of shame and remorse, still others believe that offenders tend to exaggerate their exploits. Also, Abel's study includes far fewer incest offenders than is typical of most studies. (See "Incest Offenders," later in this chapter.)

Abel's Findings

Sex and Age

All of the subjects were male. They were predominantly young; none was over 40, and about two-thirds were between 20 and 39 years of age. Eighty percent admitted to having committed their first offense before the age of 30, and 5% had committed their first offense during adolescence.

Race
Sixty-two percent were white, 23% were black, and 11% were Hispanic.[2]

Sexual Preference
The majority of the sample were heterosexual; in fact, many were involved in adult relationships at the time of the offense. Those who were characterized as being homosexual were either exclusively pederasts or had once functioned as heterosexuals.

Marital Status
Of the 504 for whom marital status was known, 47% were single. The rest had formed significant relationships with adult partners, leading to marriage or an ongoing "living with" arrangement.

Intelligence and Psychological Profile
The offenders studied were of average intelligence; none was retarded or otherwise mentally impaired. They were also normal psychologically; fewer than 5% displayed any psychotic characteristics at the time of the offense. (See also the following discussions on "Impulsivity" and "History of Abuse.")

Education
Nearly half the offenders had completed high school; 21% had also completed one year or more of college.

Employment/Socioeconomic Status
The offenders came from a broad range of socioeconomic levels. Sixty-four percent were fully employed.

Religion
Thirty-four percent of the subjects were Catholic; 28% were Protestant.[3]

Alcohol and Drug Use
Less than one-third of Abel's sample could be characterized as drug or alcohol dependent. The majority of the offenders were not under the influence of drugs or alcohol when they committed the abuse.

Acts Committed
In all, the population of 561 subjects completed a total of 291,737 acts. On average, each subject committed 2.02 types of offenses, or paraphilias (e.g., exhibitionism, fondling, oral sex, etc.). By type of offense, the numbers of completed acts ranged from 7.2 acts per rapist to 1,139.2 acts by masochists.[4] High-frequency acts included masochism, frottage (rubbing or fondling), transvestism, exhibitionism, and voyeurism.

In comparison, child molesting was *relatively* infrequent, comprising 21.9% of the acts of abuse reported. The average number of acts ranged from 23.2 times by a female-target offender to 281.7 times by a male-target offender (nonincest offenses only). Of the four categories of child molester—male target, female target, incest, and nonincest—the greatest number of offenses was committed by subjects targeting young boys outside the home (281.7 acts, or 14.8%). The second greatest number of offenses involved incest with a female family member (4.4%); the third and fourth greatest numbers of offenses involved female-target/nonincest (1.8%) and male-target/incest (.9%), respectively.

Incestuous offenders were also likely to abuse the same victim repeatedly, from an average of 36.7 acts per boy victim to 45.2 acts per girl victim. Thus, the ratio of acts to victims is higher for child molesters than other paraphiliacs.

Program Participation/Treatment
Nearly two-thirds of the offenders said that they felt slight or no pressure from others to participate in the study, which led Abel to conclude that more offenders would seek treatment if it were available on a confidential and nonprosecutorial basis.

In Sum

Abel's findings challenged some long-held assumptions about sexual abuse. First of all, the frequencies with which given offenses were committed were significant. Despite public awareness and media attention, rape was surprisingly infrequent compared to other offenses. (Abel qualified that this finding did not minimize the seriousness of the offense but rather put it in context with other offenses.)

There were similar surprises in the findings about child molesters. While earlier data on incarcerated offenders have reported that, on average, pedophiles have been found guilty of fewer than three acts each (Gebhard, Gagnon, Pomeroy, & Christenson, 1965), Abel found that nonincarcerated child molesters had committed an average range of 23.2 to 281.7 acts each.[5]

The findings about how frequently boys are sexually abused in comparison to girls are also surprising, contradicting other research as well as general public opinion. Certainly, the media portrayal of the typical child sexual abuse scenario includes a girl victim.

Abel concludes that these discrepancies suggest that "information regarding paraphiliacs and their behavior can be obtained from various sources but that self-report information may be exceedingly helpful in providing a better understanding of the true nature of paraphilia because the source of this information is the offender himself (p. 21)."

Additional Psychological Characteristics

Abel's study did find that, in general, child sexual abusers are not mentally ill in the sense that they are psychotic or schizophrenic; in fact, most seem surprisingly normal. Other researchers have supported this notion but found that offenders do have personality disorders that may account for their behavior.

Child molesters are often characterized as being psychosexually immature and lacking self-esteem and authority. This immaturity may lead to alienation and even fear of age peers, particularly in terms of sexual interests. Perhaps this is why an adult would turn to a child for sex: Children are accessible and controllable, making them easy targets. Abusing children may also give the offender feelings of power and domination, increasing his or her self-worth, at least in his or her own eyes (de Young, 1982).

In addition to these general findings about the psychological make-up of adult offenders, two topics have been explored in some detail: impulsivity and history of abuse.

Impulsivity

Many psychological profiles of sexual offenders suggest that these individuals have difficulty controlling their impulses. With regard specifically to sexual impulses, this lack of control may be a significant factor in why some individuals are able to overcome normal inhibitions and have sex with children.

Robert A. Prentky and Raymond A. Knight (1986), of the Massachusetts Treatment Center (MTC), studied impulsivity in the lifestyle and criminal behavior of a sample of 230 incarcerated rapists and child molesters (all men). Each individual was scored on three measures of impulsivity: (1) the relative amount of forethought and planning involved in the offense committed; (2) the degree of general life-style impulsivity; and (3) the tendency toward transiency.

The investigation focused on how these three measures were interrelated and how they were significant causal or contributory factors in juvenile and adult criminal behavior. In particular, the research examined whether general impulsivity and impulsivity in sexual offense (ISO) were correlated, a notion that has some empirical support in the psychopathology literature (see also Cleckley, 1976; Hare, 1980).

Prentky and Knight drew the following conclusions:

1. ISO was uncorrelated with life-style impulsivity but covaried with individual sexual and aggressive motivational factors.
2. General life-style impulsivity was characterized by childhood behavioral problems that were followed by poor achievement in education, the military, and interpersonal and professional domains throughout life.
3. Aimlessness and unstable employment history were particularly significant for child molesters—more so than for rapists. A lifetime of alcohol abuse was also characteristic.

As they discovered, "ISO taps a rather complex domain of behaviors" (Prentky & Knight, 1986, p. 159). Offenses that are very much planned are more compulsive than impulsive and have a sexual motivation (e.g., compensation, sexual sadism). Those offenses that are less planned reflect a predatory-type motivation, perhaps due to anger or opportunity, and are more determined by situational events.

A comparison of ISO with general life-style impulsivity revealed that, "not only were these two aspects of impulsivity statistically independent, they also correlated with different sets of life events and criminal behavior, suggesting that separate domains of behavior were tapped by the different measures" (p. 161).

History of Abuse

Perhaps no other notion about offenders has received as much popular attention as the notion that these individuals were themselves physically or sexually abused as children. This theory, the so-called vampire theory, asserts that the offender was victimized as a child and has become the aggressor as an adult in an attempt to act out his or her own victimization or because he or she has simply learned abusive behavior.

Another MTC study of incarcerated rapists and child molesters, conducted by Theoharis K. Seghorn, Robert A. Prentky, and Richard J. Boucher (1987), examined the incidence of childhood physical and sexual abuse in the lives of sexually aggressive offenders (all men). Their purpose: "In a population where the manifest adult pathology is explicitly, albeit not exclusively, sexual in nature, it is psychologically meaningful to posit that one of the important antecedents of such pathology lies rooted in early childhood sexual experiences" (p. 262).

The four most compelling conclusions drawn from this study of sex offenders' backgrounds were:

1. The incidence of sexual assault in childhood among child molesters was higher than that reported for the general population in the professional literature (almost six times higher).
2. The incidence of sexual assault in childhood among child molesters was more than twice that among rapists.
3. Rapists were three times more likely than child molesters to have been assaulted by a family member.
4. When sexual assault did occur, for both rapists and child molesters, it was indicative of general family dysfunction and instability.

What has not been established is the functional relationship between the incidence of childhood sexual assault and the outcome, or the severity of pathology. In other words, exactly what about the childhood assault contributed to the adult committing a particular offense? For example, rapists were more likely than child molesters to have been assaulted by family members. Since the closeness of the relationship between the offender and the victim is related to the severity of the psychological damage done, perhaps this helps explain the motivation to rape, especially given the violence and rage demonstrated by most rapists.

Theories of Adult Offenders

A good deal of research has addressed the question we posed at the beginning of this chapter: Why would anyone sexually abuse a child? Many of the theories proposed are psychologically based and look at such factors as arrested development, mental deficiency or illness, personality disorders, and so on. Other theories are physiologically based and examine such factors as impotence, degenerative disease (e.g., alcoholism, senility), cerebral trauma, and so on. Still other theories classify sexual offenders according to the type of victim they choose (i.e., age, gender), the type of act they commit, the amount of force they use, how they are related to the victim, and the situational characteristics of the offense.

Dichotomous Classifications

According to Howells (1981), the classification scheme most pervasive in the sexual abuse literature is one that provides two classes of individuals: "offenders whose deviant behavior is a product of a deviant sexual preference for children and those whose deviant behavior is situationally induced and occurs in the context of a normal sexual preference structure" (p. 76). Howells uses the terms *sexual-preference mediated* and *situational* to describe these offender types, while others use *pedophile* and *nonpedophile* (Finkelhor, 1984).

Nicholas Groth (1978), among others, has suggested a two-group classification of offender types: (1) the *fixated pedophile*, whose sexual involvement with children shows a persistent pattern, or a fixation, and (2) the *regressed pedophile*, for whom the sexual activity is new or a change in his or her normal sexual orientation.

The fixated pedophile has always been sexually attracted to children, regardless of what other sexual experiences he or she has had. This sexual pattern began in adolescence, when he or she probably avoided usual dating, sports, and other socialization activities. There was no precipitating stress or event that triggered the behavior, nor is there usually any history of alcohol or drug abuse.

The fixated pedophile maintains a persistent interest in children and is prone to compulsive behavior. His or her offenses are usually preplanned and premeditated. Groth describes the fixated pedophile's feelings about his or her sexuality:

For the most part, these pedophilic desires are not disturbing to the fixated offender; that is, he [or she] is comfortable and satisfied with such activity and experiences no intense feelings of guilt, shame or remorse in this regard. Even when the fixated offender is distressed by such desires, he [or she] experiences the attraction as compulsion, something that cannot be resisted or avoided. . . . The offender appears sexually "addicted" to children. (1978, p. 7)

The second category, the regressed pedophile, is someone who originally had appropriate sexual interest in his or her age peers but who has deviated at some point due to an inability to handle life stresses. Some sort of personal crisis during adulthood, such as marriage or financial problems, is typically the catalyst.

The regressed pedophile's initial offense may be impulsive, not premeditated, and the involvement may be episodic and irregular. Alcohol consumption is often a factor in the incident. Again, quoting Groth, the regressed pedophile is "quite often distressed by this behavior; that is, he [or she] may experience feelings of guilt, shame, disgust, embarrassment, remorse or dissatisfaction about what he [or she] has done, but these feelings occur after the fact" (1978, p. 9).

In sum, the fixated pedophile suffers from a chronic sexual condition, whereas the regressed pedophile is experiencing an acute situational problem in his or her sexual life-style. The fixated pedophile has little or no meaningful involvement in peer-age or adult sex and has no interest in achieving such relations. The regressed pedophile does have such involvement and interest, but his or her sexual impulses have been displaced for some reason. Because of these differences, Groth suggests that the regressed pedophile is more likely to respond to treatment than the fixated pedophile.

Groth also found some similarities between the two subtypes. He estimated that there were equal numbers of fixated and regressed pedophiles and that recidivism was common for both types. Also, both types chose female victims twice as often as males and had specific preferences for certain victim characteristics. Both fixated and regressed pedophiles usually committed a specific act consistently, and most acted alone. Interestingly, neither group was particularly distressed about what they had done, especially in worrying about the victim; more were concerned with what they had done to their own lives. Groth felt that some of this lack of self-blame could be attributed to offenders simply lying about their feelings or rationalizing as a sort of defense mechanism to deny or minimize their actions.

Alternative Theories

Although Groth's theory remains popular, other researchers have criticized his two-group typology as being simplistic and perhaps even misleading. For instance, research has documented that only a small number of adult offenders (25% to 33%) can be labeled as fixated pedophiles. The majority are regressed and involved with children for transient reasons. What's more, Groth's typology does not examine or qualify what motivates individuals to offend, even individuals within the same category. Again, the question, Why do they do it?

In reviewing Groth's theory, Finkelhor suggested that, rather than establish two dichotomous categories, a continuum of behavioral characteristics should be examined, allowing a range of behavior. At one end of the continuum would be the strength of the offender's sexual interest in children, and at the other end would be the exclusivity of that interest. Certainly, a two-dimensional theory, examining a range of behavior between two variables, is more realistic and comprehensive than a single-factor theory (Finkelhor, 1984).

The Child Molester Classification System

Prentky and colleagues, working at the Massachusetts Treatment Center (MTC), developed a Child Molester Classification System that set up a number of decision-making criteria for assessing offender subtypes (MTC, n.d.). On one axis, they examined two separate constructs: the offender's degree of fixation on children and his level of social competence. On a second axis, they divided offenders into groups based on (1) how much contact they had with children, (2) their motivation for the contact, and (3) the amount of physical injury they caused to the victim. (All offenders were male.)

We will review Prentky's classification scheme but will not go into detail about selection and rating factors. For such information, refer to the original Prentky publication (MTC, n.d.), as well as others by the MTC group (see "References and Suggested Readings").

Axis I. In this domain, two variables were considered.

1. The *degree of fixation* assessed the strength of the individual's pedophilic interest, or "the extent to which children are a major focus of the offender's thought and attention." The individual was rated as having *high fixation* if children were demonstrated to be the primary focus of his sexual and interpersonal thoughts and fantasies for at least six months. The individual was rated as having *low fixation* when such evidence was lacking and/or when he was over 20 years old and all of his sexual encounters with children occurred within a six-month period.

2. The *level of social competence* assessed a number of characteristics that typically demonstrate individual responsibility and social participation, including (a) length and regularity of employment; (b) involvement in an ongoing sexual relationship with an adult; (c) significant responsibility in parenting; (d) active membership in an adult-oriented organization; and (e) involvement in a normal, ongoing friendship with an adult (not involving marriage or cohabitation).

After rating the individual as high or low on both these factors, one of four type assignments would be possible: (1) high fixation/low social competence (Type 0); (2) high fixation/high social competence (Type 1); (3) low fixation/low social competence (Type 2); and (4) low fixation/high social competence (Type 3).

Axis II. In this domain, the primary variable was the *amount of contact with children.* This is a behavioral measure of the time the individual spends with children, including both sexual and nonsexual activities but excluding activities that involve parental caretaking. (It is important to distinguish the amount of *contact* from the degree of *fixation;* the *contact* measure refers to a quantity of involvement, whereas the *fixation* measure refers to the strength of the attraction.)

1. The *high-contact offender* spends a significant amount of time in "close proximity" to children, in both sexual and nonsexual contexts. Two other issues addressed here are the motivation of the high-contact offender (interpersonal or sexual) and the nature or aim of the sexual offense (nongenital or phallic).

2. The *low-contact offender* has had little or no contact with children in either his work or leisure activities. His only contact has been sexual assault. A secondary issue here is the degree of injury the low-contact offender inflicts on the victim and his motivation for aggression (i.e., sexual or nonsexual).

Again, refer to Prentky's publication (MTC, n.d.) for additional information on scoring.

Special Offender Groups

Several specific groups of offenders—including women, incest, and homosexual offenders—have been studied in isolation, an approach that is debated among researchers. For instance, the topic of father/daughter incest has been studied extensively, particularly by family-systems theorists. While this study may provide information regarding how the nature of the family and personal relationships contribute to abuse, it still does not address the specific issue of why the offender offends.

When the goal of the study is to examine motivation, there is an inherent problem in isolating the incest offender or any other type of offender, for that matter. Certainly, each offender type is different in certain ways, but the question is, How different and in what ways? Following this logic, a number of researchers prefer to study special offender types in the context of the general offender group. And current empirical evidence does not disprove that such a unified theory is workable (Finkelhor, 1984).

Brief discussions follow on women, incest, and homosexual offenders. These discussions are by no means conclusive and complete but rather point out what may be uniquely characteristic of the particular subtype. The concluding discussion of Finkelhor's theory and model is also relevant to these special groups.

Women Offenders

There is a "male monopoly" on child sexual abuse: 90% of all reported cases of abuse are committed by men (Finkelhor, 1986a; Finkelhor & Hotaling, 1983). More specifically, it's estimated that 95% of all girls and 80% of all boys are abused by men (Finkelhor & Baron, 1986).

Most research takes this monopoly for granted and even ignores the possibility that the sex of the offender may contribute to the abuse (i.e., Why are men so much more likely to abuse than women?). Granted, reported instances of women abusing children are rare, although perhaps not as rare as was once believed. Nonetheless, when reports of abuse by women surface, they are often taken less seriously than reports of abuse by men. Women offenders are less likely to be investigated or prosecuted as fully as men offenders, and when they are charged, the offense is often reduced to a misdemeanor (Finkelhor, 1979).

A degree of child compliance or lack of reporting may also be involved. Children react differently to being abused by a woman than by a man. Some believe that sexual abuse by a woman is less traumatic and may even stir some sexual interest in the child regarding the nature of the experience. Child victims of women are usually less fearful and display fewer negative effects after the incident. The primary reason for this difference is that women are most often less forceful and intimidating than men. In cases where the degree of force is significant, children are more traumatized (Finkelhor, 1979). (See also Chapter 4 on victims.)

Many still find the so-called initiation concept, by which a mature woman leads a naive youth to manhood, appealing. In 1978, a 23-year-old housewife was charged with contributing to the delinquency of a minor when she had actually had intercourse with a 15-year-old boy. Worse yet, the charges were dismissed in court when the judge proclaimed that the case was "nothing more than sex education, essential and necessary in his growth toward maturity and subsequent family life" (*The Boston Globe*, 10 Feb. 1978, p. 28, reported in de Young, 1982).

This blatant sexism is a strong indication of the social views that surround this topic. In short, society sees women differently than men, particularly with regard to sex and parenting. Women are supposed to be loving and nurturing; men, aggressive and dominant. As parents, women are believed to have a natural edge over men, being guided by some sort of mothering instinct.

Are these views nothing more than stereotypes, or do they illustrate actual gender-role differences between men and women? If gender does affect men's and women's attitudes about sex and parenting, it could explain why women are less likely to abuse children. Consider the following observations (based on Finkelhor 1979; 1986a).

1. Women are socially conditioned to prefer larger, older, and more powerful partners; men are conditioned to prefer smaller, younger, and vulnerable partners. Men would therefore be more likely to find children sexually attractive.

2. Women are less likely to play the dominant, aggressive role in sex; therefore, they are less likely to initiate sex. And since children would rarely initiate sex, woman/child encounters are unlikely. Men, on the other hand, are expected not only to initiate sex but to be dominant and overcome any resistance their partner may show.

3. Men are more promiscuous than women, which some researchers have attributed to biological reasons (Symons, 1979). Men also typically have more sexual experiences as youths than women do. Since women are more monogamous, they may be less likely to seek relationships with other partners, children included.

4. Men are more aroused than women are by sexual stimuli that are "divorced from any relationship context" (e.g., pornography). Women are more attuned to the subtleties of the relationship and the nature of their partner, which may preclude interest in a child.

5. Men sexualize the expression of emotion more than women do. Thus, women are better able to distinguish between situations of sexual versus nonsexual affection and intimacy. They are less likely to sexualize feelings between themselves and children.

6. Men and women react differently when sexual opportunities are unavailable. Sexual contact seems to be more important in maintaining self-esteem for men than for women (Person, 1980). Assuming this is true, when normal sexual avenues are blocked, men may turn to children for sex.

7. Women, as mothers, are more concerned with the well-being of children than men are, which may prevent women from inflicting harm on children (Herman, 1981). A related notion is that women interact with children much more than men do, such that a kind of bonding takes place between women and children. Few men have the opportunity to develop this sense of protectiveness and responsibility toward children.

8. As victims of sexual abuse themselves, women are more empathetic to children. They may therefore control their erotic impulses more than men do.

9. Sexual contact with children may be more condoned by male subculture than by female subculture. Research has documented that sex between men and children has been accepted and even encouraged throughout Western history. This social pattern does not exist for women (Rush, 1980).

Is it possible that women offenders are less likely to be discovered or reported because of their unique relationship with children? Finkelhor pointed out that women would have a difficult time concealing sexual abuse because abusive acts are very different than normal mothering behaviors. For instance, having a child fondle her mother's genitals could not be passed off as normal mother/child interaction. Also, the child would be able to distinguish between normal caretaking and sexual advances.

There is also other evidence to discount the notion that a so-called maternal bond prevents women from sexually abusing children. Research has shown that women are more likely to physically abuse children than men are. Besides, not all women are mothers, and not all abuse is intrafamilial (Finkelhor, 1979).

Although the questions remain, we do know something about women offenders. Statistically, they are not much different than men offenders: the age of their victims is about the same; they commit intrafamilial and extrafamilial abuse in about the same proportion; the acts they commit are similar; and they use force about as often.

There are also two qualities that distinguish women offenders from men offenders:

1. On average, women offenders are slightly younger than men offenders: 22.1 years for women versus 29.4 years for men.
2. Women offenders are more likely to be homosexual. In one study, 67% of the women were homosexual compared to only 14% of the men (Finkelhor, 1979).

Finkelhor has examined women offenders in some depth and has applied his four-factor theory, which we will discuss later in this chapter, to the male monopoly concept. (For more information, see Finkelhor 1986a, pp. 128-129.)

Genesis II Typology

Regardless of questions of reporting or rationalizations about why women do or do not offend, there are women offenders. In fact, increasing numbers of women are being prosecuted and treated in therapy programs. One of the most successful of such programs is Genesis II, based in Minneapolis. Ruth Mathews and Jane Matthews (1987) and colleagues at Genesis II have created a preliminary typology of female sex offenders. (Also see the section on female adolescent offenders at the end of Chapter 3, which parallels this discussion.)

At the first level, the Genesis II typology examines whether the offense was self-initiated by the woman offender or whether a man was somehow involved in committing the offense (i.e., encouraged or coerced the woman offender into acting). The reason for this initial classification—self-initiated or male-involved—is that nearly half of all acts of child sexual abuse committed by women do involve a male co-offender. At the second level, the self-initiated and male-involved classifications are subdivided, as follows:[6]

I. *Self-initiated offenses*
   A. *Exploration/Exploitation*—This female abuser is 16 years old or younger. She is frequently described by her parents as being a loner, nervous, and active. Her school performance ranges from average to excellent. Psychological testing characterizes her as being extremely sensitive and respectful regarding sexual acceptance. She tends to be self-deprecating and socially detached; her general social skills are poor.

Her victim is usually a young child, age 6 or younger, and is usually a boy who is not a sibling. She generally commits just one abusive act, usually fondling; older offenders may perform oral sex on the victim. It is significant that the young female offender rarely has the victim sexually stimulate her. Thus, she is detached and unemotional, and there are no feelings of intimacy about the sex. Her motivation for exploring sex is not ego, as is the case with many young males; rather, her feelings are mechanical and fragmented. She often seems unaware of her own sexual arousal or her ability to deny participation.

B. *Personality disordered/Severe abuse history*—This offender may be an adolescent or an adult female. Most significantly, she is characterized by a history of severe sexual and physical abuse, often committed by male family members. Presumably because of this history, she has poor personal and social skills, is prone to aggression and substance abuse, and is apt to have deviant sexual fantasies. In particular, she is likely to eroticize adult/child relationships and is unable to see why her abusive behavior is wrong. Psychological testing indicates severe psychological distress.

The victim is usually someone with whom the offender is in regular contact: her own child or a relative, foster sibling, or neighbor. The victim is often female, and she is generally of the age at which the perpetrator was herself first sexually abused. Clearly, there is some acting out here, perhaps identifying with her own aggressor or attempting to somehow validate her own abuse.

The abuse committed is generally ongoing, involving more than one act, but is limited to a single victim at a time. Again, fondling is common, as is exhibition, particularly with a younger victim. Older victims may be subject to more physical and forceful sex, such as oral sex and finger or object penetration.

C. *Developmentally arrested or regressed*—This offender is an adult female. She may be married, divorced, or single and has clearly heterosexual interests. She uses deviant fantasies and projection as a sort of defense mechanism, denying any wrongdoing. In fact, she may describe the abuse as a love affair and assume that her victim is a willing and satisfied participant. About half of these women offenders were themselves sexually abused; most are socially isolated and not self-sufficient.

This woman's victims are teenage males, ages 11 to 16, again, youths with whom she has regular contact: children, stepchildren, friends of children, neighbors, or so-called young friends. When the victim is the woman's son, a family history of abuse is likely.

II. *Male involvement in commission of offense*
   A. *Male-accompanied*—This female offender, generally an adult 17 to 45 years old, has not been coerced by anyone to commit the offense, but a male co-offender is involved. The act may be initiated by either the man or the woman.

   This type of offender typically has an adolescent history of psychological problems, often resulting in hospitalization, and severe conduct and antisocial disorders. She is of low or average intelligence and has performed poorly in school and work; again, social isolation is common, as are substance abuse and a personal history of abuse. Most importantly, these women are psychologically unstable at the time of the offense.

   The victim of the male-accompanied offender is generally an adult female acquaintance, often within several years of the offender's age, or she is the offender's child. In this latter case, allowing or encouraging the sexual abuse of her children may be the offender's attempt at attracting or keeping a boyfriend.

   The acts of abuse committed by this offender are more violent and may involve rape. When the male initiates the act, the female offender is usually also sexual with the victim. But when the female initiates the act, she usually is not involved in a relationship with the victim. Because of the severity of these offenses, these women are more likely to be discovered and convicted of sexual abuse.

   B. *Male-coerced*—This type of offender may be either an adolescent- or adult-aged woman, but the profiles of the two groups are very different. The adolescent offender is coerced by a male into committing the behavior; the victim is generally a peer, and the abuse is a one-time event. Most often, the abusive behavior is described as being very uncharacteristic of the offender. Her psychological profile is fairly normal, perhaps indicating some problems with dependency and peer security.

The adult offender in this subtype is generally involved in the abuse after it has been initiated by a husband or boyfriend. Because of her own isolated and dependent nature and low self-esteem, she feels powerless and participates in the sexual abuse. Also, she may be threatened with abuse or abandonment if she does not participate. These women are often characterized as being passive-aggressive.

The adult offender's victim is usually her child or a relative or neighbor child. While the sex of the victim is generally decided by the male offender, both boys and girls are victimized. Again, violent acts such as rape are common.

Incest Offenders

Incest, as a type of sexual abuse, is unique in that it cannot be studied solely from an individual perspective. Both offender and victim analyses must include the family and overlying social dynamics (Mayer, 1985). Our focus here will be on the incest offender. Consult Chapters 4 and 5 for specific discussions of victims and family dynamics, respectively.

It was once believed that incest occurred only in poor, degenerate families, but researchers now believe the problem is rampant and affects all levels of society. In a sample of 530 women, just over 1% reported having been victimized by a father or stepfather. And although 1% may sound like a small rate, this means that over 16,000 girls are abused by their fathers each year (Finkelhor, 1979). When actual parents are distinguished from functional parents, the statistics are even more alarming: Father/daughter incest is five times more likely in stepfamilies than in families in which both biological parents are present (Finkelhor, 1979). It's estimated that 1 out of 6 girls living with a stepfather will be sexually abused by him, compared with 1 out of 43 girls living with a natural father (Russell, 1986).

In general, the incestuous family is highly disturbed. All roles and relationships are somehow affected, even if not overtly. A cold, controlling atmosphere is common; communication and affection are strained if not nonexistent. And the discovery of incest causes even more disturbance, even more than the discovery of extrafamilial abuse, because it may also involve the breakup of the marriage and other family relationships (Groth, 1978).

Nearly all incest offenders are male (97% to 99%), and nearly all incest victims are female (92% to 95%) (Mayer, 1985). The incest offender usually abuses one child at a time, although he may have several victims over an extended period (i.e., daughters of various ages over the years) (Groth, 1978).

His motivation is usually emotional satisfaction, not sexual satisfaction. He usually does not physically harm the children but controls them with threats and coercion (Mayer, 1985). A stepfather may be more likely to abuse than a biological father because he does not have strong, traditional feelings of parenting and protecting for his stepdaughter. In fact, he may be attracted to the younger, vulnerable woman, perhaps even out of resentment for his wife. Mother/daughter rivalry, which is common during the daughter's adolescence, may also be misinterpreted as the daughter's interest in the stepfather, encouraging his advances (Finkelhor, 1979).

Another factor—alcoholism—also has special significance for incestuous families. Perhaps as many as three-fourths of all incestuous fathers are alcohol or drug dependent. Abusive incidents often occur after the father has been drinking, presumably because normal inhibitions have been lowered. For this reason, alcohol or other substance abuse may be cited as a *contributing* but not a *causal* factor in incest (Mayer, 1985).

Finally, the so-called vampire theory seems to have especially strong relevance for incestuous families. Abusing parents most often have a severe history of abuse of all kinds. In one sample of 100 mothers of abused children, 24% had themselves been victims of incest, compared with 3% of the normal population (Goodwin, 1982). Gebhard et al. (1965) found that, in a sample of imprisoned incestuous fathers, 12% had had sex with an adult before reaching puberty, compared to 5% of the normal population and 28% of the overall prison population (in Goodwin, 1982). Other estimates run as high as 70% to 75% (Mayer, 1985).

The vampire theory asserts that the pattern repeats because of a learned coping mechanism that is developed through personal experiences, family background, and social values. The victim may also become the victimizer in an attempt to address his or her repressed trauma (Goodwin, 1982).

Incest has been described as the "ultimate taboo" or the "universal taboo," since sex with blood relatives and children are both forbidden by Western values. Still, incest is joked about, as are wife abuse and rape, which suggests an undercurrent of acceptance or at least tolerance (Finkelhor, 1979). It is still believed that incest is grossly underreported. (See also Chapter 3 on sibling/adolescent incest.)

Homosexual Offenders

The general public attitude toward homosexuality can be described as homophobic. The topic of homosexual child abusers is particularly volatile, due in part to exaggerated and stereotyped reports of homosexuals luring children into sex. The Save Our Children crusade of the late 1970s, made famous by Anita Bryant in Dade County, Florida, was not alone in spreading such rhetoric. Quoting Bryant, "Because homosexuals cannot have children, they can only recruit children. And that is what they do" (de Young, 1982).

In reality, homosexuals make up only a small proportion of child sexual offenders. As mentioned earlier, women offenders are more likely to be homosexual. For offenders overall, statistics range from 19% to 33% of the total offender population (Revitch & Weiss, 1962; Swift, 1977; de Young, 1982). And although one in three sounds high, consider that children are still at far greater risk from the heterosexual population (de Young, 1982).

Three points should be made about the background of homosexual offenders:

1. Of all offender groups studied, homosexuals had the worst family and parental relationships (Gebhard et al., 1965). Two-thirds were from broken homes, and the majority had experienced or witnessed various types of abuse (physical, verbal, and sexual) during their childhood. Homosexual men were especially fearful of their fathers and felt emotional rejection early on; they were more likely to be very close to their mothers (de Young, 1982).

2. The emotional atmosphere of the family is also telling. Most homosexual offenders described a cold and rejecting atmosphere. The parents displayed rigid and intolerant attitudes about sex, which meant that the youths had to learn about sex elsewhere, making them prone to abuse by others (de Young, 1982).

3. Homosexual offenders also had considerably more homosexual experiences as children (Gebhard et al., 1965). While some of this could be characterized as playful and mutual experimentation among children (which is typical among male children especially), a

good deal was coercive sex forced by an adult. In a small sample of nine homosexual offenders, all of them had experienced such abuse as children (de Young, 1982).

Finally, homosexuals should be distinguished from pederasts, or "boy worshipers." Pederasts do not consider themselves homosexual, although they have always been attracted to boys. However, they seek "companions," not victims, and solicit boys who willingly participate in sex.[7] Ironically, pederasts have a sort of "code of ethics" that dictates careful and even exalted treatment of the boys.

Regardless of pederasts' supposedly pure and loving feelings for boys, sex with children is against the law, which makes pederasty criminal behavior. For this reason, pederasts have been forced underground, where they maintain a sophisticated network and have developed a sexual subculture. They support a good deal of pornography and are responsible for newsletters and apologist-type promotions on the topic. Pederasts have also been linked to sex rings in which a single adult may form a group of boys with whom he engages in sex; the boys participate for an extended time and know of one another's involvement. The pederast leader obviously has strong control over the boys and even their parents, since the contact is often made through scout or church groups (de Young, 1982).

In sum, a pederast is not a typical sex offender. Unfortunately, many of the individuals are able to escape criminal prosecution because they get lost in the pederast underground.

A Model of Child Sexual Abuse

To conclude this chapter, we return to the work of Finkelhor and perhaps his most recurring theme: "There is a pressing need for new theory in the field of sexual abuse. What theory we have currently is not sufficient to account for what we know. Nor is it far-reaching enough to guide the development of new empirical research" (1984, p. 53).

Finkelhor cites several problems with the current state of child sexual abuse theories:

1. Current theories are not useful in synthesizing what is known about offenders with what is known about victims and their families. Research on offenders is conducted in isolation from and by different groups than that on child victims. There is no overlap, no attempt at producing a coherent theory that puts together the whole picture.

2. Current theories are not comprehensive. Two general theoretical domains have emerged: (a) theories based on studies of men who molested multiple children outside their own families and (b) family-systems theories based on studies of father/daughter incest. Other situations and types of offenders are simply not explained by these theories.

3. Current theories neglect sociological factors while centering on individual factors. Historically, pedophilia has been seen as an individual psychopathology, a behavioral deviance, because of the standard use of incarcerated sexual offenders as the sample population. But given the scope of the problem, it is clear that sociocultural factors are involved and must be addressed.

The Four-Factor Framework

Finkelhor conducted an exhaustive review of the literature on child sexual abuse to assess the current state of knowledge and synthesize the numerous theories offered. He found that these various theories could be organized around a framework of four factors:

1. *Emotional congruence*—Why does the individual find relating sexually to a child emotionally gratifying and congruent (in the sense of the child fitting the adult's needs)?
2. *Sexual arousal*—Why is the individual capable of being sexually aroused by a child?
3. *Blockage*—Why is the individual frustrated or blocked in his or her efforts to find sexual and emotional gratification from more normatively approved sources (i.e., adults)?
4. *Disinhibition*—Why isn't the individual deterred by conventional social restraints and inhibitions against having sex with a child (Araji & Finkelhor, 1986)?

While other theorists have seen these factors as competitive, Finkelhor sees them as a "complementary process, . . . many or all of which come into play in the creation of one particular person's pedophilic interest." These factors may work antagonistically or synergistically to explain the diversity of sexually abusive behavior (Araji & Finkelhor, 1986, pp. 92-94).

The Four Preconditions for Child Sexual Abuse

Beginning with these four factors, Finkelhor (1984) developed a model of sexual abuse that incorporates information about victims, families, and offenders and also addresses both individual and sociological/cultural levels. This model proposed that there were four preconditions that must be met in order for sexual abuse to occur (see also Table 2-1 and Figure 2-1).

Precondition 1: Motivation to Sexually Abuse

The offender must have some reason to have sexual contact with a child. Most often, that motivation may be based on (1) emotional congruence, (2) sexual arousal, and/or (3) blockage. (Note that these are three of the four factors mentioned above. The fourth factor, disinhibition, is a separate precondition, for reasons explained in Precondition 2.)

These three components are not preconditions by themselves; thus, all three do not have to be demonstrated for the abuse to occur. For instance, an offender may abuse the child out of some need to degrade others yet feel no sexual satisfaction from doing so. However, it is common to find a mixture of the three elements in evaluating motivation, perhaps explaining the variety of reasons for abuse.

Precondition 2: Overcoming Internal Inhibitors

The offender must not only be motivated; he or she must also overcome internal inhibitions against acting on those motivations. (This assumes that most people have such inhibitions, obviously.)

In essence, this precondition is the same as the disinhibition factor (factor 4) discussed earlier. It has been separated from the other three factors and established as a precondition for two reasons. First of all, emotional congruence, sexual arousal, and block-

Figure 2-1 *Model of Sexual Abuse*

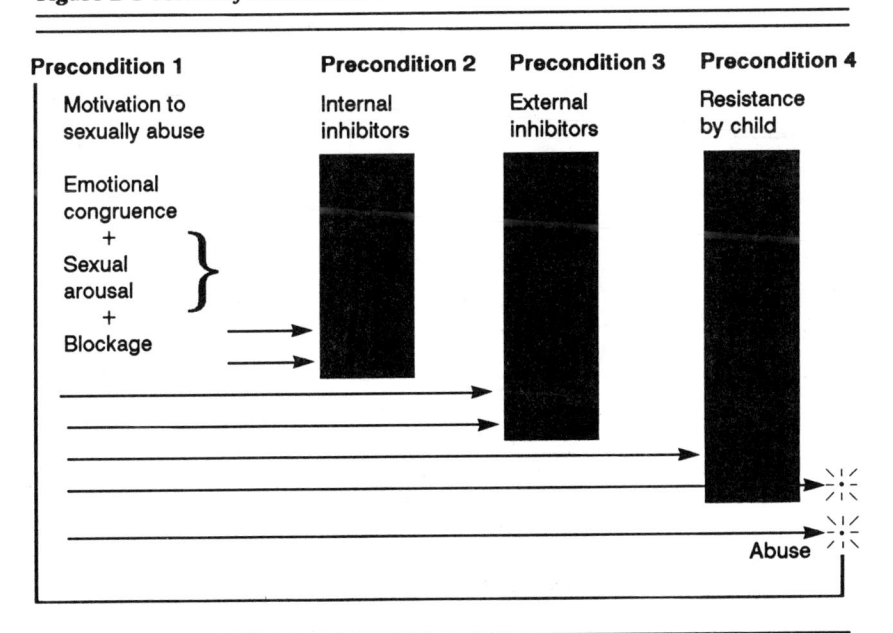

Precondition 1	Precondition 2	Precondition 3	Precondition 4
Motivation to sexually abuse	Internal inhibitors	External inhibitors	Resistance by child

Precondition 1:
Emotional congruence
+
Sexual arousal
+
Blockage

Abuse

Source: Reprinted with permission of The Free Press, a Division of Macmillan, Inc. from *Child Sexual Abuse: New Theory and Research* by David Finkelhor. Copyright (c) 1984 by David Finkelhor.

age are *sources* of motivation, whereas disinhibition is the *reason* the motivation leads to action. It follows then that disinhibition, unlike the other three factors, is by itself a requirement for sexual abuse. The motivation may exist, but unless inhibitions are overcome, the individual will not act.

Precondition 3: Overcoming External Inhibitors

The first two preconditions address the behavior of the offender: Why does he or she act? Preconditions 3 and 4 address those external inhibitors that affect the offender and his or her interactions with children. Precondition 3 examines external inhibitors outside the offender and the child, including third-person supervision, general public scrutiny, and the absence of physical opportunity to be alone with the child.

Table 2-1 *Preconditions for Sexual Abuse*

	Level of Explanation	
	Individual	*Social/Cultural*
Precondition I: Factors Related to Motivation to Sexually Abuse		
Emotional congruence	Arrested emotional development Need to feel powerful and controlling Reenactment of childhood trauma to undo the hurt Narcissistic indentification with self as a young child	Masculine requirement to be dominant and powerful in sexual relationships
Sexual arousal	Childhood sexual experience that was traumatic or strongly conditioning Modeling of sexual interest in children by someone else Misattribution of arousal cues Biologic abnormality	Child pornography Erotic portrayal of children in advertising Male tendency to sexualize all emotional needs
Blockage	Oedipal conflict Castration anxiety Fear of adult females Traumatic sexual experience with adult Inadequate social skills Marital problems	Repressive norms about masturbation and extramarital sex

A Model of Child Sexual Abuse

	Level of Explanation	
	Individual	*Social/Cultural*
Precondition II: *Factors Predisposing to Overcoming Internal Inhibitors*	Alcohol Psychosis Impulse disorder Senility Failure of incest inhibition mechanism in family dynamics	Social toleration of sexual interest in children Weak criminal sanctions against offenders Ideology of patriarchal prerogatives for fathers Social toleration for deviance committed while intoxicated Child pornogaphy Male inability to identify with needs of children
Precondition III: *Factors Predisposing to Overcoming External Inhibitors*	Mother who is absent or ill Mother who is not close to or protective of child Mother who is dominated or abused by father Social isolation of family Unusual opportunities to be alone with child Lack of supervision of child Unusual sleeping or rooming conditions	Lack of social supports for mother Barriers to women's equality Erosion of social networks Ideology of family sanctity
Precondition IV: *Factors Predisposing to Overcoming Child's Resistance*	Child who is emotionally insecure or deprived Child who lacks knowledge about sexual abuse Situation of unusual trust between child and offender Coercion	Unavailability of sex education for children Social powerlessness of children

Source: Reprinted with permission of The Free Press, a Division of Macmillan, Inc. from *Child Sexual Abuse: New Theory and Research* by David Finkelhor. Copyright (c) 1984 by David Finkelhor.

Precondition 4: Overcoming the Resistance of the Child

Since most research is done on children who have already been victimized, the issue of the child's ability to avoid or resist abuse is often overlooked. This is not simply a question of the child's saying no to a likely abuser; it is much more complicated. However, it seems that abusers can pick out children who will succumb to abuse. The child's willingness to play along, keep a secret, or be intimidated are all part of his or her "front of invulnerability." Children who are generally insecure, needy, or unsupported, as well as those who are young, naive, or uninformed, are all at especially high risk. (See also Chapter 4 on victims.)

In situations involving force or coercion, what the child did or said obviously had no effect. Nonetheless, the ability of children to avoid or resist sexual abuse should not be discounted.

Operation of the Model

The four preconditions operate in a logical sequence: Only some individuals have a strong motivation to have sexual contact with children. Of those individuals who do, only some overcome their internal inhibitions against acting on their motives. And of those who overcome their internal inhibitions, only some overcome the external inhibitions and actually act on their motives.

Once the first three preconditions have been met, three things can happen:

1. The child victim may resist and avoid the abuse. (See Figure 2-1; this is shown by the arrow that stops before Precondition 4.)
2. The child victim may fail to resist and be abused. (This is shown by the lowest line in the figure.)
3. The child victim may resist but be overcome by force or coercion. (This is shown by the line drawn through Precondition 4.)

All four preconditions must be met in order for the abuse to occur. Any other combination of three or less preconditions is not sufficient. "Theories from only one level of the model will never accurately discriminate between those who engage and those who do not engage in such behavior" (Finkelhor, 1986a, p. 125).

Application of the Model

Finkelhor's model is useful in categorizing and synthesizing many other theories of individual, family, and cultural factors that lead to child sexual abuse. It is also general enough to account for many different types of abuse, such as incest, and it is comprehensive enough to integrate other models of sexual abuse, such as the family-systems model (see Finkelhor, 1984, pp. 62-63). Finally, Finkelhor's model is flexible enough to adapt to new developments in research about child abuse. In sum:

> *One thing this model should do is remind us that sexual abuse is a complex phenomenon. Factors at a number of levels, regarding a number of individuals, come into play in determining its occurrence. Keeping such a model in mind should keep us from being seduced by simple explanations.*
>
> *At the same time, this model should help us to keep from getting discouraged by that complexity. Sexual abuse is a problem with causes and explanations. Many of these we do not yet fully understand. The four-preconditions model is open-ended; new findings and new ideas can be added to it. By having given some structure to what is already known, this model enables us to use that knowledge. (1984, p. 68)*

Summary

What do we know about the adult sexual offender? He or she is very seldom mentally ill in a true clinical sense, but certain personality disorders—such as psychosexual immaturity, feelings of alienation, and depression—may be diagnosed. Although impulsivity has generally been discounted as a contributing factor, the offender's own history of abuse is believed to have important bearing. This so-called vampire theory is currently a major research topic and also a popularly held notion among the media and general public. Although it does have some validity as a contributing factor, it cannot be singled out as a cause of deviancy.

The key topic in research on sexual offenders is motivation: Why do certain individuals sexually abuse children? Numerous theories have been offered, examining victim type, use of force, situational characteristics, individual psychopathology, social values, and so on. A great deal of research is based on the fixated/regressed pedophile typology. Others have elaborated on this single-factor, two-type classification and offered subtypes that examine more complex and individual factors. Work by Prentky and his Massachusetts Treatment Center colleagues has done this, examining not only sexual motivation but degree of fixation, social competence, amount of contact, nature of abuse, and degree of injury caused to the victim.

One of the most comprehensive and useful theories is that of Finkelhor, whose four-factor classification examines emotional congruence, sexual arousal, blockage, and disinhibition as complementary and synergistic factors. This classification is able to synthesize what is known about offenders, victims, and the family, offering a view of the whole picture of child sexual abuse. Also, Finkelhor's classification addresses both individual and sociological psychology, since child sexual abuse cannot be described as a purely individual problem, given its social scope today.

Finkelhor's four-factor theory has been applied in creating a working model of child sexual abuse. There are four preconditions for abuse to occur: (1) motivation to sexually abuse; (2) overcoming internal inhibitors; (3) overcoming external inhibitors; and (4) overcoming the child's resistance. These four preconditions operate in logical sequence to explain the child sexual abuse scenario.

Perhaps the greatest testimony to Finkelhor's work is that it is able to accommodate other theories of sexual abuse and may be applied to all types of offenders, including women, incest, and homosexual offenders. What's more, Finkelhor's model has important implications for treatment of offenders, offering four levels at which to evaluate and intervene in the problem.

Notes

1. Abel's sample included all types of sexual offenders. Child molesters, or pedophiles, were examined as a subgroup.
2. Racial demographics are representative only of the area in which the research was conducted.
3. Likewise, religious demographics are representative only of the area in which the research was conducted.

4. Other researchers have argued with how Abel tallied the number of offenses, since offenders who committed multiple acts were placed into multiple categories; thus, there is likely a good deal of overlap among categories. Moreover, since acts were counted individually, a single act of exhibitionism was counted or weighted the same as a rape. This is a good example of how incidence statistics—reflecting the total number of acts counted—are somewhat misleading. Consider that, although the *mean* number of acts committed by each offender in Abel's study was 218.7, the *median* was only 10.1.

5. Again, other researchers have argued against these high totals.

6. The summary of the Genesis II offender typology is presented with permission from Ruth Mathews and Jane Matthews, Genesis II, Minneapolis, MN. Copyright 1987.

7. *Willingness* is a relative term here. There is some degree of cooperation, since the boys know of one another's involvement and do not usually report the ongoing activity. However, the pederast certainly has some psychological hold on the children and perhaps even their parents, so there is some type of coercion at work.

Chapter Three

Adolescent Sexual Offenders

It has only been within the last 10 to 15 years that adolescent sexual offenders have been identified and studied as a group separate from adult offenders. And as this topic has emerged, we have learned not only that adolescent offenders have unique characteristics but that the dynamics of their offenses are also unique for the victim and the family.

In this chapter, we will describe the adolescent offender. First, we will examine general characteristics: age, sex, race, socioeconomic background, and criminal history. Then, we will discuss two typologies of adolescent offenders that have been produced by therapists at PHASE, a treatment program for adolescent sexual offenders.

Characteristics of Adolescent Offenders

Unfortunately, little is known about adolescent sexual offenders, in part, because the topic is relatively new, considering the longitudinal needs of most social science research. Other factors compound the problem, as well, making it difficult to gather and evaluate valid data.

As we discussed in Chapter 1, adolescent sexual offenders have historically not been taken seriously. Myths about sexual play and experimentation, along with stereotypes about supposedly normal male aggression, have been used to rationalize all but the most abusive and aggressive sexual offenses.

These misconceptions have been gradually dispelled as surveys of adult sexual offenders have revealed that the majority committed their first sexual assault as teenagers. In one study of 83 convicted rapists and 54 convicted child molesters, as many as 60% to 80% reported offending as adolescents. Most had been convicted more than once and admitted anonymously to having committed two to five times as many sexual offenses for which they were not arrested (Groth, Longo, & McFadin, 1982).

Myths about sexual experimentation were disproved even more when studies of adolescent sexual offenders provided alarming evidence about the numbers and types of offenses committed.

- In California in 1983, 2,575 people under 20 years old were arrested for felony sexual offenses; this constituted 24% of all felony arrests for sexual offense. Nearly 1,000 of these arrests were for forcible rape (Department of the Youth Authority, 1986).
- In Michigan in 1985, of 1,178 total referrals alleging child sexual abuse by a youth, 731 were substantiated (about 60%). This accounts for about 20% of the total number of substantiated sexual abuse cases in 1985 (Michigan Adolescent Sexual Abuser Project, 1988).
- In St. Paul in 1983, juveniles committed 40% of all sexual offenses, excluding prostitution (O'Brien & Bera, 1986).

What conclusion can be drawn from this information? Michael O'Brien and Walter Bera of PHASE make the point well: "Adolescent sexual offenders represent a serious social problem. Not only do they commit a relatively large number of sexual crimes . . . but these often represent the early stages of a developing sexual deviance that the adolescent carries into adult life" (O'Brien & Bera, 1986).

Early Research

Some of the first research on adolescent offenders dates back to the mid 1960s. Gebhard, Gagnon, Pomeroy, and Christenson (1965) studied nonadult victims and offenders in research that was more descriptive and less theoretical than previous work. They characterized the nonadult offender as alcoholic, mentally impaired or ill, and of low socioeconomic status. (As we will see later in this chapter, none of these conclusions is considered valid today; in fact, these observations are probably indicative of the type of adolescent who was reported for sexual offenses in the 1960s.) Gebhard et al. also found, however, that the nonadult offender was antisocial, impulsive, opportunistic, and prone to other criminal activity, conclusions that generally remain valid today.

Mohr, Turner, and Jerry (1964) and Amir (1971) looked at an overall age breakdown for sexual offenders and found that there were three general groupings: (1) adolescents, (2) middle adults, and (3) senescents. When the groups were studied according to victim type, the researchers found very different motivations and meanings for each age group. This research shattered the stereotype of the "dirty old man" sexual offender.

Later work by Kempe and Kempe (1984) and Schlesinger (1982) established that pedophiles are more active at certain ages. The first age group was from late adolescence into the early twenties. The adolescent pedophile was characterized as being sexually and psychologically immature; this delayed maturation may prevent him or her from seeking sexual experience with age peers and promote interest in sex with younger children.

During the 1980s, a number of studies of adolescent sexual offenders have been conducted by legislative and social service agencies of several states. Although their primary goal usually has been treatment oriented, they have also provided a wealth of descriptive information.

Demographics

To provide a sort of statistical picture of the adolescent offender and the crime he or she commits, we will review demographic information from two of the most recent and significant studies, *Sexual Offenses by Youth in Michigan* (Michigan Adolescent Sexual Abuser Project, 1988) and *Adolescent Sex Offenders in Vermont* (Wasserman & Kappel, 1985). In the next section, we will draw more general conclusions about individual and family variables.

The Vermont study was conducted by the state's Department of Health and surveyed adolescent offenders who became part of the caseload of either the Department of Social and Rehabilitation Services (SRS) or the Department of Corrections during 1984. Those juveniles had committed a sexual offense but had not necessarily been adjudicated or convicted of one. (The Vermont report acknowledges that its data are biased toward severity of offense—since most of the youths who come to the attention of the SRS and Corrections have committed serious acts of sexual abuse—and therefore the data cannot be applied to a general adolescent population.)

The methodology for the Michigan study was developed by the state's Adolescent Sexual Abuser Project and its advisory board. Data were obtained from three sources: Department of Social Services Children's Protective Services supervisors, court juvenile officers, and Department of Social Services community service workers. The adolescents involved were known to have committed sexual abuse and were on the active caseload of a Department of Social Services community service worker or a court juvenile officer during the summer/fall of 1986. (Again, the survey admits to a bias toward severity of offense and cannot be applied to adolescents in the general population.)

In both studies, offenders were placed in one of four categories based on the type of offense committed:

1. *Penetration*—The Vermont study specified penetration of the vagina or anus using the penis, a finger, or an object. The Michigan study included attempted penetration.

2. *Oral-genital acts*—Cunnilingus and fellatio

3. *Fondling*—Any touching of genitals, breasts, or other intimate parts of the body

4. *Noncontact offenses*—Obscene phone calling, voyeurism, exhibitionism, fetish burglary (e.g., stealing underwear), and sexual exploitation

In both studies, sexual offenses were categorized according to their degree of *invasiveness* (Vermont) or *intrusiveness* (Michigan): the more invasive or intrusive the act, the more serious. An offender who committed more than one type of act was placed in the "most serious" category.

The Vermont study used data on 161 offenders, ages 19 and younger (the youngest offender was 5). The Michigan study used data on 681 offenders, all under 18. Despite this slight difference in age definition, both report remarkably similar findings.

Offender Sex/Age

Over 92% were males (95% in the Michigan study). The median age was 14 (Michigan) or 15 (Vermont). In the Vermont study, the female offenders were slightly younger (median age = 13); in the Michigan study, there was no age difference between male and female offenders. The Michigan study also reported that the number of offenders increased rapidly between the ages of 9 and 14 and then declined quickly to age 17, after which offenders were legally adults.

Victim Sex/Age

The Vermont study found that over one-fourth of all victims were male. Male offenders chose female victims in over three-fourths of their offenses, while female offenders chose male victims in 11 out of 12 incidents. The Michigan study found that 36% of the victims age 10 and under were males; 14% of the victims over 10 were males.

The median age of victims in both studies was 7. In addition, in the Vermont study:

- Victims ranged in age from 2 to 60.
- Over two-thirds of the victims were 9 years old or younger.
- Offenders chose victims younger than themselves "almost exclusively."
- Offenders chose same-age victims in just 2% of the incidents.
- Victims were older in only 7% of all cases, and in 90% of these, a weapon or physical force was used by the offender (see "Use of Coercion" below).

Other findings in the Michigan study included:

- Two-thirds of the victims were 10 or younger.
- Offenders were older than victims in 85% of all cases.
- In nearly one of two cases, offenders were 7 years or more older than their victims.
- Where there was no age difference or the offender was younger, the threat or use of a weapon or force was present 70% of the time. Offenders who assaulted younger victims were more likely to use verbal threats.

Type of Offense

In both studies, penetration—the most serious act—was also the most common. Nearly 60% of the reported cases involved penetration; in the Vermont sample, more than half of these involved penile penetration. The incidences of the four categories of offenses were as follows:

	Vermont	Michigan
Penetration	59.2%	56.4%
Oral-genital	12.1%	18.2%
Fondling	16.5%	17%
Noncontact	12.1%	8.4%

The Vermont study found that the incidence of penetration—both in number and percentage of offenses—increased with the age of the offender. Over 60% of the offenses committed by 15- to 19-year-olds were acts of penetration. The Michigan study found no variation with the age of the offender.

Both studies found that the incidence of penetration did vary with the victim's age. The highest rate of penetration was committed against the youngest victims. Based on Vermont data, nearly 60% of the acts committed against victims 10 years and younger were acts of penetration. The Michigan study found a fairly steady proportion of penetration cases for victims aged 3 to 10; the incidence of penetration peaked with 11-year-olds and then declined unevenly.

Relationship to Victim

In the overwhelming majority of cases, the adolescent offender knew his victim (92% in the Vermont sample, 95% in the Michigan sample). The friend/acquaintance victim was the most common in both studies; about 40% of victims were relatives, either immediate or extended family members. The Vermont study found that the most common abusive familial relationships were brother/sister, stepbrother/stepsister, and cousin/cousin. Other data from the Michigan study are shown in Figure 3-1.

Use of Coercion

Coercion ranged from verbal threat to the threat or use of a weapon or force. Verbal threat, the most common method, was used in 56.9% of the cases in the Vermont sample. As mentioned above, offenders

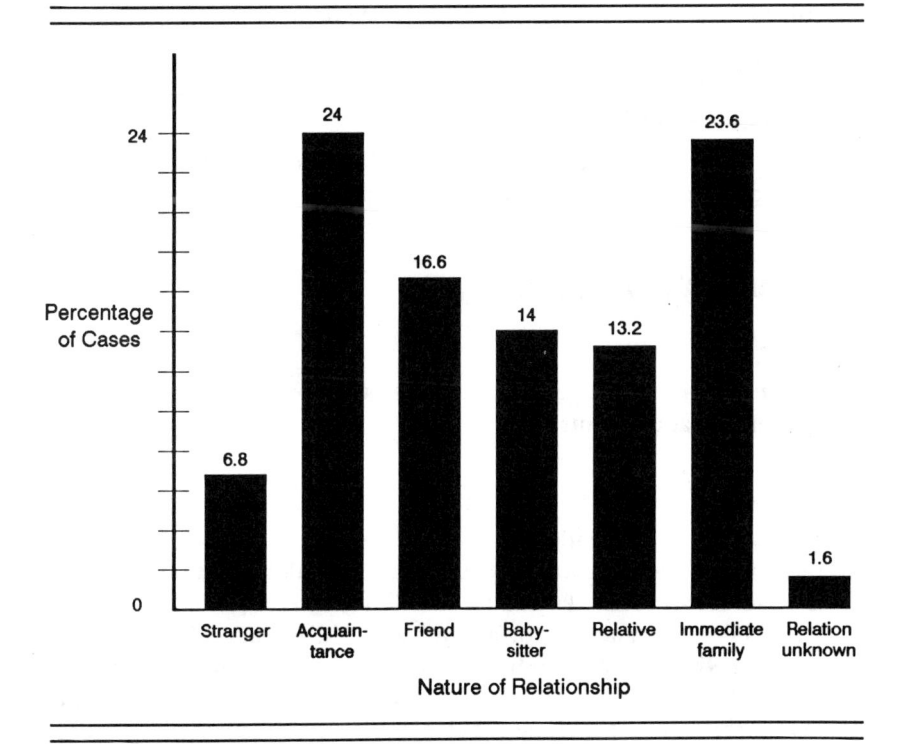

Figure 3-1 *Relationship of Offender to Victim*

[Bar chart: Percentage of Cases by Nature of Relationship]
- Stranger: 6.8
- Acquaintance: 24
- Friend: 16.6
- Babysitter: 14
- Relative: 13.2
- Immediate family: 23.6
- Relation unknown: 1.6

Source: Adapted with permission from Michigan Adolescent Sexual Abuser Project, *Sexual offenses by youth in Michigan: Data, implications, and policy recommendations* (Detroit: Safer Society Resources of Michigan, January 1988), Figure 6, p. 15.

who assault young children were more likely to use verbal threats, according to the Michigan study.

A weapon was used in 7.6% of the Vermont cases; of these 10 cases, 4 required hospitalizing the victim for major injury. Again, as mentioned above, offenders who assault older or same-age victims were very likely to use a weapon or force, according to the Michigan study.

Location of Offense

Only the Vermont study reported on this factor. Three-fourths of the incidents took place in a home. Of these, about 55% occurred in the victim's home, 22% occurred in the offender's home, and 16% occurred in a home they shared. The remainder (approximately 7%) took place in the homes of others.

Drug or Alcohol Use

Only the Vermont study reported on this factor. Alcohol or drugs were rarely involved, about 10% of the time.

Personal and Family Variables

Biological Traits

To date, no biological factors have been truly proven to cause sexual deviance in adolescents.

Psychological Traits

Most adolescent offenders are not mentally ill but emotionally troubled. Judith Becker and colleagues surveyed adolescent offenders at the New York State Psychiatric Institute; 97% reported they had never been hospitalized for a psychiatric illness, and 88% reported that immediate family members had never been hospitalized for such an illness (Becker, Cunningham-Rather, & Kaplan, 1986). A California task force report concluded that high-risk sexual offenders display addictive and compulsive tendencies (Department of the Youth Authority, 1986).

Academic Achievement

Many adolescent offenders are academic underachievers (de Young, 1982; Schlesinger, 1982). In a study of adolescent offenders in the PHASE program (see p. 72), 14% performed above average in school, 37% were average, and 49% were below average. Twenty-eight percent of these youth had repeated a grade, and 52% had been involved in some type of special education. In addition, 34% were classified as learning disabled and 8% were mentally retarded. (PHASE tries to exclude youths with known learning problems, so these figures are surprising.) Nineteen percent of the PHASE sample were diagnosed as having an attention-deficit disorder (ADD) (O'Brien, 1988).

Social Skills and Development

Most adolescent offenders display poor social skills and are unable to develop and maintain normal relationships, particularly heterosexual ones (Department of the Youth Authority, 1986). Many are loners who may prefer the company of children to that of age peers or adults, as children are not as intimidating (de Young, 1982). O'Brien (1988) found that, in the PHASE sample, 54% were unsocialized or undersocialized, 9.3% were pseudosocialized, and 25% were normal.

Becker has also described the cognitive distortions that characterize adolescent offenders. Erroneous and confused attitudes about sexuality, power, and relationships may lead to deviance when a youth suffers no consequences for wrongful behavior. Becker includes cognitive distortions as an element in her model of the development of deviant sexuality patterns (Becker, 1988).

Sexual Beliefs and Development

Many argue that it is difficult, if not impossible, to characterize normal adolescent sexuality. Problems with parental consent and personal confidentiality certainly do make it difficult to study the issue. Moreover, differences in cultural, social, and family norms all affect what constitutes normal sexuality.

We can, however, discuss adolescent sexuality in fairly broad terms. Sexual development is characterized by identifiable physical, emotional, and psychological changes. Although not all youths experience the same changes at the same time in their development, the general pattern is there. And because we can identify this pattern, we can also identify deviancy, again, in broad terms.

Adolescent offenders tend to be psychosexually immature, ignorant of normal sexual development and behavior. Their beliefs about sexuality are rooted in distorted myths and misconceptions that are promoted by their family and culture. Such distorted thinking is the root of sexual deviancy. Eventually, it may lead to acting on these thoughts, often through masturbatory aggressive fantasies, which "rehearse and heighten the offense" (Department of the Youth Authority, 1986, p. 8).

For more information on adolescent sexuality, consult the following resources: Blyth (1981); Burt and Meeks (1985); Katchadourian (1972); Santrock (1987); and Sarafino (1980).

Family Situation

Little research has been done on the families of adolescent offenders. In fact, most of what is available is based on studies of families in which sibling incest has occurred (intrafamilial abuse) (Becker, 1988; de Young, 1982; Finkelhor, 1980; Goldman & Wheeler, 1986; Meiselman, 1978; O'Brien, 1988). Although we must be careful about making generalizations to all adolescent offenders, several conclusions can be drawn about their families:

1. The parents are typically absent in one way or another. The father is often dead or gone as a result of divorce or separation or incapacity due to mental illness, alcoholism, or some other dysfunction. The mother is typically passive and ineffectual and completely unable to supervise her children. In cases where the mother is dead or absent, she is usually replaced by a stepmother or adoptive mother who never establishes a maternal bond with the children.

2. The parents lack any authority or supervisory ability. On the other hand, they may be very protective overall, even in light of their child's offenses; this protective pattern promotes denial and prevents the child from suffering the consequences of his or her behavior.

3. The family is often described as being *enmeshed, chaotic, dysfunctional,* or *disabled.* Communication among family members is poor, relationships are obscured, and little support is available for individual members.

4. The pervasive sexual attitude is puritanical and rigid; the mother is often especially rigid. However, children may be confused by promiscuous behavior or attitudes of family members.

5. Brothers often act as fathers, becoming demanding, argumentative, and coercive in using the power provided by the role reversal. Bribery, threats, or violence are frequently used against sisters to initiate incest. Finkelhor cites this as the most common type of family violence.

6. Paternal incest with a female sibling often precedes sibling incest, as the sons imitate their fathers. Daughters may be imitating weak, submissive mothers, as well.

7. The offenders themselves have often been abused, either physically or sexually. Becker cites prior physical and sexual abuse as

the two most consistent variables in the adolescent offender's profile. This may be part of a family history of abuse, in which the parents were abused as children, too.

The degree of family dysfunction usually correlates with the severity of the offense committed. Thus, in cases of minor offenses (e.g., a 13-year-old boy has been making obscene phone calls), the family may appear only slightly dysfunctional, perhaps unnoticeably so. Factors 4, 5, and 6 are especially descriptive of the incestuous family. We will discuss family dynamics in depth in Chapter 5.

Prior Criminal Involvement

The Vermont study found that only 16% of the youths had committed a previous *reported* sexual offense, most of which were either similar or less serious in nature. But this figure was believed to be a gross underestimate of actual previous offenses, due to reporting problems (Wasserman & Kappel, 1985).

Becker and colleagues surveyed 67 adolescent offenders. Nearly 72% said they had never committed a prior *nonsexual* crime. Nearly 80% reported being arrested once before for a *sexual* crime (Becker et al., 1986). O'Brien found that 42% of the PHASE adolescent sample had some type of previous delinquency: 31% had committed status offenses, 42.5% had committed property offenses, and 20.6% had committed crimes against persons (O'Brien, 1988).

Adjudication and Conviction

About one-fourth of the offenders in the Vermont sample were either adjudicated delinquent or convicted for a sexual offense (Wasserman & Kappel, 1985). The Michigan study considered adjudication in relation to the intrusiveness of the offense and found that, as the intrusiveness of the offense increased from noncontact to oral-genital to penetration, the percentage of cases adjudicated as sex-offense charges also increased. For instance, of the noncontact offenders, only 20% were adjudicated on sex-offense charges, while 70% of those who committed oral-genital and penetration offenses were adjudicated on sex-offense charges (Michigan Adolescent Sexual Abuser Project, 1988).

Treatment

Both the Michigan and Vermont studies reported an alarming lack of treatment for adjudicated and convicted adolescent sexual offenders. Less than 12% (about 20 of the total 161) of the Vermont sample received specialized treatment for having committed a sexual offense. Over 25% (40) received no treatment at all (Wasserman & Kappel, 1985). Over 60% of the Michigan sample were reported to have received no specialized treatment services. In over two-thirds of the cases, probation officers reported dissatisfaction with treatment options offered to the adolescent (Michigan Adolescent Sexual Abuser Project, 1988). In the Becker et al. study, 69% did admit to part or all of the deviant behavior for which they were referred. Becker speculated that that might mean adolescent sex offenders would be willing to participate in treatment (Becker et al., 1986).

Adolescent Offender Typologies

The PHASE Typology

The first typology we will examine was developed by Michael O'Brien and Walter Bera based on their work with over 350 male adolescent offenders at PHASE, the Program for Healthy Adolescent Sexual Expression.[1] PHASE was created in 1981 "in response to the increased awareness of the prevalence and seriousness of adolescent sexual offenses" (O'Brien & Bera, 1986, p. 2). It is an outpatient, family-centered program designed to assess and treat adolescents who have displayed sexually inappropriate or abusive behavior. PHASE's dual purpose is to treat and prevent sexually abusive behavior.

O'Brien and Bera observed that the adolescents at PHASE could be placed in seven separate categories. The PHASE typology, as it has become known, is intended as a therapeutic and research tool, providing concrete behavioral descriptions, personal and family variables, and motivations for each of the seven categories. It is a framework from which to develop appropriate treatment strategies for each type of offender.

Each of the following sections will begin with a short case study that illustrates the offender type. A discussion of the general characteristics of the type will follow.

Type 1: The Naive Experimenter

Johnny is a 13-year-old boy who had been asked to babysit a neighbor girl, age 5, named Nicky. Johnny had been babysitting for only a short time and the situation was still new to him. While there he discovered a Playboy magazine hidden under the couch and Johnny found the explicit photographs arousing. While helping Nicky change into her pajamas he wanted to see what it was like to kiss and touch her in the way depicted in the photographs. After a short time he felt guilty and stopped. Later that week Nicky told her mother and Johnny was arrested for criminal sexual conduct. (p. 2)

The naive experimenter is usually young, 11 to 14 years old. His social skills and peer relationships are adequate. He is sexually naive and has little history of acting out behaviors. The abuse seems to have been situationally determined (i.e., occurred during babysitting, family gathering, camping, etc.).

This type of offender may be involved in a single or a few isolated acts of sexual exploration with young children (2 to 6 years old). He does not usually use force or make threats. His primary motivation is to explore and experiment with newly developing sexual feelings.

Type 2: The Undersocialized Child Exploiter

Jerry, age 16, had no close peer relationships and only a few school acquaintances. He could be considered a loner, and he spent a good portion of his time watching television or playing video games at home. He was well-liked by his parents and was no trouble at home or at school. When playing outside he was often by himself or with considerably younger children.

In the course of playing with younger children he became involved with them sexually and required fondling and oral-genital contact as an initiation rite for membership in a club he had formed. No threats or force were used, but he did maintain secrecy with the children by telling them not to tell their parents. One of the children told a teacher and Jerry was arrested for criminal sexual conduct. (p. 2)

The undersocialized child exploiter suffers from "chronic social isolation." He has few friends his own age and seeks out younger children who admire and accept him. He is controlled by feelings of inadequacy and insecurity. He has little history of acting out socially.

His family is often characterized by an overinvolved mother and a distant father.

The abusive behavior of this type of offender may involve a chronic pattern of activities, including the use of manipulation, trickery, enticement, and rewards. Typically, the victim is a young child who is available in a babysitting, neighborhood play, or family situation. The offender is motivated by the need for intimacy, self-importance, self-esteem, self-identity, or autonomy.

Type 3: The Pseudo-Socialized Child Exploiter

Norm was a 17-year-old boy, the youngest of six children. He was an exceptional achiever: an A student and in the top bracket of students completing the SAT. This religious and college-bound youth had also engaged in kissing, oral-genital sex and penis-vaginal rubbing with a niece 6 years younger than he.

The abuse events occurred regularly over a three-year period and it appeared he had trained her into a victim role and coaxed her to remain silent. Vaginal redness led to questions by the girl's physician and her final disclosure. The entire family was grievously shocked when Norm was arrested for criminal sexual conduct. (p. 3)

The pseudo-socialized child exploiter is usually an older adolescent. He has good social skills and is comfortable but not intimate with his peers. He appears confident and secure in most arenas; he is often intellectually gifted and a hard worker. He has little or no history of acting out socially. He may be a victim himself of early childhood abuse—physical, sexual, or emotional—or neglect. His role in the family is often that of a "parentified child."

The pseudo-socialized offender often goes undetected and unreported for several years. He is able to rationalize his abusive behavior and feels little remorse or guilt. In particular, he characterizes the sexual activity as being mutual, intimate, and noncoercive. His motivation for sex appears to be "a guiltless and narcissistic exploitation of a vulnerable child to gain sexual pleasure" (p. 3). It is very possible that the pseudo-socialized child exploiter will become a lifelong pedophile or pathological narcissist if appropriate treatment is not provided.

Type 4: The Sexual Aggressive

> Troy, age 15, was a victim of severe physical abuse at the hands of his stepfather, his mother's third husband. The mother was passive and often suffered from physical beatings from her husband as well. Troy had a history of fire-setting, theft, vandalism and truancy over several years.
>
> Very social and flamboyant, he took a 14-year-old girl out on a date and when she refused to "go all the way," Troy slapped her and forced her to perform oral sex by threatening her with a screwdriver. When Troy released her, she made her way home and told her mother what happened. Troy was arrested later that evening by police for first-degree criminal sexual conduct. (p. 3)

The sexual aggressive is typically from a disorganized and abusive family. He has good peer-age social skills and may even be charming and gregarious. But he also has a long history of antisocial behaviors and impulse-control problems; he often fights with family members and friends. He is likely to abuse chemicals, as well.

This type of offender usually employs threats or violence against his victim, who may be a peer, an adult, or a child. Results from psychological tests usually portray an antisocial and character-disordered youth. He uses sex to gain personal power through dominating, humiliating, and expressing anger toward his victim. In extreme cases, the sexual aggressive may actually have a learned sexual response to violence, such that violence alone is sexually arousing and committing violence enhances sexual pleasure.

Type 5: The Sexual Compulsive

> David, age 16, was a football player and a good student. His mother was a traditional homemaker and his father was often gone, working two shifts in a hospital. David committed a series of exposing incidents in front of high school girls near his school and was identified and arrested by the police. In the course of therapy it was discovered that he had exposed himself numerous times to his older sister who kept it a secret and just yelled at him. The total abuse history spanned a two-year period. (p. 3)

The sexual compulsive is often caught up in a family that is rigidly enmeshed. The parents are emotionally repressed and unable to show intimacy. The offender is unable to express negative emotions in a clear, straightforward manner. He often engages in a repetitive, sexually arousing behavior that is compulsive or addictive. He usually commits noncontact offenses, such as window peeping, obscene phone calling, exhibitionism, and fetish burglary (e.g., stealing women's underwear).

The sexual compulsive usually acts alone; his offense has been planned. He may enjoy a reinforcing mood swing while committing the offense; he may also feel that some ongoing anxiety or tension has been relieved. He often masturbates during or after the incident to achieve orgasm.

Type 6: The Disturbed Impulsive

>Bill, age 15, was living with his father who had won custody of him and his sister after bitter divorce proceedings. He had grown up in a house where there was always tension and anxiety as a result of the marital discord, and he generally learned to keep to himself. One day while taking the vacuum cleaner from his sister's closet he turned to his sister who was sitting in her underwear and attempted to mount her while she screamed "Stop! Stop!" Finally she pushed him off and he seemed to "come to his senses," grabbed the vacuum cleaner and left to complete his household chores. Because of the family tension the sister kept the event quiet.
>
>A second incident occurred with a girlfriend of his sister's, whom Bill accosted suddenly while ice skating with her, grabbing her breast and buttocks. This incident was reported to the police and he was questioned and left to the custody of his father. He was finally arrested after accosting an adult female in the laundry room of his mother's apartment building. Again, the assault was sudden and unpredictable. He was subsequently placed in a psychiatric hospital. (p. 4)

The disturbed impulsive often has a history of problems involving psychological factors, severe family discord, substance abuse, and severe learning difficulties. His sexual abuse is highly impulsive, "reflecting an acute disturbance of reality testing" (p. 4). It may be a single, unpredictable, uncharacteristic incident, or it may be part of a series of bizarre or ritualistic acts against adults, peers, and/or children. The disturbed impulsive may abuse because normal inhibitory mechanisms fail, due perhaps to mental disorder or chemical abuse. His motivation is highly complex and must be individually determined.

Type 7: The Group-Influenced Offender

Greg, age 13, was a lonely boy whose only friend was Travis, age 14. One evening they went to a neighbor's house after the parents had left. While there, Travis encouraged the group that included Greg, a 12-year-old boy and his 11-year-old sister to engage in a game of "strip poker." The boys began kissing and fondling the girl when her brother went to the bathroom. Both boys told her not to tell but the next morning she told her parents. Both Travis and Greg were arrested for sexual misconduct. (p. 4)

The group-influenced offender is typically a younger teenager who has not been involved with the juvenile justice system before. The abuse occurs with a group of peers present; the victim is usually known by the offenders. The offender defers responsibility for the incident to the victim and/or to his peer participants.

This type of offender is clearly motivated by peer pressure. He may be a "follower" and act to meet others' expectations, or he may be a "leader" and act to gain others' approval or attention.

Conclusion

O'Brien and Bera stress that the PHASE typology is a "working typology" that has been expanded and refined from an initial two-type classification and will certainly continue to be refined further. Nonetheless, it remains a useful, tangible guide for those individuals working with adolescent offenders in a variety of situations.

The Female Adolescent Offender Typology

Ruth Mathews and Jodie Newell Raymaker, also associated with the PHASE program, have developed a typology of female offenders based on their work as therapists over the past several years. Their typology examines offenders who are self-initiated versus those who are manipulated or coerced into offending by others.[2]

Self-Initiated Offenders

Type 1: Exploration/Exploitation. The exploring/exploiting adolescent female offender is 16 or younger. She is nervous, self-deprecating, and socially isolated. She is extremely sensitive and respectful of sexual acceptance concerns. Although she lacks social skills, her school performance is typically average to excellent.

The exploring/exploiting offender most often commits just one act of abuse. Her victim is usually a young male nonsibling (less than 6 years old), perhaps someone she is babysitting. The abuse is detached, nonintimate, and nonemotional; she may fondle the child but is unlikely to ask for stimulation in return. The offender's exploration is mechanical and "fragmented from [her] sense of self." That is, the offender is unaware of or denies her sexual arousal, often out of fear of where sexual interest will lead her (i.e., feeling aroused may make her unable to resist male sexual advances).

Type 2: Severe Abuse History/Personality Disordered. The female adolescent offender with a history of abuse has usually been physically and/or sexually abused by male family members. As a result, she has developed a number of personality problems (e.g., low self-esteem, inhibitedness, alienation, paranoia) and has often followed a self-destructive course that includes drinking, drug abuse, running away, and even attempted suicide. Given the dysfunction that characterizes her family, she is usually without security or care. For all these reasons, this girl is likely to be a poor student.

The abused/personality disordered offender typically abuses a child with whom she has a relationship: a relative, foster sibling, or neighbor. The victim is usually female and under 10 years old. The type of abuse may range from fondling or exposing to more forceful acts of oral sex or digital penetration. This type of offender has few victims, but the abuse usually occurs more than once with the same victim and may be ritualized. The abuse is a reenactment of the offender's own abuse as a child, it seems, as the youth identifies with her aggressor or perhaps somehow attempts to validate her victimization through abusing others. The abused/personality disordered offender is likely to self-report the abuse, often during therapy for other problems.

Manipulated/Coerced Offender

Type 3: Male-Coerced. This female offender is intimidated into commiting sexual abuse by a male, usually a peer. Often, she resists and is coerced and threatened by the male until she agrees to participate. The behavior is uncharacteristic of the young woman, who is fairly normal in psychological and social terms. She may be somewhat dependent and struggling with issues of peer security.

The male initiates the sexual abuse and involves the female in assisting him. The victim is usually a peer. Because this type of behavior is so uncharacteristic of the offender, it usually occurs just once.

Summary

It has only been within the last 10 to 15 years that adolescents have been recognized as a unique group of sexual offenders. Studies of adults, which indicated that their deviance typically began before or during adolescence, as well as increases in the number and severity of offenses committed by youths have been significant factors in dispelling the myths and stereotypes historically used to rationalize and deny the problem of adolescent sexual offenders.

A general demographic profile can be provided. Typically, the offender is a male youth, age 14 or 15. His victim is 7 years old, on average, and is usually female. The victim is usually a friend or acquaintance; sometimes she is a sister, stepsister, or cousin. The most common offense is penetration; verbal threat is used most often as a means of coercion.

A number of personal and social variables also characterize the adolescent offender. He or she is not usually mentally ill but emotionally troubled. He or she is usually not of below-average intelligence but performs poorly in school. And he or she is generally immature, particularly in social skills and sexual development, which leads to social isolation and difficulty interacting with age peers.

Family variables are also significant. The family situation is often described as *dysfunctional* or *chaotic*. The father is typically absent from the family; he may be dead or simply gone due to divorce or separation; or he may be incapacitated from alcoholism or mental illness. The mother is typically passive and ineffectual and unable to control her children. A family history of abuse—sexual and physical—is often identified.

The adolescent sexual offender often goes undetected and unreported. And when he or she is reported, incarceration rarely results. In fact, in the majority of cases, the youth receives no treatment at all or at least no treatment specific to the nature of the offense.

Moving beyond statistics and general characteristics, two typologies from the PHASE program classify adolescent offenders. The first typology, by O'Brien and Bera, includes seven categories of adolescent offenders: (1) the naive experimenter; (2) the undersocialized child exploiter; (3) the pseudo-socialized child exploiter; (4) the sexual aggressive; (5) the sexual compulsive; (6) the disturbed impulsive; and (7) the group-influenced offender. The second typology, by Mathews and Raymaker, characterizes three types of female adolescent offenders: (1) the exploring/exploiting offender; (2) the abused/personality disordered offender; and (3) the male-coerced offender.

Notes

1. The section on the PHASE typology was excerpted from an article written by Michael O'Brien and Walter Bera entitled "Adolescent Sex Offenders: A Descriptive Typology" that originally appeared in *Preventing Sexual Abuse* in the Fall of 1986, ETR Associates, Santa Cruz, CA. All rights reserved by Michael O'Brien and Walter Bera.

2. The summary of the adolescent female offenders typology is reprinted with permission from Ruth Mathews and Jodie Newell Raymaker, PHASE Program, Maplewood, MN. Copyright 1987.

Chapter Four

Victims of Child Sexual Abuse

On the surface, much of the information available about the victims of child sexual abuse seems to make sense. That is, the shared assumptions about these victims—that they are mostly girls, that they come from all socioeconomic levels, that they will be affected by being abused throughout their lives in predictable ways—seem to be understood and accepted by most people as reasonable explanations for the causes and effects of abuse. These generalized assumptions about who is likely to be victimized and how they are likely to be affected are treated as truth and communicated and accepted as facts. But, in fact, few of these assumptions have been proven. And although research does not prove that they are completely invalid, it is premature to accept these observations as anything more than that.

Our purpose in this chapter will be to review the available information and determine its empirical validity. We will describe those characteristics, or risk factors, that are common to sexually abused children. A discussion of boy victims will conclude the victim-description section. In the next section, we will look at risk factors for trauma, a topic of some research concern. We will then move to a discussion of the commonly observed effects of sexual abuse, both immediate and long term. To conclude, we will present another model of sexual abuse by David Finkelhor, this time looking at a series of traumagenic factors.

Description of Victims: Risk Factors for Child Sexual Abuse

While many people still believe that only specific groups of children are at risk for sexual abuse, the reality is that sexual abuse is found consistently in most social classes and family circumstances. Because sexual abuse is so prevalent, researchers have devoted a good deal of study to characterizing the typical victim, in part to help identify and prevent future sexual abuse.

Before we proceed, a caveat: Most of the data about victims of child sexual abuse are based on females—actual girl victims or women who were victimized as children. Unless boys are specified in the discussion of victims in this chapter, assume that the information applies to girls. As mentioned, we will discuss boy victims specifically later in this chapter.

The Victim

Sex

More girls than boys are sexually abused. Some researchers estimate that four times as many girls as boys are abused (Murphy, 1985), while others estimate only $1\frac{1}{2}$ times as many (Fritz, Stall, & Wagner, 1981). Still another group feels that boys are victimized as often as girls (Kempe & Kempe, 1984; Plummer, 1984), but their beliefs have not been verified. A representative or average estimate is that $2\frac{1}{2}$ times as many girls are victimized as boys, which means that nearly three-fourths of all victims are girls (Finkelhor & Baron, 1986). The number of boy victims has increased somewhat in recent years, but this is believed to demonstrate a change in reporting and not necessarily incidence.

Age

The most vulnerable age for children is between 8 and 12 years, the preadolescent period.[1] In addition, vulnerability increases dramatically at the ages of 6 or 7 years and 10 years. The most acute age, however, is 10 to 12 years, during which time the rate of sexual abuse is nearly double the average rate (Finkelhor & Baron, 1986).

Surveys in which the sample is actual reported cases of sexually abused children generally report a slightly higher median age than those in which adult samples are used. However, the age reported is the age of the child at the time of the report, which was made sometime after the abuse occurred. Moreover, older children are more likely to report (especially girls), so they will be more represented in samples of reporting victims (Finkelhor & Baron, 1986).

The risk of abuse for adolescent girls may actually decrease at puberty (age 12 or 13), at which time girls may have the knowledge and ability to react to and resist victimization. This assertiveness may also explain increased reporting by adolescent girls. Not only do these girls want to protect themselves from abuse, but their fears of venereal disease, pregnancy, and other health problems may prompt them to seek help (Chandler, 1982).

Findings about victims younger than 6 or 7 years old may be questionable because these children lack the cognitive framework to understand what happened. Also, since many victim samples are adults looking back, it is likely that memories of that early age may be vague. The adult may also have repressed or forgotten what happened (Finkelhor & Baron, 1986).

Socioeconomic Status

One of the most popular stereotypes about the victim of sexual abuse is that he or she is from a lower-class family. While sexual abuse is not limited to any socioeconomic group, it is not necessarily unrelated to class. The conditions of poverty, unemployment, and broken homes may contribute to the problem even if they do not directly cause it (Finkelhor & Baron, 1986).

The consensus of most research is that there is no correlation between socioeconomic status (SES) and child sexual abuse. Some studies that employ reported victims as samples show that low-SES children are at slightly more risk, but remember that such samples typically overrepresent the poor and underprivileged (Finkelhor & Baron, 1986).

Ethnicity

Finkelhor has described child sexual abuse as being highly "democratic," in that it does not discriminate racially. In short, there are no black versus white differences. The prevalence of black victims is equal to the percentage of blacks in the U.S. population (approximately 11%) (Finkelhor & Baron, 1986).

There are also few black/white differences in the types of abuse that are committed and the effects it has on the children. Interestingly, there are some risk factors for white children that are not risk factors for black children, including separation from father, change in caretaker, and mother working (Peters, 1984).

Little research has addressed child sexual abuse in other ethnic groups, but Russell (1986) did consider race in her study of incest victims. Child sexual abuse (and especially incest) was slightly higher for Hispanics. Rates were lower for Jewish and Asian samples.

See also the discussion of multicultural concerns for treatment at the end of Chapter 5.

Social Isolation

The issue of social isolation is interesting for two reasons: (1) high rates of child sexual abuse are frequently reported in rural areas, and (2) social isolation has correlated in some research with other types of child abuse and neglect.

The research on sexual abuse in rural areas is definitely divided. Finkelhor (1984) found a high rate (44%) of child sexual abuse in his survey of college women who grew up on farms. Russell (1986) also found rates of incest to be higher in rural areas and small towns (17% and 20%, respectively) than in urban areas (14%). But other researchers have found lower rates in rural areas (Miller, 1976; Wyatt, 1985), which means that no strong conclusions can be drawn here.

The general concept of social isolation, in the sense that certain children are loners and withdrawn, has also been examined. Finkelhor (1984) found that women who reported having fewer than two friends at the age of 12 were more likely to have been abused. Other studies have supported the notion that sexual abuse victims are isolated from their peers and that they may lack close relations with their siblings, as well. Children with few friends will most likely seek attention from adults and thus have greater contact and chance of being abused (Finkelhor & Baron, 1986).

It is also possible that victimized children may have fewer friends as a *result* of their abuse. Feelings of shame and guilt, as well as threats from the offender about contact with others (as is common in incest cases), may lead to self-isolation (Finkelhor & Baron, 1986).

Family Background

Income Level. Reported child abuse (the general category, not specifically child sexual abuse) has been described as "a heavily lower-class phenomenon" (Finkelhor, 1984, p. 163). According to a 1979 NCCAN study, the average income of families in which child abuse was reported was $8,435, which was well below the national average of $19,661.

Sexual abuse is the most middle-class type of child abuse. The average income of families in which sexual abuse was reported was $9,285, some 10% higher than that for general child abuse families. The median income for families in which father/daughter incest was discovered was even higher, making this perhaps the most middle-class type of sexual abuse (Brown & Holder, 1980).

Social Isolation. Sexually abusive families are often socially isolated from the community. The parents have few interests or relationships outside the home, and they often discourage the children from outside involvement, as well. The isolated family operates as a closed system and shuts out the types of social support normally available. Such a family may view the outside world as hostile, which makes intervention for any reason difficult (McCabe, Cohen, & Weiss, 1985).

Parental Relationships. Characteristics of parental relationships, which describe the child victim's background, are believed to be the strongest predictors of sexual abuse. Four factors are significant:

1. *Parental absence and availability*—Girls who live without their natural mothers and fathers are more likely to be abused at some time during their childhood. Separation from the mother is especially critical; the risk is three times greater (Finkelhor, 1984). Regarding incest, separation from the natural father has been found to be critical (Finkelhor, 1984; Fromuth, 1983; Peters, 1984).

Parental availability covers a number of issues. Children whose mothers are employed outside the home are at greater risk for abuse than those whose mothers remain home (Fromuth, 1983; Landis, 1956; Peters, 1984; Russell, 1986); this is especially predictive when a stepfather is present (Russell, 1986). Several factors may be involved here. For instance, the mother may work long or odd hours, leaving the children alone or in someone else's care, or perhaps her work demands a lot of her attention and energy, such that she is unaware of problems at home. The real issue, however, is the amount of supervision the child receives and not just whether the mother works outside the home (Finkelhor, 1984).

The parents' health is also a factor. Children with disabled, sick, addicted, or emotionally dysfunctional mothers are at greater risk (Finkelhor, 1984; Peters, 1984).

2. *Poor parental relationships*—One of the most consistent research findings to date is that a poor relationship with the mother is predictive of child sexual abuse. In addition to the emotional trauma such a distant relationship creates, there is the problem that a girl who is not close to her mother will lack important communication about sex and protecting herself from abuse (Landis, 1956). This does not mean specifically a lack of sex education, since girls who have been abused versus those who have not received the same amount of instruction (or lack thereof, according to Finkelhor) from their parents (Finkelhor, 1984).

Also regarding sex education, repressive sexual attitudes and practices backfire in terms of protecting children from abuse: Girls whose mothers are repressive and punitive about sex are more vulnerable to abuse. "It is possible that girls most bombarded with sexual prohibitions and punishments have the hardest time developing realistic standards about what constitutes danger" (Finkelhor, 1984, p. 27). Children who are forbidden normal sexual exploration are easy prey for opportunistic adults.

A higher rate of child sexual abuse is also observed in families in which the father is very strict and conservative regarding male/female roles; girls who are raised to be subordinate and obedient will have a hard time resisting abuse even though they know it is wrong. This type of father is probably unaffectionate and physically distant, as well, which may make the girls starved for affection and ignorant about what is appropriate (Finkelhor, 1984). Finally, children who have fathers who are physically abusive are also at greater risk for sexual abuse (Fromuth, 1983).

Sexual abuse may also be a factor in creating poor parent/child relationships. The sexually abused child may become estranged from his or her family because of feelings of shame and even betrayal (i.e., no one protected him or her). This is very likely in cases of incest, especially if the offending parent has been removed from the home (Finkelhor & Baron, 1986).

3. *Conflicts between parents*—Children of parents who are not happily married and who show little affection for one another will most likely be emotionally disturbed, to some degree. In particular, they may have low feelings of self-worth and crave attention from any source. Given the parents' marital dysfunction, it is likely that these children lack supervision, which makes them even more vulnerable. Finally, if the general family atmosphere is cold and closed, children are not likely to receive much instruction and guidance at home, and they are not likely to report abuse for fear of not being supported.

The marital conflict that may result after incest is discovered may be very traumatic for the child. He or she may feel responsible, especially if the offending parent has been removed and the parents break up (Finkelhor & Baron, 1986).

There is an interesting correlation between parents' educational levels and child sexual abuse. Namely, in families where the wife is much less educated than the husband, the daughters are much more vulnerable to sexual abuse, even more so than in families where both parents are poorly educated (44% versus 30%). In theory, a woman who is much less educated than her husband will be oppressed and dependent and will serve as a negative role model for her daughters, who will learn to be passive and obedient (Finkelhor, 1984).

4. *Presence of a stepfather*—There is no doubt that the presence of a stepfather increases the chances for all types of child sexual abuse (Finkelhor, 1980; Gruber & Jones, 1983; Miller, 1976). Most notably, the chance for father/daughter abuse increases dramatically. Russell (1986) found that just over 2% of the surveyed women who lived with their natural fathers had been abused by them, compared with nearly 20% of those who lived with and were abused by their stepfathers. Finkelhor (1984) concluded that the presence of a stepfather more than doubled a girl's chance of being sexually abused. What's more, the type of abuse committed becomes more serious, including more acts of intercourse, oral sex, and anal sex. There are several theories about this phenomenon.

    a. The lack of strong social taboos and protective paternal feelings reduces a stepfather's inhibitions about having sex with his daughter. Stepfathers are five times more likely to abuse their daughters than are natural fathers.

    b. Girls living without their natural fathers are often in contact with more men. Mothers may bring home opportunistic dates, and stepfamily relationships involve contact with more relatives and acquaintances, few of whom may have any genuine interest in the child's welfare. Girls living with stepfathers are five times more likely to be abused by their parents' friends than are girls living with their natural fathers.

    c. A certain type of mother—one who is continually in and out of relationships and who becomes involved with sexually predatory men—may place her children in jeopardy. Even if the mother remarries, her selection of a partner will probably fit this pattern (Finkelhor, 1984).

Refer to Chapter 5 for a more thorough discussion of family dynamics.

The Nature of the Abuse

A 1986 study by Conte, Berliner, and Schuerman surveyed 369 children from a sexual assault center in order to assess the early effects of abuse on children and to identify factors associated with variations in those effects. In response to questions about the nature of the abuse, the following data were gathered.

The Offender

- Ninety-five percent of the children had been abused by a male offender, 4% by a female offender, and 1% by both male and female offenders.
- The offender was a stranger to the child in only 3.8% of the cases. In 12.5% of the cases, the offender was a friend of the victim or his or her family. In 10% of the cases, the offender was a neighbor. In 16% of the cases, the offender was the child's natural parent.
- At the time of the abuse, nearly half the child victims lived with the offender. In 28% of the cases, other children in the household were known to have been abused, as well.

The Abuse

- Twenty-four percent of the child victims were abused just once, 43% were abused over a limited period of time, and 25% were abused chronically (over an extended period of time).
- On average, each child was exposed to 3.5 types of sexual behavior. Only 20% were exposed to only one behavior.[2]
- A threat of harm to the victim or others was made in one-third of the cases. The victim was told the behavior was acceptable in one-fourth of the cases. Sixty percent of the children feared negative consequences to themselves if they revealed the abuse.

- In 52% of the cases, the child passively submitted to the abuse; in 39%, the child made an effort to resist; and in 27%, the child pretended the abuse was not happening.
- The children suffered no medical problems in three-fourths of the cases.
- Half the children believed the abuse was the offender's responsibility, not theirs. But nearly the same proportion of children claimed partial responsibility.

Reporting

- The abuse was reported to some child protective service in 83% of the cases and to the appropriate police agency in 93% of the cases.
- Most children reported the abuse and were interviewed quite soon after the last assault: nearly one-third came in between two days and two weeks afterward, and one-fourth came in two weeks to six months afterward.
- In 32% of the cases, the adult/parent elicited the report from the child, and in 30% of the cases, the child initiated the report to the adult/parent.
- Nearly all the primary parents (90%) believed the child. In only 30% of the cases was the child pressed to recant.

Boy Victims

Very little research has been done on sexually abused boys, primarily because so few cases are reported. Not only, then, is there little data available to study, but there is also little pressure to conduct research because it *appears* that boys are rarely abused.

Another reason for the lack of research on boy victims is that much of the investigation of sexual abuse of all types has been sponsored by the women's rights movement, which means that the emphasis has been placed on the abuse of females by males. Boys have been similarly neglected by the large body of research that has focused on incest; the goal of such research has been to develop a classic model of abuse, which has identified a girl victim (Finkelhor, 1984).

More cases of boy victims have been reported in recent years, however, and there appears to be new interest in studying these youths. Research on boys addresses two questions in particular: (1) How widespread is the sexual abuse of boys? and (2) How does the sexual abuse of boys compare to that of girls?

Defining Sexual Abuse

Researchers hesitate to define *sexual abuse* for boys in the same way that they define it for girls, namely, because two presumptions are made: (1) that boys play a part in initiating the sex and (2) that abuse does not affect boys as negatively as girls.

Neither of these conditions should be assumed, since there is little evidence to support either. The offender initiates the sex in an estimated 91% of boy-target cases (versus 98% of girl-target cases), and although boys generally rate less trauma than girls (38% versus 66%), most describe their abuse as a negative experience. More boys than girls do cite feelings of sexual interest and even pleasure from the abuse, but the long-term effects of being abused are comparable for both sexes or perhaps even greater for boys (Finkelhor, 1984).

We are dealing once again with stereotypes. The presumption that boys initiate and enjoy the sex is rooted in the male sex ethic, which portrays youthful sexuality as being positive, exploratory, and adventuresome. Boys who adhere to this ethic may not report their abuse, and if they do, the incident may be interpreted according to this standard and dismissed as normal.

What's more, the stereotype of the seductive boy may be perpetuated as part of a weak attempt to vindicate homosexual pedophilia. Granted, there have been reports of boys who have been willingly recruited by pedophilic networks or who have initiated the seduction of adult males, but stories such as these are greatly exaggerated. Passive compliance cannot be interpreted as consent (Finkelhor, 1979).

Prevalence

It is understandably difficult to estimate the prevalence of sexual abuse among boys. Studies that have included boy victims have estimated the prevalence to be anywhere from 2.5% to 8.7% (Bell & Weinberg, 1978, 1981; Finkelhor, 1979). When these figures are adjusted for definitional differences, an average range of 2.5% to

5% is produced. This means that, each year, between 46,000 and 92,000 boys under the age of 13 are sexually abused (Finkelhor, 1984).

Reporting

All sources who report child sexual abuse encounter boy victims, but general population surveys and police reports include more boys than do clinical or social service agencies. The likely explanation for this is that social service agencies and hospitals see a lot of incest cases, which involve primarily girl victims. Girls more commonly receive medical attention after abuse to substantiate rape and test for disease and pregnancy. Finally, girls are more often referred for treatment, so they will show up more in clinical samples.

Boys, on the other hand, seldom report, and when they do, it is most likely to the police. The police are usually called in to investigate the most serious incidents of extrafamilial abuse, most often by a stranger. The number of cases of boys being referred to clinics has increased, however. Before 1980, most clinics saw just a few boy victims each year, but in 1984, the proportion of boy victims was estimated at one-third (Finkelhor, 1984).

Why is the sexual abuse of boys so underreported? Once again, consider the male sex ethic and its credo of self-reliance. When boys are hurt, they are less likely to get help because they are supposed to be able to take care of themselves. This applies to being sexually abused, as well, so the rule is not to complain and not to ask for help. Only one-fourth of abused boys tell someone of their abuse versus one-third of abused girls.

The stigma of homosexuality is another substantial pressure for boys. The victim will question his masculinity, afraid that being molested by a man has made him homosexual or that he must already be homosexual if he has attracted a man's sexual attention. He will be reluctant to report because, should his peers find out, he would be labeled a homosexual. Parents have these fears, too, which they may repress by refusing to discuss the issue or report the abuse. As a result, the boy is never given the information or assurance he needs to work through this trauma (Finkelhor, 1984).

The Victim

Age. There are mixed data describing the average age of the sexually abused boy. In an American Humane Association study (AHA, 1981),

32% of the boy victims were less than 6 years old, compared to 18% of the girls. Only one-fourth of the boy victims were 13 or older, compared to nearly half of the girls. The median age of boy victims was 8.46 years versus 12.4 years for girls.

Finkelhor has estimated that almost 40% of boy victims are less than 6 years old when the abuse is reported (1984). In his Boston public survey, the median ages of children who reported abuse to their parents were 7.9 years for boys and 8.9 years for girls. But the median ages found for the parents who reported having been abused as children were 11.4 for boys and 9.7 for girls (reported in 1984). Finkelhor's college survey (1979) also found the median age for boys to be older than that for girls: 11.2 years versus 10.2 years.

These discrepancies can be explained in part by differences in definitions used by researchers. Some studies report the age of the victim at the time the case was investigated, not when the abuse occurred or first began. For example, in the AHA study (1981), girl victims had typically endured intrafamilial abuse for a number of years and were thus older when their cases were evaluated. Boy victims were more often abused by someone outside the family, so if their abuse was discovered and reported, it was at an earlier age.

Boy/girl reporting differences also help explain the discrepancies. As mentioned earlier, older girls are more likely to report being abused, for several reasons: self-assertiveness, fear of pregnancy or disease, and a desire for help and support. Older boys, on the other hand, are less likely to report because the sexual ethics and fears mentioned above become more pronounced with age (Finkelhor, 1984).

In sum, the difference between the median ages of sexually abused boys and girls may be the result of reporting differences. Before such a difference can be identified with certainty, we need more information on how a child's age and sex affects his or her risk for sexual abuse and likelihood to report.

Family Background. Sexually abused boys are more typical of the general abuse family than the more specific sexual abuse family (see "Family Background" in the earlier discussion of victim characteristics). Sexually abused boys more often come from poor, broken homes: Over 60% of these families receive public assistance (versus 40% of girls' families), and nearly half are headed by single parents (versus one-third of girls' families). Many of these single parents are women who have never married or who are divorced or separated; most are poorly educated and work at low-paying jobs, which explains their lower-class status (reported in Finkelhor, 1984).

Sexually abused boys also suffer more physical abuse. Twenty percent of the boys reported physical abuse in their families, versus just 5% of the girls. The investigation of physical abuse often leads to the discovery of sexual abuse (Finkelhor, 1984).

The Nature of the Abuse

The Offender. The AHA study cited earlier (1981) found that boys were sexually abused by women in 14% of reported cases (versus 6% for girls). And women were named as co-perpetrators, which means that they somehow contributed to the abuse (i.e., by leaving the child alone), in 41% of reported cases. (Men actually committed the abuse in these cases.)

In the AHA study, nearly one-fourth of the boys were abused by someone outside their family (versus 14% for girls). Most often, the offender was someone well known to the child: a coach, teacher, babysitter, neighbor, mother's boyfriend, and so on. Finkelhor has found much higher rates of extrafamilial abuse for boys, ranging from 77% to 83% (reported in Finkelhor, 1984).[3]

The AHA study also found that boys were less likely to be abused alone, especially in intrafamilial situations. In nearly two-thirds of the incest cases involving boys, another victim was also involved, usually a sister. In cases involving girls, only one-third described multiple victims. It is difficult to assess whether this is a pattern or just another discrepancy due to reporting differences. For instance, we know that girls are more likely to report, so if a boy and a girl are abused together, a report is more probable than if a boy is abused alone (Finkelhor, 1984).

When boys are abused alone, the circumstances are very different than those for girls or for boys and girls together. Boys are 2 1/2 times more likely to be sexually abused by someone outside their family; they are also at risk for abuse by offenders who are less than 25 years old, such as an older brother, a babysitter, or a young neighbor. Finally, as mentioned earlier, almost 40% of boy victims are less than 6 years old when the abuse is reported (Finkelhor, 1984).

Incest. In intrafamilial abuse, boys are more frequently victims of their fathers than of their mothers. Boys abused by their fathers are on average four years younger than girls abused by their fathers.

When boys are abused by their mothers, they are usually very young; evaluation of the four incest pairings (mother/daughter, mother/son, father/daughter, father/son) revealed that the youngest victims were in the mother/son pairing. Mothers are also likely to abuse several siblings, boys and girls, and they more often combine physical and sexual abuse (in over half of all cases). Both the mother and father usually abuse the oldest child (Finkelhor, 1984).

Refer to Chapter 5 for more information on incest and family dynamics.

Risk Factors for Trauma

One of the earliest theories of what creates trauma for the child victim was postulated in 1978 by Nicholas Groth, who outlined four risk factors:

1. *The relationship between the offender and the victim*—The closer the emotional relationship, the greater the risk of some traumatic psychological effect to the victim.

2. *The duration of the sexual relationship*—An ongoing abusive relationship, involving repeated contacts over an extended period, is more traumatic than a single abusive incident.

3. *The type of sexual activity that occurred*—Sexual abuse involving no physical contact, such as exhibitionism or voyeurism, is less traumatic than that involving physical contact. And acts of penetration are potentially more traumatic than those involving noncoital activity (e.g., fondling, masturbating, oral sex).

4. *The degree of physical aggression directed toward the child during the sexual activity*—Incidents that are marked by an excessive use of force or violence against the victim are more traumatic than those in which nonphysical means of persuasion are employed (e.g., verbal coercion or threats).

Also in 1978, Kee MacFarlane added three more risk factors to Groth's list:

5. *Degree of victim participation*—If the child feels he or she participated in or enjoyed the experience, he or she will be more traumatized than the child who has no such feelings.

6. *Parental reaction*—Strong and highly emotional reactions by parents—especially unsupportive reactions—increase the trauma to the child.

7. *Age of the victim*—The older and more mature the child, the greater the degree of trauma.

These early theories by Groth and MacFarlane laid the groundwork for later studies of victims. In fact, most of these risk factors were assumed to be valid and therefore became widely accepted and communicated. Certainly, they seemed to be based on common sense and were simple to understand.

However, what has been proven? Browne and Finkelhor (1986) have reviewed the research on risk factors, including those postulated by Groth and MacFarlane, from an empirical standpoint and have made the following evaluation. Their review shows that the early theories of risk factors, though appearing reasonable and complete, must be constantly revised and updated based on what research demonstrates about abuse. (We will return to Finkelhor's work on trauma later in this chapter, in "A Model of Child Sexual Abuse.")

The Offender

Relationship to the Victim. The most systematic studies of sexual abuse victims have found no correlation between the victim/offender relationship and the degree of trauma that followed the abuse, except in cases of father/daughter incest (Finkelhor, 1979; Peters, 1985; Russell, 1986; Tufts, 1984). The trauma created by father/daughter incest is consistently more severe than that created by any other offense.

Consider that the type of relationship does not necessarily reflect the degree of betrayal or violation felt by the victim. For instance, the child who has been abused by a father from whom she has been estranged or of whom she has always been distrustful will not feel as betrayed as will the child who felt close to and loved by her father. Thus, the quality or closeness of the relationship seems to be more significant (Browne & Finkelhor, 1986).

Age. Victims are more traumatized by adult offenders than adolescent offenders (Fromuth, 1983; Briere & Runtz, 1985). In fact, Finkelhor (1979) found the offender's age to be the second most predictive factor in trauma. Russell (1986) also found less trauma when the offender was less than 26 or older than 50.

Sex. There is very little research on offender sex, because there are so few women offenders. But adults who have been surveyed rated sexual abuse by a male offender as being more traumatic than that by a female offender (Finkelhor, 1984; Russell, 1986).

The Nature of the Abuse

Duration of the Relationship. Researchers generally agree that there is a positive correlation between the duration of the relationship and the trauma that follows (i.e., the longer the relationship, the greater the trauma), but the agreement is not unanimous. In Russell's survey (1986), 73% of the victims who had been abused for five years or longer were described as being extremely or considerably traumatized, compared to 62% of those who had been abused for one week to five years and 46% of those who had been abused just once.

Several significant studies have found no correlation (Finkelhor, 1979; Tufts, 1984), and several others have found a negative correlation (Courtois, 1979; Seidner & Calhoun, 1984), suggesting that individuals have an ability to tolerate or somehow reduce the trauma over time (Browne & Finkelhor, 1986).

Multiple Offenders. In examining the impact of multiple offenders over time, Peters (1984) found that the number of different offenders was the most important single factor related to psychosocial problems. This finding has been confirmed by others (Briere & Runtz, 1985; Bagley & Ramsay, 1985).

Type of Sexual Activity. There are no consistent findings regarding the type of abuse and the impact it has. Certainly, there is evidence that the more serious and aggressive types of abuse are more traumatic for the victim. For instance, Russell (1986) found that victims who were forced to have intercourse (or attempted intercourse), oral sex, or anal sex were three times more likely to be extremely traumatized by the incident than those who were kissed or touched on their clothed bodies.

Bagley and Ramsay (1985) reached the conclusion that penetration was the single most powerful factor in predicting trauma and other mental health impairments. Again, however, other researchers have found no relationship between abuse type and trauma (Anderson, Bach, & Griffith, 1981; Finkelhor, 1979; Fromuth, 1983).

Degree of Physical Aggression. The relationship between use of force and resultant trauma has been demonstrated by a number of studies. Finkelhor (1979) concluded that severe trauma caused by the use of force is the most predictive factor in assessing the effects of the abuse on the victim. A study by Tufts University (1984—also see p. 104) also found that force is one of few predictors of initial reactions to abuse. Quite understandably, physical injury contributes to the trauma experienced by the victim, as well.

While contradictory findings have been offered, this factor is generally supported.

Disclosure

Much of the trauma that results from sexual abuse is due not to the abuse itself but to the general reaction of others after disclosure. Remaining silent may be torturous, but reporting the abuse often brings another level of trauma, one that includes social isolation and stigmatization. The Tufts study (1984) found that children who took a long time to disclose their abuse suffered the least anxiety and least hostility of all victims. Other studies have verified that not telling does not necessarily add to the trauma.

This variable is difficult to measure because even though we know child sexual abuse is underreported, we don't really know by how much. Moreover, since we can't evaluate victims who don't report, we don't know the effects the abuse and/or reporting has on them. "Undoubtedly, the decision to disclose is related to many factors about the experience, which confounds a clear assessment of its effects alone" (Browne & Finkelhor, 1986, p. 173).

Parental Reaction. An unsupportive parental reaction, particularly an angry, punishing reaction by the child's mother, contributes to trauma (Tufts, 1984). Anderson et al. (1981) found $2\frac{1}{2}$ times more negative emotional symptoms in children whose parents were unsupportive of their disclosure. It is interesting that a strongly positive parental response did not have any positive effects on the victim (Tufts, 1984).

The Victim

Age. Studies about victim age must be interpreted carefully, because often the age being referred to is the age of the victim at the time of the report, not at the time of the abuse. Also, if the abuse continues for an extended period of time, there is the issue of whether the age reference is to the child's age at the onset of the abuse or at the last incident of abuse.

Meiselman (1978) found that younger children were more vulnerable; more than twice as many prepubescent victims as pubescent victims were seriously disturbed by being abused (37% versus 17%). Finkelhor (1979) and Russell (1986) also found younger children (less than 9 years) to be slightly more vulnerable. But Peters (1985) found older girls to be more depressed after the incident.

The Tufts study (1984) did not qualify age groups as more or less traumatized. However, it concluded that the age of onset of abuse was not significant in predicting trauma, but the age of the victim at the time of disclosure and evaluation was clearly related to the degree of trauma experienced.

Developmental Stage. Child development has been touched on in various topic discussions within this section, but it has not been addressed specifically. Because this topic is so involved, we will only review general information as it relates to child sexual abuse. Also see Table 4-1 for an overview of the stages of child development.

Overall, the developmental stage the child was at during the abuse (or the stages he or she passed through during an extended period of abuse) is significant in predicting trauma (Browne & Finkelhor, 1986). Younger children, who do not have the cognitive or psychosocial capacity to understand all the implications of sexual abuse, will be traumatized differently than older children, who do understand.

We must be wary of qualifying trauma using terms like *more* or *less*, however. Consider that, even though the younger child may be too immature to understand issues of sexuality and power, he or she will likely be very traumatized by fear and violation of trust, given that these basic emotions have been so severely violated at such an early age. For the older child, however, sexuality will certainly be an issue, given his or her understanding of and concern with sexual identity. In addition, older children are likely to feel enormous guilt and responsibility for their abuse, which will severely damage their self-image. Much of the research examining child development and sexual abuse considers reporting by and interviewing of children at various ages.

- Preschool children (ages 5 and younger) are generally limited conceptually, both in thought and expression. They will therefore need a good deal of guidance to relate their abuse in sufficiently specific and complete terms. However, for the same reason, they are unlikely to lie, at least convincingly, and they are unlikely to feel guilty or responsible for the abuse. Their inconsistencies during an interview can be attributed to confusion more than intentional deception.
- Elementary-age children (ages 6-11) better understand what abuse involves, so they are more likely to feel some guilt and self-blame. As a result, they may be somewhat inhibited during an interview. On the other hand, elementary-age children are fairly trusting of adults and not completely subjective to peer pressure, which will improve their responsiveness. Finally, at this age, children have an incredible ability to remember facts and details, and although they are able to lie, they are unlikely to do so about anything significant.
- Adolescents (ages 12-16) present the biggest challenge. The primary issue to address will be self-image, since the youth is likely to feel enormous embarrassment and guilt. The influence of peer pressure is severe and will affect what the youth tells to whom. Adolescents are able to deceive adults quite convincingly and may deny or recant being abused if they are pressured (Rubin, 1987).

The child who was well-adjusted and developmentally healthy prior to being abused will deal with the ensuing trauma better than the child who had developmental problems to begin with. However, it is important that any assessment of effects of abuse also reviews

Table 4-1 *Stages of Child Development: An Overview*

Ages	Developmental Tasks	Developmental Tasks
Infancy (0-18 months)	Social smile (3 months) Differential response to specific people Stranger anxiety/separation anxiety Sit alone Crawl, walk	Establish social bonds with caregivers (attachments) Acquire sense of trust and security
Toddler (1-3 years)	Speech Toilet training Physical independence Self-assertion Object permanence	Develop sense of autonomy Separate from caregiver to explore environment; continuing to use caregiver as source of support Impulse control
Preschool (4-6 years)	Acquisition of social/sex roles Assimilation of social values/beliefs	Integrate perceptual and motor control Improve communication skills Master self-care activities Establish peer relationships Learn right versus wrong
School age (7-12 years)	Elaboration of intellectual skills Establishment of same-sex peer relations Game playing	Increase domain of social and intellectual competence beyond home and family to school, clubs, sports, and so on Acquire sense of productivity Acquire sense of mutuality/reciprocity in social realms
Adolescence (13-19 years)	Physiological changes accompanying puberty Transition from same-sex peer groups to mixed-sex peer groups Future orientation	Achieve a sense of identity Achieve independence from family Elaborate system of values Develop intimate relationships

Dimensions of Supportive Environments	Eriksonian (psychosocial) Piagetian (cognitive)
Warm, sensitive, and responsive caregivers	Basic trust versus mistrust Sensory motor intelligence
Tolerance for self-assertion Consistent limit setting Structured environment	Autonomy versus shame Preoperational thought
Exposure to a variety of sociocultural situations	Initiative versus guilt Preoperational thought
Opportunities to experience success Opportunities to interact with peers Intellectual stimulation	Industry versus inferiority (competence) Concrete operational thought
Consistent expectations Willingness to let go Respect and encouragement of individual and autonomy	Identity versus role diffusion Formal operational thought

Source: Adapted from R. ten Bensel (1986), Child sexual abuse: Improving the system's response [Special issue], *Juvenile & Family Court Journal*, 37:2. Used with permission.

the child's psychosocial nature before and after the incident. To observe a series of effects without placing them in any context is fairly useless in planning treatment. How the child has changed is the issue.

The Effects of Child Sexual Abuse

David Finkelhor, in *A Sourcebook on Child Sexual Abuse* (1986c), conducted an extensive review of the sexual abuse literature and summarized his findings, offering an overview of what truly has been proven about the effects of sexual abuse on its victims. Perhaps not surprisingly, Finkelhor demonstrated that very little has actually been proven, in an empirical sense, but enough research has produced similar findings that we do have a good idea of what effects are common and even predictable.

Most research categorizes the effects of child sexual abuse according to the period of time in which the effects are manifested. The labels *short-term* and *long-term* are commonly used to describe those effects that are observed directly following the abuse (within two years of the abuse incident) versus those that may affect the child through his or her development and into adulthood.

Some researchers have taken issue with the label *short-term*, arguing that it reduces the seriousness of the observed effects and implies that, once this time period has passed, the effects will have passed, as well. This reflects the so-called adultocentric view of child sexual abuse, discussed in Chapter 1. Disclaiming this view, Finkelhor prefers to call these *initial effects*, while others use terms such as *immediate*. We will also use these more appropriate terms.

A second issue among researchers is whether the effects of child sexual abuse are actual and observable. Some researchers argue that they are not and that certain studies have exaggerated supposedly supportive findings, finding causation where none exists (Finkelhor, 1979). Other researchers are concerned with what they consider to be an alarmist reaction to what is supposedly normal child sexual development. These individuals have tried to minimize the effects of sexual exploitation by portraying child sexuality as exploratory and purposeful (Finkelhor, 1984). (Even the most open-minded, however, find it difficult to place abuse in this context.)

The majority of researchers do agree that sexual abuse is a significant predictor of a wide range of physical, psychological, and social pathologies. We will discuss each of these types of effects as it is observed both immediately and in the long term.

Initial Effects

Physical Effects

Injury. Proportionately more injuries result from child sexual abuse than from other types of reported physical abuse. Children who have been raped or sodomized are most likely to display physical injury, including vaginal or rectal tears that cause inflammation, bleeding, and discharge. Extreme pain and significant blood loss often result, as well (Kempe & Kempe, 1984). Rape and sodomy victims should receive medical attention and be tested for sexually transmitted diseases and pregnancy.

Somatic Symptoms. Most sexually abused children display physical evidence of anxiety and stress (Browne & Finkelhor, 1986). Disturbances in sleep patterns are common, as are changes in eating habits (5% to 20%) (Anderson et al., 1981, and Peters, 1976, respectively).

Psychological/Emotional Effects

An early study by DeFrancis (1966), who interviewed abused children whose cases were in court, found that two-thirds were emotionally disturbed by the sexual abuse. Fifty-two percent were mildly to moderately disturbed; 14% were severely disturbed. Less than one-fourth of the children were found to be emotionally stable following their abuse.

A 1981 study by Anderson, Bach, and Griffith had similar findings: 63% demonstrated psychosocial complications. These complications were described according to whether they were manifested internally or externally.

- *Internalized* psychological sequelae included sleeping and eating disorders, excessive fears and phobias, depression, and feelings of guilt, shame, and anger. Sixty-seven percent of the victims of intrafamilial abuse demonstrated such effects, compared to 49% of the victims of extrafamilial abuse.

- *Externalized* psychological sequelae included more overt behavioral problems, such as difficulties in school, disruptions with peers and family, and running away. Sixty-six percent of the victims of intrafamilial abuse demonstrated such effects, compared to 21% of the victims of extrafamilial abuse.

One of the most significant studies to date was done by the Tufts University New England Medical Center in 1984. What is unique about this study is that it interviewed victims and families in a treatment program who had been abused or had revealed their abuse within six months prior to treatment. Well-established test measures were used, such that standardized norms were available for comparison. Furthermore, this study divided the victims, ages infant through 18 years, into three age groups: preschool, latency, and adolescent. The purpose for doing this was to observe whether the effects of being sexually abused were different for children of different ages (Tufts, 1984). The Tufts study found that 17% of the 4- to 6-year-old preschool group displayed significant clinical pathologies. But in the latency group (7- to 13-year-olds), 40% displayed serious disturbances (Tufts, 1984).

Using the internalized/externalized scales mentioned earlier, another study found that children less than 5 years old were more likely to display internalized effects, while those 6 to 12 years old were prone to externalized trauma (Friedrich, Urquiza, & Beilke, 1986).

Self-Esteem. The effect of being abused on a child's self-esteem is open to some argument due to lack of empirical evidence. DeFrancis (1969) found that 58% of his subjects admitted to feeling inferior or unworthy as a result of their abuse. However, the Tufts study found no evidence of lowered self-esteem in any of the age groups (1984).

Sgroi and colleagues (Porter, Blick, & Sgroi, 1982) maintain that self-esteem is very much affected by sexual abuse. They have described this effect as the "damaged goods" syndrome, in which the child feels he or she has literally been spoiled or ruined by the abuse. This feeling may be demonstrated by a fear of actual physical damage or injury (regardless of whether the child was injured in the abuse), by the child's response to the social stigma that comes with disclosure, and by eroded feelings of self-control and self-confidence) (see also "Social Functioning").

Sexually abused children may also have a poor visual self-image, such that even the most attractive children feel ugly and odd. In order to prove their desirability, abused children may become promiscuous (Porter et al., 1982) (see "Sexuality," below).

Fear. The most prevalent emotion felt after being sexually abused is fear. The Tufts study found that nearly half the 7- to 13-year-old group expressed a severe level of fear, compared with 13% of the 4- to 6-year-olds. In the adolescent group (14- to 18-year-olds), 36% expressed "ambivalent hostility" or a strong fear of being harmed (Tufts, 1984). Sgroi and colleagues confirm this understandable fear of physical harm in their "damaged goods" assessment (Porter et al., 1982).

Children are also afraid of being abused again and even that the offender will seek reprisal. The unknown consequences of the abuse, the disclosure, the treatment, and the legal proceedings are also intimidating for most children. The fear of being separated from their families is especially traumatic (Porter et al., 1982).

Anger/Hostility. The Tufts study (1984) measured anger and hostility as they are manifested both internally and externally. About half the 7- to 13-year-olds (latency group) scored high on the scale measuring internal aggression/antisocial feelings, and just over one-third scored high on the scale measuring hostility directed outward. The scores were lower for both the other age groups: internal versus external scores were 17% and 25% (respectively) for the preschool group; the external score was 23% for the adolescent group.

Sgroi observed that most victims had repressed their anger and hostility; although they appeared to be passive and compliant, on the inside they were seething with emotion. This anger is typically directed at the offender, the child's parents, the child's family, and anyone else on whom the child had depended. Very few children actually act out their anger, but the repression may produce emotional problems as well as aggressive fantasies and behavior (Porter et al., 1982).

Boys, who must address the male socialization issues of power and control, may feel a need to dominate; girls may face other socialization issues that cause them to be angry and hostile. Both boys and girls may become bullies and even offenders themselves in order to act out their own abuse, victimizing other children in an attempt to regain feelings of control and power. Anger may also serve as a defense mechanism of sorts, an effective means of avoiding relationships and thus protecting oneself (Finkelhor & Browne, 1986).

Guilt/Shame. Although guilt and shame are believed to be some of the strongest emotions the sexually abused child feels, empirical evidence shows that this belief is not necessarily true. DeFrancis (1969) found that 64% of the victims felt guilty about what had happened, but their feelings were due more to the problems that resulted after reporting than to the nature of the abuse itself.

Sgroi and colleagues had similar findings. In fact, they observed children who did not feel guilty until after they disclosed what had happened. These feelings of guilt were attributed to claiming responsibility for the abuse, the disclosure (and perhaps betraying the abuser), and the disruption that the abuse had on the family, the offender, and others who were involved (Porter et al., 1982).

Trust. In very young victims, the loss of trust and security may be demonstrated by their extreme dependency on and clinging to parents and other protective figures. Older children may have impaired judgment about who to trust, which may lead to problems in forming relationships (Finkelhor & Browne, 1986).

Sgroi and colleagues have tied the victim's ability to trust with the identification of the offender and the nature of the relationship: How much betrayal is involved? The effects of the disclosure—including the amount of pain and humiliation that is endured—will also have an impact on the child's ability to trust. Again, the issue is betrayal—that individuals who were supposed to protect the child let him or her down (Porter et al., 1982).

Depression. Like guilt, depression may be observed before and/or after disclosure. Some children may display overt depression, acting sad and withdrawn; others may mask their troubles but frequently be tired or sick. In severe cases, children may be self-destructive or suicidal (Porter et al., 1982). Finkelhor suggests that depression may be an "extended grief reaction" over losing a close, trusted person (Finkelhor & Browne, 1986).

Sexuality. In the Tufts study (1984), scores for sexuality were high for both the preschool (4-6 years) and latency (7-13 years) age groups. Twenty-seven percent of the preschool group and 36% of the latency group demonstrated abnormal levels of sexual activity, open masturbation, excessive sexual curiosity, and frequent exposure of genitalia. Friedrich et al. (1986), in a study of victims aged 3 to 12 years old, found that 70% of the boys and 44% of the girls had abnormally high sexual pathologies. Younger girls and older boys were particularly prone to such problems.

Sgroi has attributed this abnormal sexuality to poor development of social skills (also see the following section). The early sexual experience and the trauma that follows interfere with age-appropriate development in childhood and adolescence. Because the child has failed to develop normally, he or she is unable to relate to peers in an appropriate childlike way and thus adopts a *pseudomaturity*, a supposedly adultlike posture that is usually highly sexual. Some children may actually try to be seductive, believing that this is an adult thing to do. Incest victims, for instance, may play the role of a partner with their offender.

Referring once again to the "damaged goods" syndrome, we can relate the need for attention and affirmation to promiscuity. Namely, victims may play a sexual, seductive role in order to prove their desirability and thus their self-worth, at least in their eyes (Porter et al., 1982).

Social Functioning

Sexually abused children are likely to have problems in all areas of social functioning.

Social Isolation. The abused child is likely to become a loner. He or she may have difficulty initiating new relationships and even maintaining old ones. Peer relationships are especially affected. It is also possible that the offender may pressure the victim to limit his or her social involvement, most likely to keep him or her vulnerable and prevent possible discovery (Porter et al., 1982).

School. Various studies estimate that between 10% and 20% of victims quit school or are frequently truant (Peters, 1976, and Anderson et al., 1981, respectively). Learning problems are also common among children who have been sexually abused.

Running Away. Data from youth treatment and delinquency programs estimate that up to half of all runaways have been sexually abused (Browne & Finkelhor, 1986). Incest victims are especially likely to leave home, presumably to escape the abuse they're facing. Up to one-third of these children attempt to run away, compared with 5% of the normal child population (Herman, 1981), and half leave home by the age of 18, compared with 20% of the normal population (Meiselman, 1978).

Family Relationships. Children who have been sexually abused are left very confused about roles and their boundaries. Previous conceptions of authority, power, love, and trust have become obscured and are not easily clarified. And although child sexual abuse—like rape—is not truly a sexual issue, the child will be unable to make this distinction. His or her attitude toward and understanding of sex will be completely confused (Porter et al., 1982).

Sexual abuse disrupts the entire family, particularly in cases of incest, which will add to the confusion the child feels. No one will play his or her previous role in the same way, regardless of his or her involvement in the abuse. So the child will no longer have the same support system at the time he or she needs it the most.

Consult Chapter 5 for a more thorough discussion of family dynamics.

Long-Term Effects

Again, we return to the question, Does being sexually abused during childhood lead to the development of serious subsequent problems in adulthood? There is not enough evidence to document that a history of abuse in fact *causes* these problems, nor is it likely that there ever will be. Quite simply, there are too many variables that influence how people turn out, and the impact of even one given variable—such as childhood sexual abuse—will be different for different people. We can say with certainty, though, that those individuals with a history of sexual abuse are at greater risk for mental health and adjustment problems as adults than are those individuals who were not abused (Browne & Finkelhor, 1986).

Physical Effects

Individuals who were sexually abused as children are likely to experience long-term anxiety or tension. In one study (Briere, 1984), over half the adults had experienced anxiety attacks (versus 28% of the normal group), and 72% had had difficulty sleeping (versus 55% of the normal group).

Eating disorders are also common. A survey of women in an eating disorders treatment program revealed 34% had been sexually abused by the time they were 15 years old. As adults, one-third of these victims were anorexic, and two-thirds were bulimic (Oppenheimer, Palmer, & Brandon, 1984). Unfortunately, there is not much other research in this area, but it appears the effects may be underestimated (Browne & Finkelhor, 1986).

Emotional/Psychological Effects

Self-Esteem. Many studies have shown that adults who were victimized as children have low feelings of self-esteem; in one study, fewer than 10% of those victimized as children were assessed as having a good self-concept (versus 20% of the normal group), while nearly 20% had a very poor self-concept (5% normal) (Bagley & Ramsay, 1985). Turning the issue around, women who are characterized by low self-esteem are four times more likely to have been sexually abused as children than women with normal levels of self-worth (Browne & Finkelhor, 1986).

As a result of this poor self-concept, many adults find that they are unable to be emotionally self-sufficient or independent, which affects their personal relationships to a large degree (see "Personal Relationships," below). Their lack of self-confidence will also be detrimental (Sgroi, Blick, & Porter, 1982).

Phobias. Many adults who were victimized as children have excessive phobias, literally being afraid of life, in some cases. Many also display psychosomatic symptoms (Sgroi, Blick, & Porter, 1982).

Depression. Research has confirmed that depression is the most common general emotional problem faced by individuals who were sexually abused as children. Studies of adults who were victimized estimate that approximately 15% are chronically depressed, which is just over double the rate for the normal population (Peters, 1984). Data from clinical samples are less clear, but they do indicate that incest victims are even more likely to suffer depression.

Self-Destruction. Data are more conclusive regarding the victim's feelings of self-destruction. Briere (1984), who surveyed individuals at a walk-in community health center, discovered that just over half the sexual abuse victims had attempted suicide (versus 34% of the comparative patient population[4]), and nearly one-third wanted to hurt themselves (versus 19%).

Dissociation. Briere (1984) also studied dissociation, relating the childhood desire to escape the sexual abuse to an adult behavior that has become autonomous. Forty-two percent of the subjects were dissociative (versus 22% of the normal group). In addition, a third of the subjects described having out-of-body experiences (versus 11%), and another third described a general feeling that things in life were not real (versus 11%).

Sexuality. The topic of sexuality in adulthood is of great research interest, especially as it relates to any effect being sexually abused as a child has on adult sexual interests and adjustment. As related to self-esteem, Finkelhor found that women who had been abused as children found themselves in awkward sexual situations with men, and men who had been abused were generally dissatisfied with the nature of their sexual experiences as adults (reported in Finkelhor, 1984).

A good deal of the research on sexuality studies incest victims. Eighty-seven percent of the women in Meiselman's study (1978) admitted to having some sexual problems during their adult life, versus 20% of the normal population. In the Briere (1984) sample, 45% admitted to sexual problems (versus 15% normal), and 42% claimed to have a lowered sex drive (29% normal). Finkelhor (1979) found victims of incest to be less orgasmic than women who were not abused.

While some women withdraw and abstain from sex, others become sexually compulsive and promiscuous. Again, in various studies of incest victims (de Young, 1982; Herman, 1981; Meiselman, 1978), an estimated 25% to 35% were described as having a "repertoire of sexually stylized behavior" (Browne & Finkelhor, 1986, p. 161) that was used to get attention and affection.

The notion that homosexuality may be caused by being sexually abused may be a stereotype, but this is often the first concern of parents of victimized boys. There may be such a connection for boys, based on studies of homosexual males (up to four times the normal rate of child sexual abuse), but only if the offender was an adult and not an age peer. The reason for this difference may be that the authority of the adult is somehow confirming or significant, or perhaps the increased trauma of being abused by an adult also produces unresolved and troubling feelings in the victim.

Studies of homosexuality suggest that one's sexual preference may be conditioned genetically or otherwise innately. If this is so, boy victims may have some interest in or curiosity about sex with men; this is not to suggest that they initiate or ask for the abuse but that somehow they are drawn or made vulnerable to it. A more reasonable explanation of the abuse/homosexuality correlation may be that the stigma of the incident is so great that a confused and traumatized youth may label himself homosexual and then eventually gravitate toward homosexual behavior.

There is little data on the correlation between homosexuality and an individual history of child sexual abuse, so no conclusions can be drawn on this topic. What's more, to presume such a connection merely perpetuates the stereotype and resultant stigma that affect the victim. One point that can be stated quite strongly, however, is that child sexual abuse is not an issue of homosexuals recruiting children, since the majority of offenders are heterosexual (Finkelhor, 1984). (Also see the discussion of homosexual offenders in Chapter 2.)

Social Functioning

Personal Relationships. In general, personal relationships are strained and dysfunctional. Women who were abused as children have difficulty relating to men; nearly half are afraid of men, compared to 15% of the normal population (Briere, 1984). Incest victims are especially likely to have problems with husbands or partners. Courtois (1979) estimated that 79% had problems with their partners (versus 40% normal); 40% were so troubled that they never married.

Adults who were abused as children will generally have difficulty trusting others, and their negative experiences may have impaired their ability to judge trustworthiness. Thus, many women end up in abusive relationships over and over again, and they may even tolerate abuse of their children because the pattern is so reinforced (Finkelhor & Browne, 1986).

Sexually abused women also have problems relating to other women and in fact may have fear and contempt for women in general. An estimated 12% are afraid of women, compared to 4% of the normal population (Briere, 1984). Incest victims are especially resentful of their mothers, even more than of their fathers, which is ironic. An estimated 60% of Meiselman's (1978) sample strongly resented their mothers, but only 40% strongly resented their fathers, who were their abusers.

Adults who were sexually abused as children are afraid of what kind of parents they will be, mainly due to the so-called vampire theory discussed in earlier chapters (Goodwin, McCarthy, & DiVasto, 1981). This fear of an innate tendency to molest children drives the parents away from their children, because they fear being close will inevitably lead to sexual abuse. Unfortunately, in this attempt at protecting their children by staying away, these parents are actually setting up their children for abuse by other parties (Browne & Finkelhor, 1986).

Later Abuse. Girls who were sexually abused continue to be at risk for abuse as adults. Russell (1986) discovered that between 33% and 68% of the adult women who were abused as girls were subsequently raped as adults (compared with 17% of the normal population). Nearly half these women had violent husbands (17% normal group), and up to 62% had been sexually abused by their husbands (21% normal).

This phenomenon has been observed so often that several reasons have been offered to help explain this risk for later abuse:

1. Girls who have been sexually abused are likely to leave home and even marry earlier, especially in incestuous situations. Thus, they are probably financially dependent and socially isolated, making them needy and vulnerable.
2. Abuse victims may have a poor sense of self-worth and independence, again, making them vulnerable targets (Finkelhor, 1984).

Men who were abused as children may feel the need to control or dominate in relationships in order to reconcile their own feelings of powerlessness over their abuse. They may become bullies or offenders as they reenact the abuse, this time being the abuser instead of the victim (Finkelhor & Browne, 1986).

Prostitution. Much of the research on social functioning has attempted to tie a history of sexual abuse with later prostitution, and there is overwhelming evidence of such a correlation. In one study, over half of a sample of 136 prostitutes had been sexually abused as children, and 65% of the adolescent prostitutes had been forced to have sex before they were 16 years old (James & Meyerding, 1977). A similar study estimated that 60% had been sexually abused before they were 16 years old and that the mean age of victimization was 10 (Silbert & Pines, 1981).

Alcohol/Drug Abuse. Adults who were sexually abused as children are also more likely to abuse drugs and alcohol. Seventeen percent of the childhood victims in the Peters study (1984) abused alcohol (4% normal group), and 27% abused at least one drug (12% normal). These rates are even higher for incest victims (Herman, 1981).

A Model of Child Sexual Abuse

Perhaps more than any other researcher, David Finkelhor has attempted to organize and evaluate the state of knowledge about child sexual abuse. He summarizes the situation:

> *The literature on child sexual abuse is full of observations about problems that are thought to be associated with a history of abuse, such as sexual dysfunction, depression, and low self-esteem. However, such observations have not yet been organized into a clear model that specifies how and why sexual abuse might result in this kind of trauma. (Finkelhor & Browne, 1986, p. 180)*

The Four Traumagenic Dynamics

Based on his study of child victims, Finkelhor (Finkelhor & Browne, 1986) has developed a model that suggests that the experience of being sexually abused can be evaluated along four trauma-causing factors, or *traumagenic dynamics*.

1. *Traumatic sexualization* describes how the trauma of being abused in effect warps the development of the child's sexuality, producing inappropriate and dysfunctional attitudes and behaviors. A number of circumstances of the abuse may prompt this trauma:
- Repeated rewards by the offender for inappropriate behavior may be reinforcing for the child.
- The exchange of gifts, privileges, attention, and affection for sexual behavior may teach the child how to manipulate others for selfish purposes.
- Fetishizing certain parts of the child's anatomy, thus distorting their meaning and importance, may affect the child's self-image and understanding of his or her body.
- The offender's inappropriate sexual attitudes and behavior may be transmitted to the child, at least confusing his or her sense of morality and self-worth.
- Frightening memories of the abuse may become directly associated with sexual activity.

Because the circumstances of sexual abuse vary greatly from case to case, Finkelhor suggests that there are varying degrees of traumatic sexualization. For instance, the child who is enticed to participate may be more sexually traumatized than the child who is forced, but that latter child may have memories of fear to address instead. The degree of sexualization may also be affected by the child's level of understanding. For instance, the very young child may be less sexually traumatized because he or she understands little of the sexuality involved.

2. *Betrayal* describes the child's feelings upon discovering that a supposedly trusted and dependable person has caused him or her harm. Betrayal may be realized in a number of situations:
- The child may realize that he or she has been manipulated through lies and misrepresentations by someone he or she trusted.
- The child may realize that someone who supposedly loved him or her has been abusive and callous.
- The child may blame family members who did not commit the abuse but who were unwilling or unable to protect or believe him or her.
- The child may blame family and peers who have changed their feelings toward him or her after disclosure, assumably because of the abuse.

Although sexual abuse committed by family members or other trusted individuals will have more potential for betrayal than that committed by a stranger, the nature of the relationship is not the sole determinant. Rather, the degree of betrayal is determined by how tricked or let down the child feels, regardless of who the offender is.

3. *Powerlessness,* also referred to as *disempowerment,* describes the general violation of the child's will, drives, and sense of self-control, which may likely result in a number of circumstances:
- Multiple, extended incidents of abuse may create the most basic kind of powerlessness, as the child's "territory and body space are repeatedly invaded against [his or her] will" (Finkelhor & Browne, 1986, p. 183).
- The offender's use of force or coercion will exacerbate these feelings.
- The child's inability to stop the abuse, along with frustration in trying to convince adults of what is happening, will reinforce feelings of powerlessness.
- Powerlessness will ultimately be reinforced when the child feels dependent and trapped in the situation.

This last item is perhaps the most significant overall. The feeling that the child is trapped may be more traumatizing than the use of force and threat by an extremely authoritarian offender. For this reason, the circumstances of the child's disclosure are significant; the child who is not believed will feel more powerless than the child who has been believed and thus effectively ended his or her abuse.

4. *Stigmatization* describes the negative connotations that the child receives and incorporates into his or her self-image. These connotations may be communicated to the child in several ways:
- The offender may blame or denigrate the child or suggest that he or she should feel ashamed and guilty.
- Pressure for secrecy by the offender may make the child feel as if he or she cooperated somehow.
- Inferred or actual sentiment by the family and the community, especially reactions of shock or hysteria, may reinforce the child's feelings of shame or guilt.
- The child may know or even sense that what happened is deviant and violates social taboos about sex, which may cause self-criticism and stigmatization.

Again, it is important to consider degrees of trauma. The child's age and social awareness will both control how much he or she understands and feels the stigma of having been abused. The reactions of those around the child to the disclosure will also affect him or her.

A final component in assessing trauma must be an evaluation of the child's experiences before and after the abuse. Abuse will affect different children in different ways, depending on their prior level of development, knowledge, and general adjustment. Of particular importance are the child's family life and personality traits prior to the abuse. Events subsequent to the abuse fall into two categories:

1. the family's response, if and when they learn of the abuse; and

2. the social/institutional response, including not only the general reaction of people around the child but also the experiences of reporting to the police, being examined in the hospital, being removed from home, testifying in court, and so on.

Review of the Model

While these four factors are not unique to child sexual abuse (i.e., they occur in other kinds of trauma, as well), their conjunction in this particular set of circumstances uniquely characterizes the trauma of being sexually abused.

In short, these four factors impact the child's cognitive and emotional orientation, changing his or her self-view and world view. And although each factor may be more or less affective, the result is the same: Victims try to cope with the world through these distorted views, creating immediate problems in childhood and long-term developmental and adjustment problems for adolescents and adults.

Finkelhor warns that these four traumagenic dynamics are not to be applied as distinct, separate factors, nor are they to be defined in narrow terms. Instead, he describes these factors as "broad categories" with which we can organize what we know about the effects of sexual abuse. However, certain traumagenic dynamics seem to be more likely associated with certain effects. While there is no one-to-one correspondence, there are clear patterns.

Table 4-2 presents these relationships, assessing both psychological and behavioral effects of each traumagenic dynamic. Note that Finkelhor has included the common initial and long-term reactions of victims, organizing them within a single framework. Note as well that certain effects, such as depression, can be related to several traumagenic dynamics.

Application of the Model

The most obvious application of this conceptual model is in making clinical assessments about the effects of abuse and planning appropriate treatment. In the past, clinicians have evaluated the victim's experiences according to a set of "unsystematic assumptions about what causes trauma" (Finkelhor & Browne, 1986, p. 191). For instance, other models have used simple dichotomies as measures of trauma, analyzing extra- versus intrafamilial abuse, whether force was used or not, whether penetration occurred or not, whether the offender was of one type or another, and so on.

This type of approach has several limitations. Most importantly, the initial assumptions that are made are largely untested, as we've learned from our own review in this chapter. In addition, the black-and-white, all-or-none nature of a dichotomous scale is overly simplistic. "Nothing about the *character* of the effect is implied. Nothing about how the trauma is likely to manifest itself is suggested" (Finkelhor & Browne, 1986, p. 194).

Finkelhor's model of traumagenic dynamics supports a more realistic and more complex evaluation of the potential for trauma. The abuse experience can be analyzed along four separate dimensions, each of which is measured in relative terms of degree and not in absolute, yes/no terms. The clinician can proceed through the model, one dynamic at a time, questioning the significance of each. In the end, the clinician should have a good idea of what is most troubling for the victim and what psychological and behavioral effects should be expected. This assessment can be the basis for an individualized treatment program.

In addition to serving a valuable intervention/treatment purpose, the four traumagenic dynamics have implications for research, as well. Specifically, Finkelhor envisions the development of testing instruments that measure the impact of sexual abuse. To date, stan-

Table 4-2 *Traumagenic Dynamics in the Impact of Child Sexual Abuse*

1. **TRAUMATIC SEXUALIZATION**
   Dynamics
   Child rewarded for sexual behavior inappropriate to developmental level
   Offender exchanges attention and affection for sex
   Sexual parts of child fetishized
   Offender transmits misconceptions about sexual behavior and sexual morality
   Conditioning of sexual activity with negative emotions and memories
   Psychological impact
   Increased salience of sexual issues
   Confusion about sexual identity
   Confusion about sexual norms
   Confusion of sex with love and caregetting or caregiving
   Negative associations to sexual activities and arousal sensations
   Aversion to sex or intimacy
   Behavioral manifestations
   Sexual preoccupations and compulsive sexual behaviors
   Precocious sexual activity
   Aggressive sexual behaviors
   Promiscuity
   Prostitution
   Sexual dysfunctions; flashbacks, difficulty in arousal, orgasm
   Avoidance of or phobic reactions to sexual intimacy
   Inappropriate sexualization of parenting

2. **BETRAYAL**
   Dynamics
   Trust and vulnerability manipulated
   Violation of expectation that others will provide care and protection
   Child's well-being disregarded
   Lack of support and protection from parent(s)
   Psychological impact
   Grief, depression
   Extreme dependency
   Impaired ability to judge trustworthiness of others
   Mistrust, particularly of men
   Anger, hostility
   Behavioral manifestations
   Clinging
   Vulnerability to subsequent abuse and exploitation
   Allowing own children to be victimized
   Isolation
   Discomfort in intimate relationships
   Marital problems
   Aggressive behavior
   Delinquency

3. **POWERLESSNESS**
   Dynamics
   Body territory invaded against the child's wishes
   Vulnerability to invasion continues over time
   Offender uses force or trickery to involve child
   Child feels unable to protect self and halt abuse
   Repeated experience of fear
   Child is unable to make others believe
   Psychological impact
   Anxiety, fear
   Lowered sense of efficacy
   Perception of self as victim
   Need to control
   Identification with the aggressor
   Behavioral manifestations
   Nightmares
   Phobias
   Somatic complaints; eating and sleeping disorders
   Depression
   Dissociation
   Running away
   School problems, truancy
   Employment problems
   Vulnerability to subsequent victimization
   Aggressive behavior, bullying
   Delinquency
   Becoming an abuser

4. **STIGMATIZATION**
   Dynamics
   Offender blames, denigrates victim
   Offender and others pressure child for secrecy
   Child infers attitudes of shame about activities
   Others have shocked reaction to disclosure
   Others blame child for events
   Victim is stereotyped as damaged goods
   Psychological impact
   Guilt, shame
   Lowered self-esteem
   Sense of differentness from others
   Behavioral manifestations
   Isolation
   Drug or alcohol abuse
   Criminal involvement
   Self-mutilation
   Suicide

Source: D. Finkelhor and A. Browne, Initial and long-term effects: A conceptual framework, in D. Finkelhor and associates, *A sourcebook on child sexual abuse*, pp. 186-187, copyright 1986 by Sage Publications, Inc. Reprinted by permission of Sage Publications, Inc.

dardized psychological tests such as the Minnesota Multiphasic Personality Inventory (MMPI) have been used on abuse victims, but they are not designed to assess factors specific to sexual abuse. Sections of tests could be designed to address each of the four dynamics, and separate instruments could be developed for completion by the child victim and by his or her parents or professionals familiar with the case.

Summary

The typical victim of child sexual abuse is a girl between 8 and 12 years old. She is not of any particular race or socioeconomic level, but her family background is telling. The family is likely to be dysfunctional, such that there is little show of affection and little communication between members. The father may be authoritarian and rigid, and the mother may be subordinate and vulnerable. The children are frequently unsupervised, and they may be physically abused, as well.

The child's relationship with his or her parents is one of the strongest predictors of abuse. Girls living without their natural parents are more prone to abuse; girls living with stepfathers are more than twice as likely to be abused, either by the stepfather or by one of the parents' friends.

Most children are abused by male offenders, usually a relative or someone who knows the child. The abuse involves multiple acts over some time, and the victim has been coerced into submission. Of the approximately 10% of those who report, most contact a child protective service or the police.

Although few data are available, boy victims are believed to differ from girls victims in some ways. They are usually younger, they are more often physically abused, they are often from poorer families, they are more often abused by strangers, and they are more often abused with other children. The lack of reporting by boy victims, especially older youths, makes it difficult to generalize about the sexual abuse of boys.

The risk factors for trauma are open to a lot of discussion, since much of what is widely accepted has not been proven empirically. Overall, however, researchers agree that, regarding offender type, being abused by an adult male is the most traumatic. The offender/child relationship is not significant per se, except where the offender is the child's father or father figure.

Abuse that lasts over an extended time period and that involves physical contact is potentially more traumatic; research is divided over whether intercourse is more traumatic than other types of contact offenses. There is clear agreement, though, that the use of force is perhaps the most predictive risk factor for trauma. The effects of reporting on victim trauma are less clear, although a negative or unsupportive parental reaction is linked to increased trauma.

It is debatable whether victim age relates to degree of trauma. Delays and differences in boy/girl reporting mean that some victims are evaluated long after their abuse, and some victims are more or less likely to report as they get older. The child's developmental level and general adjustment are perhaps more significant predictors than age.

A good deal of research has examined the impact that being sexually abused has on the child immediately and on the adolescent and adult in later life, categorizing the effects as initial and long term. While general patterns have been observed in the initial term, researchers do not agree about what effects are common enough to be considered likely or predictable. And in the long term, findings of psychosocial problems may be more consistent, but there is a dangerous tendency to establish cause and effect.

Commonly observed initial effects include feelings of fear, anxiety, depression, anger, and hostility and inappropriate sexual behavior. Researchers disagree as to whether being sexually abused causes feelings of shame and guilt and lack of self-esteem. Some suggest that the trauma of disclosure may be more responsible for these effects than the abuse itself.

Long-term effects of child sexual abuse include a whole range of psychosocial problems: poor self-concept, depression, self-destructive and dissociative tendencies, feelings of isolation and stigma, and proclivity for alcohol and drug abuse. Problems with sexuality and relationships are very common. In particular, women who were sexually abused as children are prone to forming abusive relationships as adults.

Finkelhor's traumagenic dynamics model evaluates the experience of being sexually abused along four trauma-causing factors: traumatic sexualization, betrayal, powerlessness, and stigmatization. This model is more realistic than others that typically employ dichotomous scales, evaluating the character of the trauma and the effects it may produce. Finkelhor's model has applications for both treatment and research.

Notes

1. The upper age limit is somewhat flexible because of different definitional procedures in research. Some studies include youths up to 18 years old, while others only include those up to 16 years.
2. Data regarding the prevalence of specific acts are varied. For instance, Finkelhor (1979) found that intercourse occurred in only 4% of the cases he studied, whereas Conte and Berliner (1981) found that 25% of their subjects were raped. Regardless of the actual numbers, fondling and masturbation are much more common than intercourse, even over extended periods (Chandler, 1982).
3. The AHA sample included a large number of public welfare cases, which means reports of incest were high. Thus, the statistics for extrafamilial abuse—for boys and girls—are probably low, as shown by the Finkelhor data (1984).
4. This is an example of what we warned against in the discussion of validity in Chapter 1: using another clinical population as a sample. It is not likely that these individuals could be considered representative, which may account for the high numbers here.

Chapter Five

Incest and Family Dynamics

In our culture, incest is treated with a good deal of ambivalence. On the one hand, it is considered taboo, a grave violation of the social order, disruptive of family roles, responsibilities, and values. The incest offender is considered a true degenerate. Moreover, in most cases, incest is considered to be child sexual abuse.

Still, not everyone takes incest seriously. In contemporary society, where lines of kinship and responsibility are less clear, incest no longer holds the same meaning. Even in the face of clear evidence of the destructive pattern and effects of incest, many people choose not to report it unless the interaction is very violent or damaging. Some believe that incest is not serious enough to warrant intervention and treatment, while others claim that what happens within the family is sacrosanct, regardless of moral and legal principles. Thus, it appears that the taboo is too weak to prevent incest yet strong enough to keep it secret (Lawton-Speert & Wachtel, 1982).

In previous chapters, we have looked at the individuals involved in child sexual abuse, namely, the offenders and the victims. In this chapter, we will look at the family, because incest is a family problem. To guide our review, we will follow the principles of family dynamics, examining the incestuous family as a dysfunctional family. We will review general family functioning, as well as individual roles of fathers, mothers, victims, and siblings. The last two sections will present a five-phase model of the incest scenario and general recommendations for treatment, based on family dynamics theory.

The Study of Incest

Definitions

We have stressed the importance of using specific and consistent definitions in earlier chapters. But nowhere is definitional preciseness more relevant than in the discussion of incest.

Finkelhor (1979) points out that incest and child sexual abuse are not the same thing. *Child sexual abuse* refers to sexual relations between an adult or adolescent and a child. *Incest* refers to sexual relations between two family members whose union is forbidden by law or custom.

Finkelhor's survey (1979) found that more acts of incest than child sexual abuse are committed. Twenty-eight percent of the women and 23% of the men surveyed admitted to a sexual experience with a family member, but only 19% of the women and 9% of the men admitted to having been sexually abused.

For an experience to be both incestuous and sexually abusive, (1) the child's partner must be older than him or her (usually four years or more) or in a position of power or authority over him or her, and (2) the child's partner must be a family member (including relations beyond the immediate family). A sexual experience with a partner who is older or controlling but is not a family member is abusive but not incestuous. And a sexual experience with a family member who is of the same approximate age is incestuous but not necessarily abusive, depending on the circumstances and the relationship.

Much sexual abuse is incestuous, though. Forty-four percent of the girls who reported having been sexually abused were abused by family members. This means that about 1 in 10 of the women had a sexual experience that was both incestuous and abusive, which is a significant amount of overlap (Finkelhor, 1979).

Another definitional topic is the types of sexual activity that constitute incest. Depending on what discipline is studying the problem, a number of definitions may be offered. Briefly, some define incest as marriage between proscribed parties, while others define it along various lines of sexual contact or contemplation. For the purposes of studying child sexual abuse, a broader definition of incest is needed, for several reasons:

1. The taboo against incest in our culture applies to all forms of sexual contact between family members, not just intercourse. Any individual who willingly violates this taboo must be considered to have committed incest, regardless of what type of activity took place. Granted, some incestuous acts are more serious than others, but they are incestuous nonetheless. Limiting incest to intercourse excludes a whole range of other sexual activities that are truly incestuous.

2. Including only blood relatives or even legally defined relatives in incestuous relationships is unrealistic, given the nature of contemporary society. The prevalence of stepfamilies and single-parent families makes traditional definitions of *family* and *relatives* obsolete. The modern-day family must be considered as a domestic and social unit, which will extend beyond blood kin.

3. Incest, as a form of child sexual abuse, is the exploitation of children by manipulative, more powerful adults or adolescents, an issue that is often overlooked. As stated in the introduction to this chapter, some consider incest a primarily biological issue, and the chief concern is genetic inbreeding. Instead, the concern should be for what incest does to the children and families involved. It is a social issue, not a biological one (Finkelhor, 1979; Lawton-Speert & Wachtel, 1982).

Guided by these considerations, Finkelhor has defined *incest* as

sexual contact between family members, including not just intercourse but also mutual masturbation, hand-genital or oral-genital contact, sexual fondling, exhibition, and even sexual propositioning. It [does] not include unconscious sexual gestures, however, such as accidental exposure or a mother's concern about a child's body. (1979, p. 84)

A final definitional question concerns which partners are "off limits." Social taboo, backed by law, forbids sex between individuals and their mothers, fathers, sisters, brothers, grandparents, aunts, and uncles. But sex with cousins, in-laws, and step-relations may or may not be considered incestuous or illegal, depending on state laws and social concerns. We will include cousins, in-laws, and step-relations with the blood-relative partners in our definition of incest. A review of these forbidden relationships follows the section on prevalence.

Prevalence

The concern with defining *incest* is more than just semantic. How incest is defined has an enormous effect on measures of prevalence. If, for instance, incest is defined specifically as intercourse between proscribed individuals, then it is quite rare, occurring perhaps in 1 in 1 million families. But if incest is defined to include any type of sexual contact, it is much more common. Estimates range from 1 in 100 to 1 in 4 families (de Young, 1985).

In Finkelhor's survey (1979) of nearly 800 individuals, a sexual experience was reported with every category of blood relative included in the classification, except for grandmothers. Even when study is limited to the nuclear family, rates are still high: 14% of the girls and 8% of the boys reported having had sexual contact with their mother, father, brother, or sister.

Finkelhor also found that incest is most common among family members of the same generation, which means between brothers, sisters, and cousins (1979). This finding supports the generally held contention that sibling incest is probably the most common type, although it is greatly underreported.

Only one-fourth of the cases reported were between members of different generations, and almost all of the cross-generational incest involved girls. Girls were four times more likely to be molested by family members than boys were. This contrasts with boy/girl rates for extrafamilial abuse, where boys report being molested at least half as often as girls. Thus, girls are at more risk for incest than boys are, especially by older family members (Finkelhor, 1979).

Incestuous Partnerships

Father/Daughter

Father/daughter incest is the most often reported type of incest, and it is certainly the most studied type of incest. In fact, the study of father/daughter incest is considered by some to be the most studied topic in child sexual abuse research. Thus, most of the information presented in this chapter is based on incest between a father (or father figure) and his daughter.

It was once believed that incest between a father and daughter was very rare and occurred only in degenerate families. Current research demonstrates, however, that father/daughter incest occurs commonly in all types of families. Again, referring to Finkelhor's survey (1979), just over 1% of the girls surveyed had sexual contact with their father or stepfather. And although this may seem like a small percentage, consider that over 750,000 women over the age of 18 have had such a relationship, and another 16,000 girls between the ages of 5 and 17 are victimized by their fathers each year.

The rates for stepfathers are even more disturbing. While only 5% of the sample had a stepfather, of that group, half had been sexually abused, although not always by their stepfather. Nearly a third of the total number of cases of incest reported were with stepfathers, however. As we have discussed in earlier chapters, the dynamics of the stepfamily are unique and place the children in contact with more people, more often, greatly contributing to their chance of being abused.

The discovery of father/daughter incest has a strong impact on the family, often causing the destruction of the marital relationship, which is usually the core of the family, and the breakup of the family. A report is likely to be made, and law enforcement and child protective services workers are likely to be involved. In such cases, it is difficult for the offender or the family to prevent disclosure.

Father/Son

There are conflicting reports about the prevalence of father/son incest. Many researchers believe it to be far less common than father/daughter incest, but others have argued that it occurs more often than we think. Although few data are available, de Young (1985) reports that the incestuous victimization of boys may be near that of girls.

Most incestuous fathers who abuse their sons deny having any previous homosexual interest or activity, although case histories often prove otherwise; such men may be maintaining a heterosexual facade. Many of these fathers were themselves sexually abused as children, and incest may be a multigenerational pattern (de Young, 1985).

Mother/Son

Despite the popular speculation about oedipal triangles and boys having affairs with their mothers, mother/son incest rarely occurs. Individual pathology is a significant factor in the few cases of mother/son incest reported. The mother is frequently impaired (severe mental illness is common) (de Young, 1982), or she may vacillate between being overprotective and physically abusive (Meiselman, 1978).

Research has shown that the son more often initiates the sex in mother/son incest (de Young, 1982); others take issue with this finding, arguing that it shifts responsibility from the adult to the child (Mitnick, 1989). Coercion and physical violence are infrequent, and the experience may be less traumatic for the boy, at least in the short term (de Young, 1982). Meiselman (1978) reported that such an experience does have a significant impact on the boy's psychosexual development, however.

Mother/Daughter

This is the rarest type of incest reported within the nuclear family. In the few cases studied, the mother and daughter were isolated from the rest of the family and formed a terribly dependent and needy relationship. The mothers had uprooted and abusive family backgrounds and seemed to want to protect and preserve their daughters from everyone else. Upon disclosure, the daughters did not feel victimized and were depressed after being separated from their mothers. The daughters remained helpless and dependent (de Young, 1982).

Siblings

Although it is not reflected in the literature, researchers agree that brother/sister incest is undoubtedly the most common type of incest. In Finkelhor's survey (1979), 39% of the incest reported by girls and 21% of that reported by boys was between brothers and sisters. What is even more surprising is the amount of homosexual incest between siblings. Brothers reported sexual contact with brothers almost as often as with sisters; one-fifth of the girls who had an incestuous experience had contact with sisters.

Combining heterosexual and homosexual sibling incest, Finkelhor found that 15% of the girls and 10% of the boys surveyed had an incestuous experience with a sibling. This accounted for about half of all the incest reported and 94% of the incest reported within the nuclear family (1979).

Much of the incest reported took place when the children were very young, usually under the age of 12 and frequently at 9 or 10 years. But we should not use these numbers to rationalize that sibling incest is nothing more than sexual exploration and play. Nearly one-fourth of those who engaged in sibling incest had partners who were more than five years older; nearly half the preadolescent girls had partners who were adolescents or adults. Thus, siblings are not always age peers, which is an important distinction (Finkelhor, 1979).

In some cases, offending brothers are imitating their fathers. These youths may have assumed the patriarchal role in the family, performing fatherly responsibilities, or they may have witnessed the abuse of either their mother or sister (Weinberg, 1955; de Young, 1982). Boys most often initiate incest, and the youngest sister is the most likely victim (de Young, 1985). The sister/victim is usually the one to report the incest, usually in retaliation against her brother. Collusion among siblings is common (de Young, 1982).

The fact remains, however, that sibling incest is grossly underreported. It may be taken less seriously, and it may be less offensive to the individuals involved and their families. Thus, it is usually less upsetting to the family order and can be handled without outside intervention (Finkelhor, 1979). The handling of sibling incest has been criticized by de Young (1985), who cites a "general social apathy" about the problem, as if it's really not that bad. Generally, only the most abusive cases are reported.

Other Types

The reporting of incest between children and more distant relatives is unlikely, because the family will almost always decide to handle the problem themselves, without outside help. In particular, they feel that they can keep the offending relative away from the child and thus avoid another incident.

Incest between uncles and nieces has been reported, but it is difficult to characterize due to the diversity of uncle/niece relationships. For instance, in some families, uncles are close and almost paternal figures who have regular contact and authority over the children. In other families, uncles are actually strangers who may visit occasionally but generally have little access to the children (de Young, 1985).

The same can be said of relationships with aunts and cousins, as well as others who are not blood kin but play the role of a relative, such as a mother's boyfriend or a close family friend. As mentioned earlier in defining incest, the family cannot be limited solely to blood relatives.

The abuse of grandchildren (usually granddaughters) by grandfathers may be taken too lightly. The "dirty old man" stereotype and the joking that goes along with it may prevent people from seriously considering the grandfather as a possible offender. Even when abuse is disclosed, there may be little concern because of feelings that an old man's advances are benign and even amusing (de Young, 1985).

Theoretical Orientations

Over the years that researchers have studied child sexual abuse, they have changed their views of the problem of incest in two ways:

1. *Initially, incest was seen as an uncommon and atypical form of child sexual abuse. That perception has changed to the extent that much current theorizing about the causes and dynamics of child sexual abuse centers on abuse within the family setting.*
2. *A long period of interest in trying to characterize the particular deviant nature of the abuser has given way to a strong focus on family dynamics and the "dysfunctional family." (Lawton-Speert & Watchtel, 1982, p. v)*

Reflecting these changes, more researchers now support what can be termed the *psychosocial model* of incest, combining aspects of sociological and characterological models to study the nature of and changes within the incestuous family. The family is considered as a system, defined by roles, relationships, and boundaries. The incestuous family is a dysfunctional system, one in which traditional roles are abandoned, relationships are controlling and harmful, and boundaries are blurred or nonexistent.

In contrast to other models, the psychosocial model—also described using terms such as *family dynamics, family systems,* or *family process*—shifts the emphasis away from the individual and to the relationships within the family. Doing so means bringing in the whole family and even friends and other significant people for therapy.

Family dynamics therapy was first used by psychiatrists on an experimental basis in treating severely disturbed individuals, such as schizophrenics. Therapists noted that, upon returning home after treatment, these individuals regressed dramatically and also created problems for other family members. When the individual's family was brought in, his or her pathology was seen as a symptom of a larger problem, the family's dysfunction (Olson, 1970). An early pioneer in family therapy, Jay Haley, describes this notion:

Psychopathology in the individual is a product of the way he deals with his intimate relations, the way they deal with him, and the way other family members involve him in their relations with each other. Further, the appearance of symptomatic behavior in an individual is necessary for the continued function of a particular family system. Therefore, changes in the individual can occur only if the family system changes, and resistance to change in the individual centers in the influence of the family as a group. (in Olson, 1970, p. 504)

Thus, the goal of therapy evolved from changing the individual to changing the social environment in which he or she lived, which is the family.

Family therapy progressed from work with schizophrenic and emotionally disturbed individuals to marital counseling to treatment of children from disturbed homes. Work with children centered on their relationship with their parents and even the parents' relationship. Another established therapist, Virginia Satir, comments, "The parents are the architects of the family and the marriage *relationship* [is] the key to all other family *relationships*. When there is difficulty in the marital pair, there [are] more than likely problems in parenting" (in Olson, 1970, p. 505).

Family dynamics therapy is a unique approach, one that blends psychiatry, psychology, social work, and a number of the other helping professions. This blending has been criticized by some who point out that family dynamics therapy has no organized theoretical base or empirical methodology. It relies heavily on psychodynamic theories, along with learning theory, small-group theory, existentialism, and humanism. Its biggest theoretical contribution has been that of systems theory, which looks at the individual in his or her natural setting. In the absence of a single, coherent theory, family dynamics therapy developed in a very experimental, functional manner (Olson, 1970).

Since its experimental beginnings in the 1960s and 1970s, family dynamics therapy has been established as a significant approach to treating troubled individuals and their families. However, the loose theoretical and methodological framework upon which family dynamics is based continued to receive criticism. In response to this criticism, David Olson developed the Circumplex Model of Families. The purpose of this model, according to Olson, is "to facilitate bridging the gaps that often exist among theorists, researchers, and practitioners" (in Olson & McCubbin, 1983, p. 47).

The Circumplex Model of Families

The Circumplex Model is organized around three dynamics of marital and family behavior: *cohesion, adaptability,* and *communication.* These three were chosen from over 50 concepts to describe marital and family dynamics because they were considered most representative of basic family dynamics. Refer to Figure 5-1, which illustrates the Circumplex Model, throughout this discussion of the three dynamics and the model itself.

Cohesion

Family cohesion is "the emotional bonding that family members have toward one another" (Olson & McCubbin, 1983, p. 48). Variables that may be used to diagnose or measure cohesion include emotional bonding, boundaries, coalitions, time, space, friends, decision making, and interests and recreation.

There are four levels of family cohesion: (1) disengaged (very low), (2) separated (low to moderate), (3) connected (moderate to high), and (4) enmeshed (very high). According to the model, the two central levels of cohesion, separated and connected, are the most conducive to family functioning. The extreme levels, disengaged and enmeshed, are problematic.

- When the cohesion level is very high (level 4, enmeshed), the family identification is too great, to the point that the individuals have lost their ability to function separately. Loyalty to and consensus within the family are absolute.
- When the cohesion level is very low (level 1, disengaged), the family has limited attachment and commitment to the group. In this case, individuation is extreme, as each member acts independently and selfishly.

Clearly, the central levels of cohesion are the most supportive of family functioning because there is a balance between individuality and family identity. This balance allows the family to deal effectively with stress and change. Individuals are able to act and think independently but still belong to and support the family unit.[1]

An additional aspect of balance is that families may move along the dimension of cohesion, depending on the circumstances. "Being balanced means a family system can experience the extremes on the dimensions when appropriate, but they do not typically function at these extremes for long periods." Olson describes families having this ability for movement as having a "larger behavior repertoire" (Olson & McCubbin, 1983, p. 59).

Adaptability

Family adaptability is "the ability of a marital or family system to change its power structure, role relationships, and relationship rules in response to situational and developmental stress" (Olson & McCubbin, 1983, p. 48). Concepts used to diagnose or measure adaptability include family power (assertiveness, control, discipline), negotiation styles, role relationships, and relationship rules.

There are also four levels of adaptability: (1) rigid (very low), (2) structured (low to moderate), (3) flexible (moderate to high), and (4) chaotic (very high). Again, the central levels, structured and flexible, are the most healthy in terms of family functioning, while the extremes, rigid and chaotic, are problematic.

Most basically, adaptability means the family system's ability to change. Olson points out that much of the early research on family systems emphasized the rigidity of the family and its resistance to change. Families were generally categorized according to a dichotomous scale that measured ability to change. *Morphostasis* described a rigid family pattern, one that resisted change. *Morphogenesis* described a family pattern that allowed for growth and development within the system. Families that could change were functional; those that could not change were dysfunctional.

Olson rejects the use of this dichotomy to evaluate functioning, stressing that a system needs both stability and change to function. Families functioning at either of these extremes are dysfunctional. Although morphogenesis sounds more positive than morphostasis, no family could function this way for an extended period of time. Again, the issue of balance is important. The family must be able to respond appropriately to life's circumstances, moving along the dimensions as needed to survive (Olson & McCubbin, 1983).

Communication

Communication is a *facilitating* dimension, which means that it is necessary for movement on the other two dimensions, cohesion and adaptability. Because it serves this purpose, communication is not included graphically in the model (see Figure 5-1).

Positive communication skills—including empathy, reflective listening, and supportive comments—are conducive to healthy family functioning because they enable members to share their changing needs and preferences. Being able to do this will affect the levels of cohesion and adaptability achieved. Negative communication skills—including double messages, double binds, and critical comments—contribute to dysfunction because they restrict the sharing needed for understanding. Again, this will affect levels of cohesion and adaptability.

Operation of the Model

Figure 5-1 depicts the relationship between the two dimensions, cohesion and adaptability. Note that each is presented as a continuum, rating low to high, which corresponds to the four levels designated for each dimension. The two sets of four levels form a 4 by 4 grid, thus specifying 16 distinct types of marital and family systems. Olson contends that certain of these 16 are more common than others, but each type can be identified and measured according to the model.

Upon examining the correspondence between the two dimensions and their respective levels, Olson formed three basic groups of family types: balanced, midrange, and extreme (see the key at the base of the graph for identification):

1. *Balanced* types have scores at the central ranges of both dimensions (four types).
2. *Midrange* types have a single extreme score on one of the dimensions (eight types).
3. *Extreme* types have extreme scores on both dimensions (four types).

Figure 5-1 *The Circumplex Model of the Family*

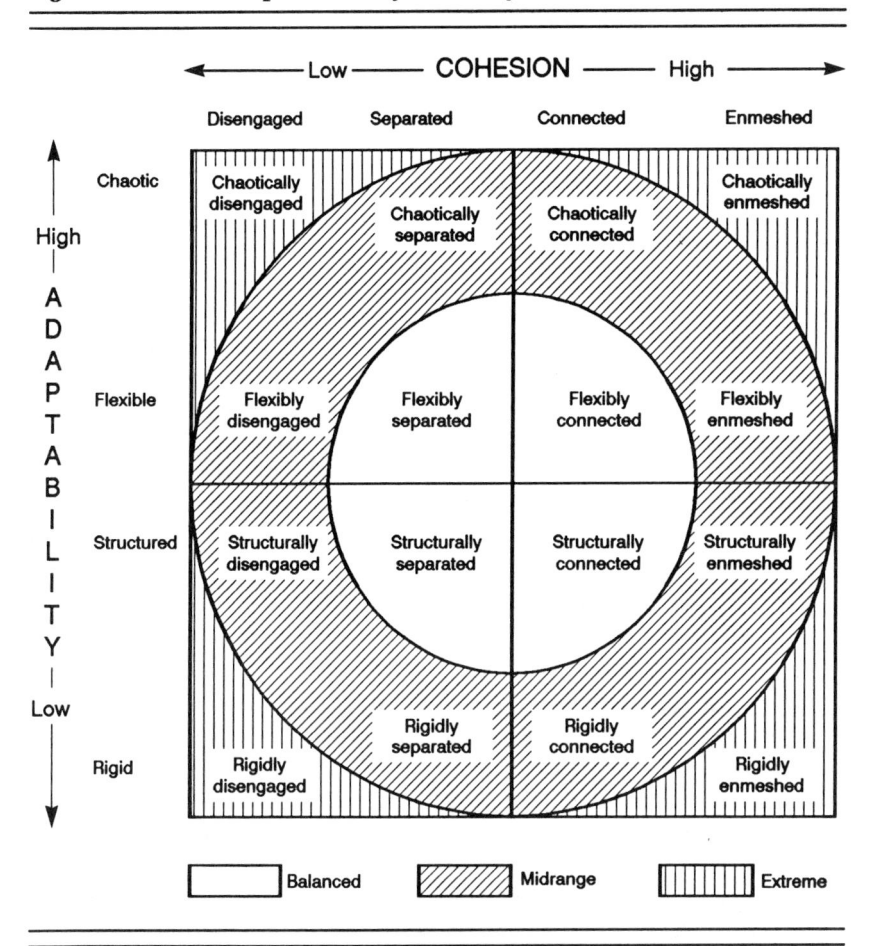

	Low — COHESION — High			
	Disengaged	Separated	Connected	Enmeshed
Chaotic (High ADAPTABILITY)	Chaotically disengaged	Chaotically separated	Chaotically connected	Chaotically enmeshed
Flexible	Flexibly disengaged	Flexibly separated	Flexibly connected	Flexibly enmeshed
Structured	Structurally disengaged	Structurally separated	Structurally connected	Structurally enmeshed
Rigid (Low)	Rigidly disengaged	Rigidly separated	Rigidly connected	Rigidly enmeshed

Balanced | Midrange | Extreme

Source: Olson and McCubbin, *Families: What makes them work?* p. 50, copyright 1983 by Sage Publications, Inc. Reprinted by permission of Sage Publications, Inc.

The Incestuous Family

According to family dynamics theory, we can't learn enough about incest by studying offenders and victims in isolation. We learn more if we study them together, and we learn a good deal more if we study them and the context in which they live. That context is the family.

The incestuous family can be called a *dysfunctional* family, but it is not the incest that creates the dysfunction. As a system, the family has operated ineffectively for some time. The incest is an "extreme symptom of family maladjustment," an observable result of the dysfunction (Lawton-Speert & Wachtel, 1982).

The family must be considered as a unit. As such, the individual members each play a part in preserving the family and furthering its supposedly common interests and welfare. Relationships are completely interdependent, and individual personalities are subordinated or even lost, as the family takes on one persona. Quite understandably, the basic motivation of everyone involved is to keep the family together. Doing so requires great energy, so much so that breaking the dysfunctional pattern may seem impossible. Thus, each member puts a lot into but gets very little out of the relationship.

It is important to understand that the family is not dysfunctional in the same way for each of its members. Although the overall aim is preservation of the unit, each individual has his or her own purposes and gains (Lawton-Speert & Wachtel, 1982). We will address these individual roles in the following section.

Family Characteristics

Resentment is a common theme in incestuous families. Individuals feel inadequate and out of control of their own lives, and they blame those around them for these problems. They may especially center on one another's weaknesses, such that they all reinforce one another's problems (Sgroi, Blick, & Porter, 1982).

Authoritarianism is another common theme. Individuals play clearly dominant or submissive roles, reinforcing in one another feelings of power and control and inadequacy and helplessness. Fathers usually play the dominant, authoritative role, and mothers and children usually play the submissive, dependent roles (Lawton-

Speert & Wachtel, 1982). Power becomes absolute. Everyone falls in line to keep the family order (Sgroi, Blick, & Porter, 1982).

Since the father is dominant in many incestuous families, themes of patriarchy and machismo are also observed. To be manly means to be strong, controlling, and dominant; feelings of weakness or dependence are suppressed and thought to be feminine. Thus, there is a strong emphasis on male and female qualities and roles, and these patterns become strongly entrenched. Such attitudes about which roles and expectations are appropriate also become justification for sexual abuse.

[The father] must delude himself into the view that his actions are not predatory but the mere expression of his rights, a natural extension of his dominant protective role. However, like the master who is faintly but inescapably aware of his dependence on his slaves (and their knowledge of that), the incestuous father is caught in the trap that he is dependent on his family in order to express the dominance he wants. (Lawton-Speert & Wachtel, pp. 35-36)

Sgroi asserts that denial is the only real coping mechanism that works in the incestuous family, perhaps because incest is so heinous. Everyone in the family denies what's going on. By avoiding reality, they can maintain the status quo (Sgroi, Blick, & Porter, 1982).

Role inversion is common in incestuous families, as well, as typical boundaries and definitions of relationships become obscured. In most cases, the mother takes on a child's role, and the daughter takes on the mother's role. In doing so, the daughter may also serve as her father's spouse. A similar pattern is observed in cases in which the son is abused by his mother. In short, both parents try to satisfy their own emotional needs through their children, clearly subverting their parental responsibilities and thwarting their children's basic development.

The incestuous family is often socially isolated in several respects. For instance, the family may live in a removed setting, a sort of "cultural backwater," in which there is little social interaction and monitoring. In addition, regardless of the geographic locale, many incestuous families are simply alienated from those around them, and this typically becomes worse as the incest continues. The sexual abuse may both result from and compensate for this alienation.

Extreme stress is also typical of incestuous families. Marital, financial, or childrearing problems may become overbearing, because a dysfunctional family will be unable to resolve them in any healthy and effective manner. Members will be unable to support one another, given the rigid and symbiotic roles they play: A dominant father will become more controlling, and a dependent mother will become more yielding. What's more, under stress, individuals are more likely to ignore the restraints they would normally feel.

Stress often results from some sort of dramatic change in the family situation, including unemployment, a major financial setback, or the serious illness or death of a family member. Many incestuous families report having undergone some type of major family crisis one or two years before the incest began (Lawton-Speert & Wachtel, 1982).

Individuals within the Family

The Father

Sgroi describes the incestuous father (the offender) as a "me-first" type of person. In short, he is a demanding, needy individual who seeks to satisfy himself without regard for anyone else. For such an individual, an incestuous relationship with a child is an easy solution: Children are less threatening and less demanding, which makes the relationship more secure (Sgroi, Blick, & Porter, 1982).

Research on incestuous fathers has also established that most come from emotionally deprived backgrounds. Their own family relationships were cold and unloving, and many of these men were deserted or somehow abandoned as youths. Not only, then, do they lack a good family model and the relationship experiences that go along with it, but they also feel a strong desertion anxiety.

Incestuous fathers have also been found to be rigid and authoritarian, heading a very strict patriarchal family. The father is all-powerful and dominant and controls the behavior of his wife and children. His need for power stems from feelings of inadequacy and low self-worth, as well as the fear of desertion mentioned above. Societal values that depict dominant male roles and submissive female roles also contribute to this pattern.

Problems including unemployment or extreme stress from work may leave men feeling hollow and emotionally cut off. They may compensate by making demands on their families (Lawton-Speert & Wachtel, 1982).

In our previous discussion of family patterns, we stated that social isolation is common among incestuous families; the father is usually primarily responsible for that isolation. He believes that the outside world is hostile and reinforces this belief in his wife and children. This belief then becomes both a reason and an excuse for having incest, and the father is likely to make such rationalizations to his victim (i.e., "You can't trust anyone but me" or "You know I would never hurt you"). Often, the father serves as the only link between the family and the outside world, establishing himself even further as the sole authority, on whom everyone else must depend (Sgroi, Blick, & Porter, 1982).

Speculation about the incestuous father would have us believe that he is psychotic, pedophilic, alcoholic, and of low intelligence. The only one of these traits that may be significant is that of alcohol abuse. A number of studies have found high rates of problem drinking but not necessarily chronic alcoholism in incestuous families. Thus, the scenario is not one in which an alcoholic father molests his daughter during repeated drunken binges. Rather, alcohol reduces the father's inhibitions, escalating the existing problem situation but not causing it. This pattern has also been observed in families in which other types of abuse are inflicted (Lawton-Speert & Wachtel, 1982).

Incestuous fathers rarely use physical force in procuring sex, although most do rely on threats, both to have sex and to keep family members in line. This is typical of the general family pattern of communication and control.

Upon disclosure, the father will be alarmed and defensive and hostile to the child and all who support him or her. The father will try to use his position of power or authority to control the situation and will likely try to make the child recant. He will also be afraid of the legal and social sanctions that are sure to follow (Sgroi, Blick, & Porter, 1982).

The Mother

The role of the mother in the incestuous family is of great interest in the research on sexual abuse. Opinions are extreme, falling at opposite ends of a continuum of responsibility. At one end, the mother is the target of blame; she has played a collusive, selfish role in setting up her children and even gaining from their victimization. At the other end, the mother is too passive to be blamed; she is just another victim of the abusive father (de Young, 1985). Regardless, the mother seems to be guilty of "commission or omission."

Most studies of mothers portray women who are either physically or psychologically absent; that is, they have withdrawn from their families. Many are weak, passive, and dependent; they are generally overwhelmed by their family responsibilities. They feel powerless and out of control; thus, they submit to the control of their husbands, and they are unable to supervise their children. Drug or alcohol abuse may contribute to the problem (de Young, 1985). Most of these women also lack basic social skills and are cut off from the outside world; they have few friends and don't know how to develop and maintain relationships. They would have difficulty supporting themselves financially (Sgroi, Blick, & Porter, 1982).

Other women may be willful and even dominant, but they have abandoned their families in favor of outside interests, such as a career or excessive involvement in volunteer work (Lawton-Speert & Wachtel, 1982). Sgroi suggests that the mother's withdrawal may be her attempt to remove herself from an unsatisfying situation (regardless of whether she knows of the incest). Many husbands in incestuous families have highly unrealistic expectations of their wives, sometimes demanding near servitude. The woman who cannot satisfy such a man may look for self-gratification elsewhere. Unfortunately, doing so often means abandoning her role as a mother, as well (Sgroi, Blick, & Porter, 1982).

A consistent aspect of this abandonment is sexual withdrawal from the husband. The helpless, dependent wife may be incapable of sexual involvement, and the husband may likely find her undesirable at this point in their relationship. A dominant woman may tease or outright reject her husband to the point that he feels emasculated (Lawton-Speert & Wachtel, 1982).

The mother often has a rigid and repressive attitude about sex. This may account in part for her lack of interest in marital sex and her inability to deal with the incest once it has been revealed. Knowing their mother feels this way will prohibit children from turning to her for help; communication will be cut off and a cold, distant relationship will be established. Restrictive attitudes about sex may have a paradoxical effect on the children, who are told one thing but observe another (de Young, 1985).

The mother/daughter roles in the incestuous family are usually psychologically inseparable. The role reversal described earlier—in which mothers act like daughters and daughters act like mothers—eventually creates mutual feelings of resentment. Mothers will resent their daughters for having replaced them, and they will frequently criticize and accuse their daughters of wrongdoing. Daughters will, in turn, resent their mothers for having put them in this position and may actually play a participatory, seductive role in an attempt to get even. And in families in which there is a generational pattern of incest, mothers who were abused as children may also be addressing unresolved feelings about their mothers as they face the current problem in their own families (Lawton-Speert & Wachtel, 1982).

Certainly, the critical question about the mother's role is, Was she aware of the incest? Could a father really hide an ongoing incestuous relationship? Would a child not tell what was going on?

It is doubtful that a mother could be unaware of incest occurring in her own family, in her own home. Mothers who say they were unaware have probably blocked the realization unconsciously, even in the face of direct evidence. And mothers who acknowledge being aware were most likely powerless to resolve the situation or maybe unconsciously avoided action for some self-serving reason (e.g., to avoid their own abuse) (Lawton-Speert & Wachtel, 1982). These mothers have practiced what may be termed *unconscious collusion* (de Young, 1985).

Sgroi reports mothers who were aware of the incest yet warned their children against disclosure, perhaps threatening them about what doing so would do to the rest of the family. The mother's own selfish interests and fear of abandonment may be very powerful. Other mothers who know what's going on try to "run interference" for their children, making it difficult for the children to be in dangerous situations with their father. This rarely works, however, even in the short term, because of the father's dominance. Regardless of their knowledge of incest, though, Sgroi concludes that few incestuous mothers are strong enough to take action alone.

Upon disclosure, the mother may be concerned primarily for the child or perhaps for herself or even for her husband. Not all mothers are able to sustain protective feelings toward their abused children throughout the entire intervention process. Some are afraid of siding with their children, which means choosing between the husband

and the child; they may fear retribution and abandonment. Others are legitimately concerned for their husbands, and they may blame or resent the victimized child for what has happened. Given the weakness of many of these mothers, it's not unusual for them to abandon all responsibility and refuse participation, clearly giving the offending husband more control (Sgroi, Blick, & Porter, 1982).

Overall, it is difficult to be fair in reviewing the role of the mother in an incestuous family. We expect mothers to be naturally caring and nurturing. They are supposed to put their children above all else, including their own interests and needs. And they are supposed to be fearless and undauntable in protecting their children, at all costs. In short, we expect too much from mothers, which makes it difficult for us to understand their very human shortcomings (Lawton-Speert & Wachtel, 1982).

The Victim

Much research has tried to explain why certain individuals are victimized: What about these individuals caused or contributed to their being abused? However, as mentioned in Chapter 4 on victims, this approach sometimes seems accusing and blaming, pointing out what's supposedly wrong with the victim. And while research on offenders has characterized them more and more as being fairly normal individuals—not perverts or psychopaths—research on victims has characterized them as being provocative and seductive (Lawton-Speert & Wachtel, 1982).

Victims are sometimes blamed for the role they play by those who insist that children are capable of seducing adults into committing incest. Some place total responsibility for incest on the children, while others view them as being less culpable but nonetheless directly involved in initiating and continuing the sex. Still others believe that the children are always the victims, regardless of the extent of their participation, because the offender, as an adult, is expected to be the responsible party. Children are not emotionally or psychologically capable of making a decision about entering into a sexual relationship. Also, on a more philosophical level, even the blatantly seductive child cannot be blamed, because his or her behavior is the result of social and family influences (de Young, 1985).

It is naive to think that children have no will, no desires, no sexual interests. They are normally curious and imitative, particularly regarding what is supposedly mature and adultlike. Researchers have found that, at least initially, children may find sex with a family member—usually a father or sibling—comfortable and even enjoyable. Unless the child is physically hurt or frightened, the early stage of sexual involvement is usually not traumatic.

As the incest continues, however, the victim will likely resent the offender's increasing demands and control, especially as the child's normal activities and friendships are curtailed. The victim may become manipulative, granting or withholding sex in return for some concession (Sgroi, Blick, & Porter, 1982). The victim may also try to end the relationship by reporting the incest to someone such as a teacher.

The Siblings

There is little actual research on the roles played by siblings in the incestuous family. Sgroi reports that siblings who have also been sexually abused may hesitate to support or help one another for fear of retaliation by the offender. In fact, a child who is being sexually abused may set up another sibling to save himself or herself from further abuse.

The other children in the family may resent the sexually abused sibling out of a sort of warped sibling rivalry. Consider, though, the general emotional neediness of the dysfunctional family. Any supposed affection is believed to be better than none, and the fact that one child has been selected over the others will be viewed as favoritism.

Upon disclosure, siblings will feel concerned and protective toward their brother or sister, but they may also be defensive and resentful. Separation anxiety will be powerful, and most children will understand the disrupting affect disclosure will have on the family. Siblings may also be angry because of the social reaction they will face when others learn of what's happened in their family (Sgroi, Blick, & Porter, 1982).

Siblings may also feel guilty about what has happened. For instance, a child who knew that his or her sister was being abused by their father may feel guilty for not having reported the abuse (Mitnick, 1989). Likewise, siblings who have also been abused may feel guilty about not reporting themselves and perhaps preventing more sexual abuse. All siblings with knowledge of the abuse will likely feel relieved that the secret is out in the open and the abuse will stop.

Five Phases of Sexual Abuse

Based on their extensive study of child sexual abuse, Suzanne Sgroi and her colleagues have outlined a typical abuse scenario (Sgroi, Blick, & Porter, 1982). Although this scenario may apply to all types of child sexual abuse, it is especially descriptive of incestuous abuse, describing how the abuse begins, how it progresses and is maintained, and what will happen upon disclosure.

1. *Engagement*—In the engagement stage, three variables are significant:
   a. Access and opportunity—The offender will create and arrange for private situations with the child if they don't occur naturally.
   b. Relationship of the participants—The offender is almost always within the family or the family circle and has normal and authorized access to the child.
   c. Inducements—The offender must be able to convince the child that what he or she is offering is fun, a "special secret" or game that they will play. The adept offender will subtly coerce the child. Physical force is rarely used in intrafamilial situations, but the nature of the family relationship may be threatening (i.e., strong patriarchal structure).

2. *Sexual interaction*—Incestuous sex typically progresses in severity. The offender may begin exposing himself or herself and then progress to masturbation and fondling, at first individually and then mutually. Next, the interaction will involve various types of penetration, including oral sex, anal sex, and vaginal intercourse. Although the order and nature of the acts are not prescribed, the general idea of progression is common.

3. *Secrecy*—"Secrecy eliminates accountability" (Sgroi, Blick, & Porter, 1982, p. 15). On a very functional level, keeping the sex secret allows for repeating it; this is critical to the offender, who is typically very needy and demanding. In terms of relationships, sex with a child is easier than sex with an adult. The relationship is clearly not mutual but rather is completely self-serving. On a psychological level, secrecy means denial, which we discussed earlier in this chapter.

Why does the child keep the secret? He or she may enjoy the rewards and the attention received from the offender, or he or she may be afraid to report, especially if the offender has made threats. Some children feel that having sex makes them mature and grown up (pseudomaturity). Many fear that, if they report, they will be separated from the family; this is especially true of very young children.

4. *Disclosure*—Two types of disclosure are possible:
   a. Accidental disclosure is effected by an external agent and without purposeful involvement by any of the participants. A third party, usually outside the family, may observe the relationship or the effects of it (i.e., physical injury or venereal disease). Accidental disclosure is always followed by some type of crisis intervention. Such intervention is incredibly traumatic because it must happen so quickly, without warning or preparation, and because of the anxiety over what's happened.
   b. Purposeful disclosure is made by one of the participants, usually the child. Younger children may want to "share a secret" with someone, while older children may simply want to be free from the abuse and the control. Planned intervention will be more orderly and less anxious than crisis intervention. More preparations can be made, and the child reporting the abuse can be encouraged and supported about his or her actions. (Also see Chapter 6 on identification and disclosure.)

5. *Suppression*—Suppression always follows disclosure, and it is especially intense in intrafamilial situations. The offender will try to retain his dominant role and even seek more power as he induces feelings of guilt and fear and tries to prevent family members from participating in treatment. The entire family may pressure the child victim into recanting or simply refuse to cooperate, hoping that doing so will stop intervention; verbal and physical abuse may be employed. If the child will not recant, the family may try to undermine his or her credibility.

Treatment Recommendations

Family therapy is the treatment of choice for families in which incest has been discovered. Sgroi (1982) recommends it as the best treatment for all families in which sexual abuse has occurred, regardless of whether the abuse was intrafamilial or extrafamilial.

As mentioned in the overview of family dynamics therapy earlier in the chapter, there is no standard set of operating procedures. However, therapists do follow several major methods:

1. *Conjoint family therapy*—This is a transactional approach in which one or two therapists see the entire nuclear family during every session.
2. *Multiple impact theory (MIT)*—A team of therapists works with the family members individually and in various combinations. Intense sessions last over two to three days.
3. *Kin network therapy*—The nuclear family, as well as significant relatives and friends, are involved in therapy as needed.
4. *Multiple family group therapy*—Three or four families are brought together in the same group for therapy, usually on a regular basis.

Most therapists prefer to work with the nuclear family in a conjoint approach. Some therapists prefer to work alone, but it is helpful to have both male and female co-therapists. This allows for better observation and control and also provides role models for both sexes.

Therapy is usually conducted in an office setting on a regularly scheduled basis, just like any other type of medical treatment. Some therapists visit the home on an occasional but usually irregular basis. There is interest in conducting therapy in the home setting because of the significance of the family's natural environment (Olson, 1970).

Little research is available on which approaches work best in which types of situations. Moreover, family dynamics therapy continues to be very experimental and innovative, so hard-and-fast rules are not likely to be produced. This appears to be the nature of the theory, as Haley saw it nearly 20 years ago: "Family therapy is not a method of treatment but a new orientation to the human dilemma. Given that orientation, any number of methods may be used" (in Olson, 1970, p. 516).

Assessment

Before treatment can be planned, an assessment of how the family situation contributed to the abuse is important. Such an assessment should address:

1. quality of parental supervision,
2. appropriateness of parental choices of caretakers,
3. inappropriate sleeping arrangements,
4. clarity of role boundaries,
5. level and types of violence between family members,
6. chemical dependency by family members,
7. individual psychopathologies, and
8. extent of direct or collusive involvement in abuse by family members.

In cases of incest, three contributing factors related to the family situation are most often cited:

1. failure to protect children, both in terms of poor supervision and inappropriate choices of caretakers;
2. failure to define roles clearly and appropriately, including the failure to set and follow limits; and
3. abuse of power and how corresponding passive/dominant patterns have become a family way of life (Sgroi, 1982).

Treatment Issues

Once an assessment has been completed, the therapist must concentrate on those issues that are most critical to the family's functioning. What is at the root of the problem?

At the risk of oversimplifying the complexity of family dynamics, there is usually a pattern, a common set of behaviors that are the basis of the dysfunction. Treatment must be designed specifically to address this pattern, because unless it can be changed, the family will continue to be dysfunctional.

Sgroi (1982) has outlined 10 problematic behaviors that have been found to be common to incestuous families. These are the issues that must be addressed for treatment to be successful.

1. *Abuse of power*—Without exception, abuse of power is a primary treatment issue. In most incestuous families, authoritarianism is so prominent that it dictates the entire nature of the family relationships. Even when the abuse of power is not forceful or coer-

cive, it is still aggressive and harmful; individuals with more power seek self-gratification at the expense of others without regard. Until the exercise of power is under control, change within individuals and the family unit will be impossible.

2. *Fear of authority*—As a result of the abuse of power they have endured, individuals in dysfunctional families see authority as destructive and controlling. Even those individuals in power will fear outside authority, which means discovery and disclosure. This is a difficult issue to address, because intervention itself is viewed as authority. The natural reaction is avoidance; when treatment is forced, a range of reactions is possible, from passive participation to aggressive resistance.

3. *Isolation*—Social isolation and the fear of authority are mutually reinforcing and must be addressed as such in treatment. The isolated family will view the outside world as hostile and punishing, and the powerful authority figure in the family (usually the father) will encourage this view, both out of his fear of authority and as a means of preventing disclosure. The other family members will become increasingly dependent and helpless, especially since they are deprived of the support and care of others.

4. *Denial*—Denial operates on two levels in the incestuous family. First, the family denies the incest in order to bear knowledge of it; this denial may be overt or unconscious. And second, to maintain their social isolation, which is critical to maintaining the status quo, the family denies the positive aspects of the outside world. Fortunately, denial generally works in the short term only. It simply takes too much energy to sustain denial over the long term.

5. *Lack of empathy*—This, like abuse of power, is a major treatment issue, because until individuals are willing to acknowledge one another's feelings and abandon the existing callous relationship, change is impossible. Developing empathy is particularly important in working with the offender, who is usually totally unaware of the victim's feelings. This is a denial mechanism that diminishes guilt and simplifies the abuse of power.

6. *Poor communication patterns*—The family's communication patterns—both within the family itself and between the family and the outside world—must be addressed in treatment. In most cases, communication has become a tool of power. The offending parent

gives orders and criticizes as a means of controlling others, and the other family members may communicate or hold back to retaliate in one of the few ways they can. Social isolation will restrict opportunities for developing needed communication skills, and lack of empathy and an attitude of denial will hinder correcting communication problems. Because communication affects so many aspects of the family relationship, it is a primary treatment issue.

7. *Inadequate self-control and limit setting*—The issue of self-control is tied to role boundaries and personal neediness, which will be addressed in the following discussions. All three of these factors relate to the offender's uncontrollable need for self-gratification and his or her abuse of power to achieve it. Regardless of whether this behavior is impulsive, as some have suggested, offenders have difficulty rationalizing their needs and setting appropriate limits for themselves. In some cases, individuals place no restrictions on their behavior, while in other cases, they may impose very rigid and unrealistic limits, trying to ensure compliance by themselves and others. The result is constant feelings of guilt and impunity.

8. *Blurred boundaries*—Inadequate self-control and limit setting inevitably lead to confusion about physical and emotional boundaries. In many cases, parents set rigid limits for others and then violate them themselves. The role conversion that is characteristic of the incestuous family is the best illustration of this problem. According to traditional family roles, this conversion is wrong; parents are supposed to provide their children with emotional gratification, not depend on them for providing it. Children cannot help but be confused about what is right and wrong when they have no appropriate role models. This pattern is self-reinforcing and difficult to correct.

9. *Extreme emotional deprivation and neediness*—All people have needs and seek to have them met; however, when these needs become overwhelming and immediate self-gratification becomes critical, behavior may become destructive and pathological. People with exaggerated needs have never learned how to satisfy themselves through normal means; thus, they become very dependent and garner a certain amount of attention. But what's worse is that this neediness may be taught and passed on to others in the social environment. This perpetuation may be a factor in intergenerational abuse, as children model their dependent parents and become vic-

tims themselves. This is another pattern that is self-reinforcing and thus difficult to correct.

10. *Magical expectations*—A final treatment issue addresses what the family and each individual member expect from treatment. Given the nature of the individuals involved and the dysfunctional relationship they are enmeshed in, it should be expected that everyone will be looking for an ultimate solution, one that will not only resolve the incest problem but that will also gratify all their individual needs and make things right. At the onset of treatment, individual expectations must be spelled out, even though this will be difficult at first, due to the collective persona of the incestuous family. It is especially important that, if the victimized child has disclosed the abuse, he or she is encouraged and supported yet made aware that there is no magical answer to the problem.

Multicultural Concerns

In planning intervention and treatment for an abuse victim and his or her family, it is important to acknowledge the family's cultural and ethnic background and values. These values will vary with each cultural group (e.g., black, Native American, Hispanic, Southeast Asian) and even within segments of the same group, so workers must be sensitive in approaching the family and assessing how this trauma has affected them. The following general issues should be considered:

1. Will the victim and/or family be uncomfortable with medical, social, and law enforcement institutions (i.e., fear insensitive or discriminatory treatment, language or religious barriers, humiliation due to financial hardship or previous experience)?
2. What specific cultural connotations does being sexually abused have for the victim and/or family (i.e., issues of virginity, suitability for marriage, general self-worth)?
3. What family dynamics are involved—in both the immediate and extended families—that may help or hinder the victim and/or family in recovering (i.e., strong matriarchal or patriarchal structure, absent or incapacitated authority figures or role models)?

4. What feelings of anger or despair does the victim and/or family have about the abuse having been committed by someone in their own race/culture *or* by someone from another race/culture (i.e., individual and cultural victimization)?

In addition to these victim/family issues, workers should consider their own personal values about minorities. They should be honest in acknowledging any biases they may hold and, if appropriate, refer the victim to another, more empathetic worker without hesitation. Even if the worker feels able to handle the case with understanding, he or she should bring in someone from the victim's culture to serve as a liaison with the victim and/or family. These so-called *cultural translators* need not be trained or professional individuals; their role is to offer information about the culture to the worker and serve as a healthy role model for the victim and family (George, 1989).

Prognosis for Success

Unfortunately, the prognosis for treatment of severely dysfunctional families is poor (Sgroi, 1982). It is very hard to change patterns and behaviors that have become a way of life, which is what has happened in the incestuous family. Even when one family member is able to change, the others will pressure him or her to revert or will minimize the change, discounting the effects of therapy. Indeed, therapy can be very frustrating.

Olson contends that the dysfunctional family will resist change because it is by nature a homeostatic system. To break through, he recommends observing what he terms *homeostatic mechanisms*, signs of the pattern of interaction between family members that sustains the negative behaviors. Simply, families have rules that govern their behavior; even the smallest set of rules can be very telling about relationships between members. There is a circular causality, a chain reaction of events from one member to another. No problem exists solely between two people; in one way or another, sooner or later, it will affect everyone. The key is to trace the pattern of movement, how each family member is touched by the same event (Olson & McCubbin, 1983).

Summary

In our culture, incest is treated with a good deal of ambivalence. On the one hand, it is, in most cases, considered to be child sexual abuse, and it is regarded to be a grave violation of the family and the social order. On the other hand, unless the interaction is very violent or damaging, many people choose not to report incest, deciding that it's not serious enough to warrant intervention and treatment.

The definition of *incest* is significant in establishing its prevalence. We have defined *incest* to include sexual contact between family members; however, *family* is defined as a social and domestic unit—including step-relations and significant others—and not strictly according to kinship.

Incest is grossly underreported, but prevalence estimates range from 1 in 100 families to 1 in 4 families. Finkelhor estimates that, just within the nuclear family, 14% of girls and 8% of boys have had an incestuous experience. Most of this contact, both heterosexual and homosexual, is between siblings. Girls are more at risk than boys from abuse by older family members.

Although incest has been reported between all family members, father/daughter incest and sibling incest are most common; there is some speculation that father/son incest may be more common than we would think, however. Mothers rarely sexually abuse their children. Incest with other family members is difficult to evaluate because of reporting problems and the diversity in family relationships.

Our review of the incestuous family is based on family dynamics theory, specifically, as described by David Olson. Olson's Circumplex Model of the Family illustrates family functioning by examining three dynamics: cohesion, adaptability, and communication. Olson stresses that the issue of balance is basic to healthy family functioning, as the family must be able to fluctuate and evolve with changing circumstances.

The incestuous family, as a dysfunctional family, has operated ineffectively for some time. The incest is not the cause of the dysfunction; rather, it is a gross symptom of the problem. The typical scenario presents a patriarchal family in which the father's power is absolute; the mother is passive and dependent, unable to care for herself and her children. Although the mother and the siblings usually know of the incest, they are too powerless to act. Feelings of resentment, collusion, and denial contribute to the secrecy that surrounds incest.

Treatment of the incestuous family, based on family dynamics theory, must address the enmeshed pattern of family interaction. Individual change is not possible without change in the family system. Primary treatment issues include abuse of power, social isolation, role boundaries, and communication, to name a few. Unless these issues are resolved, the family will continue to be dysfunctional. Unfortunately, the prognosis for seriously dysfunctional families is poor, since the patterns of interaction have become a way of life.

Note

1. Olson points out that what is considered appropriate family cohesion is very much cultural. The levels described in the Circumplex Model and the assessment of how they contribute to family functioning are based on mainstream U.S. culture. Families in other cultures may function well at extreme levels of cohesion, but this is not likely for American families (Olson & McCubbin, 1983).

Part Three

The System

Chapter Six

Reporting Child Sexual Abuse

One of the most consistently posed theories about child sexual abuse is that it is grossly underreported. It's estimated that only two-thirds of all victims report being molested to anyone, due to feelings of helplessness and guilt and fears of separation and retaliation. And it's difficult to establish how many parents, teachers, coaches, or other adults have been told of abuse or have observed likely symptoms but have failed to report. Some say they weren't sure enough to report; some didn't believe the children; others were ignorant of what to do and where to go; others empathized with the family's desire for privacy and control; and still others feared involvement or retaliation.

Hopefully, increased knowledge about child sexual abuse—including knowledge of what to look for and how to report—will lead to increased reporting. What's more, increased knowledge about reporting—including documenting and "packaging" the report—will lead to improved determination and more successful intervention.

In this chapter, we will begin with a discussion of mandated reporting, giving an overview of the basic principles of Minnesota's reporting law. The remainder of the chapter will be instructional, outlining how to be a proactive reporter: how to prepare for making a report, how to influence the impact the report has, and what will likely happen after the report is made.

Mandated Reporting

The legal concept of a *mandated reporter* is relatively new. There were no national or state laws enforcing reporting of child abuse prior to 1960. And the original interest was in physical abuse; thus, initially, physicians were the only mandated reporters. Sexual abuse was addressed only in those cases where the child was severely injured, which constituted physical abuse.

National legislation was enacted in 1974 (Public Law 93-247), addressing the prevention and treatment of child abuse and neglect, including sexual abuse. And by 1975, every state had instituted some sort of mandated reporting law. Minnesota first passed such legislation in 1963, providing protection for children from physical abuse, which included sexual abuse. In 1978, child neglect was added to the statute, and over the last 10 years, a number of provisions have been added to the law, making it more specific and inclusive.

General Provisions of the Minnesota Reporting Law

The law that mandates reporting of child abuse is Minnesota statute 626.556, the Reporting of Maltreatment to Minors Act. This law is part of the state criminal code, not the juvenile code.[1]

The law has three general purposes, as described by the first subdivision outlining public policy:

1. to protect children whose health or welfare may be jeopardized through physical abuse, neglect, or sexual abuse;
2. to strengthen the family and make the home, school, and community safe for children by promoting responsible child care in all settings; and
3. to provide, when necessary, a safe temporary or permanent home environment for physically or sexually abused children.

In order to ensure that these purposes are fulfilled, the law does the following:

1. it requires the reporting of neglect, physical abuse, or sexual abuse of children in home, school, and community settings by the person responsible for them;
2. it provides for the voluntary reporting of abuse or neglect;
3. it requires the assessment and investigation of the reports; and
4. it provides protective and counseling services in appropriate cases.

As can be expected, the law itself contains a number of subdivisions and specific details regarding definitions and legal provisions. We will review only the basics of the reporting law, in essence, outlining who is mandated to report, how they should go about making that report, and what they can expect after reporting. Also, we will discuss the law in terms of reporting child sexual abuse only, although the same guidelines apply to reporting child neglect and physical abuse, as well.

Mandated versus Voluntary Reporters

In Minnesota, a number of professionals are mandated reporters, including those engaged in:

- health care, or the "healing" arts (physical, psychological, psychiatric, and health administration);
- education (teachers, administrators, aides, and staff);
- child care;
- clergy;
- social services; and
- law enforcement.

Individuals in these professions are required to report if they *know or have reason to believe*[2] that a child is being neglected or physically or sexually abused or has been neglected or abused within the last three years. People who are not working in these professions may voluntarily report if they *know, have reason to believe,* or *suspect* that a child is being neglected or abused. Thus, one does not have to be a mandated reporter to make a report.

How to Make a Report

Mandated reporters who know or believe that abuse has occurred must report the information immediately (within 24 hours) to the local child protective services (CPS), police department, or county sheriff's office. The agency receiving the report—CPS or law enforcement—must notify the other agency within 24 hours, both orally and in writing. Therefore, it is not necessary for the reporter to report to more than one agency.

The reporter should make an oral report first, in person or by telephone. A mandated reporter (but not a voluntary one) must follow up with a written report to the same agency within 72 hours (excluding weekends and holidays). Again, the agency receiving the information will share it with the other agency immediately.

The written report from the mandated reporter must contain the following information:

1. the identity of the child,
2. the identity of anyone believed to be responsible for the abuse or neglect if it is known,
3. the nature and extent of the abuse or neglect (as much as is known), and
4. the name and address of the person making the report.

Along with the written report, the mandated reporter should submit any documentation he or she has made of the abuse, such as notes in a log or student record. Doing so will enhance his or her credibility and thus the likelihood that the report will be followed up. (See "Documentation" and "Packaging Your Report," later in this chapter.)

Confidentiality

The identity of a mandated or voluntary reporter is essentially confidential. Only the CPS worker, prosecuting attorney, and law enforcement personnel involved in the case will know who made the report. The only exception is that, in accordance with disclosure rules, the prosecutor can reveal the identity of a reporter who is called as a witness. In such a case, the reporter's identity would be disclosed to the defense and may be entered into public record.

The reporter may allow the release of his or her name, if desired. And if a court establishes that a report was false and made in bad faith, the reporter's name will be released and civil or criminal action may be taken against him or her.

If the child has been abused by a family member or adult caretaker, local CPS and law enforcement agencies have the authority to interview the alleged victim and other minors living with him or her (or who have resided with him or her in the past) without parental consent. If the offender is outside the family unit, parents will be notified prior to the child's interview. However, if the parents are unavailable and the interview is deemed to be urgent, workers may proceed without parental consent. The parents are to be informed as soon as possible after the interview. If the parents or caretakers refuse to let their child be interviewed, CPS and law enforcement may get an order from the juvenile court and proceed with the interview.

Children are usually interviewed in a familiar location, one in which they are normally found, such as school. When the meeting is to be conducted on school property, the agency will notify the school of the need for an interview. School officials are expected to comply with this request within 24 hours, setting up a time and place for the interview that interferes least with normal school operation. School officials are also instructed not to disclose this information or other relevant details regarding the report or the interview to the parents or guardians, should the alleged offender be a family member, or to others in the school who have no need to know.

The parent or legal guardian is to be notified of the interview by the agency no later than the completion of the assessment or investigation, unless the juvenile court agrees that doing so would bring harm to the child. Under such circumstances, notification may be withheld indefinitely, generally until necessary intervention plans have been formulated.

After the assessment or investigation is completed, records will be maintained depending on the determination made.

- If it could not be determined that maltreatment occurred and protective services are not determined to be necessary, the records may be maintained for up to four years. If the alleged offender desires, however, the records must be destroyed within 30 days after his or her request for destruction. The

exception is that law enforcement may maintain records permanently.
- If it has been determined that maltreatment occurred and/or that protective services are needed, the records will be maintained for seven years after the last entry is made in the record.

Liability and Retaliation

Both voluntary and mandated reporters are immune from any civil or criminal liability for having made a report, provided that they have acted in good faith. Employees of schools and other facilities that may assist in the assessment and investigation of abuse or neglect are also immune. No supervisor or employer may penalize any employee or child for making a report.

The key point regarding immunity is that the report was made in good faith. Anyone who knowingly or recklessly makes a false report is liable for both civil and criminal damages. A mandated reporter who fails to report abuse, whether it is ongoing or has occurred within the past three years, is subject to criminal prosecution by the county attorney for a misdemeanor offense.

Along these lines, retaliation against the reporter, the facility, or the child involved is prohibited. For instance, an employer cannot discharge, transfer, demote, or suspend an employee because he or she reported abuse or neglect, nor can a child in a facility be restricted or prohibited access to school or other activities because a report has been made about him or her.

Follow-Up

After a report is made, it must be validated. If the report alleges neglect or abuse of a child by a parent or another adult caretaker within the family unit or a facility, local CPS will conduct an assessment, determining whether maltreatment occurred and if protective services are needed. (Services may be recommended regardless of the disposition of the report. See Chapter 8.) If the report alleges a criminal violation (i.e., severe physical abuse), the local law enforcement agency may conduct an investigation.

In most cases of sexual abuse, both CPS and law enforcement will be involved, since the child's well-being is in question and a crime has allegedly been committed. Ideally, both agencies will coordinate their actions and cooperate in fact-finding to avoid duplication of efforts and repeated interviews with children. However, each agency will conduct its own assessment/investigation[3] and produce its own disposition of the case. (See Chapter 8.)

A mandated reporter may request from CPS that he or she receive a summary of the assessment and/or any services recommended, unless releasing the information would somehow be detrimental to the child. A voluntary reporter is entitled to receive a concise summary of the findings of the assessment, again, unless doing so would be harmful to the child. Keep in mind, however, that it's up to the reporter to request the assessment summary. It will not be made available automatically. (Also see "Packaging Your Report," later in this chapter.)

Proactive Reporting

The responsibility of reporting child abuse or neglect is one that must be taken seriously. To some, this is intimidating, particularly in this era of malpractice and similar litigation. Indeed, some may wonder if reporting is worth the risk: Why go out on a limb, especially when it's possible that ultimately nothing will be done?

Fern Sepler (1988), executive director of the Minnesota Crime Victim and Witness Advisory Council, has spoken of this attitude, describing reporters whose chief concern is to "cover their butt." A good reporter must be a *proactive reporter,* someone who strives to follow his or her instincts, make observations, ask questions, and get involved with children on an ongoing basis. Such a professional doesn't wait for the child to come to him or her but knows how to tell if something's wrong.

Sometimes, the proactive reporter must be covert, for instance, picking up questionable bits of conversation between a child and parent. And sometimes, he or she must be overt, perhaps asking a parent a direct question about how a child got hurt or why a child is acting differently. This is not to say that a good reporter must be a spy or an investigator or that he or she should be unethical. Rather, a good reporter must be able to employ all of the information that is available to him or her within a professional setting.

Who Reports?

In its 1988 report *Child Maltreatment in Minnesota: 1985-86,* the Minnesota Department of Human Services revealed that, of all the reports it received in 1986 (including neglect, physical abuse, and sexual abuse), 46% came from nonmandated reporters, 46.4% came from mandated reporters, and 7.2% came from both. Among the mandated reporters, educators and those employed in other work with children (e.g., child care, counseling, social services) made the most reports (15.4% and 16%, respectively), followed by law enforcement professionals (9.6%) and medical professionals (9.4%).

How many of the cases that were reported in 1986 were actually substantiated (i.e., it was determined that maltreatment occurred)? Approximately 30% of the cases reported by voluntary reporters were substantiated, versus 43% of those reported by mandated reporters. When both voluntary and mandated reporters reported, approximately 60% of the cases were substantiated. National statistics on substantiation are comparable to these figures (Swanson Broberg, 1988).

Douglas Besharov, former head of the National Center on Child Abuse and Neglect, is critical of what he feels is an excess of mandated reporting. He cites what many feel are disturbingly low substantiation rates as evidence that too many invalid reports are made. Besharov condemns the unnecessary and unfounded intrusion of the state into personal and family domains, a view that has a good deal of support. (Besharov's views on the dysfunctioning system are also discussed in Chapter 9.)

Others would argue that it's better to report, even when uncertain, than not to report a potentially abusive and dangerous situation. After all, a child's welfare is at stake. Reporters cannot be expected to have the experience and judgment necessary to assess and validate cases of abuse; however, they should have the knowledge necessary to recognize the likely symptoms of abuse and how to go about reporting it.

Identification

Refer to the statistics just cited about which professionals most often report child abuse and neglect. They say a lot about who has the best opportunity to observe children and know when something's wrong. Teachers, for instance, see children on a daily basis for the better part of a year. They know each child, what's normal for him or her, and they will likely have some insight into the child's family situation, as well. So, when the normally gregarious child suddenly becomes depressed and withdrawn, the teacher will know something's wrong. *Sudden change* is the key in identifying sexual abuse. Understand that children change all the time. Look for children to be different, usually dramatically and suddenly different, and to continue to change over time, regressing or deteriorating.

Physical Signs

In past years, investigators emphasized the importance of physical evidence in recognizing and verifying child abuse, both physical and sexual. As we discussed earlier, this is why the first reporting laws mandated only physicians; it was assumed that they had the best opportunity to discover and report abuse. However, as the study of child sexual abuse progressed, it was soon realized that there is often little physical evidence of sexual molestation. Unless the abuse is terribly violent, most children will not display overt physical signs of having been abused. Thus, once again, only the most severe cases will come to the attention of authorities.

A proactive reporter will be aware of physical signs of abuse, including the following:

1. Difficulty walking or sitting
2. Torn, stained, or bloody underclothes
3. Complaints of pain or itching in the genital area
4. Bruises, bleeding, swelling, or lacerations in the external genitals or vaginal or anal areas (or trauma to the breasts, for girls)
5. Symptoms of sexually transmitted disease, including sores and discharge; boys may also have pain during urination
6. For girls, signs of pregnancy
7. Bruising around the mouth, especially for young children and infants
8. Complaints of illness or injury that have no apparent basis, such as headache, backache, or stomachache
9. General signs of physical abuse, including bruises or scratches from having been restrained or struck[4]

Behavioral Signs

Professionals working with children should also be aware of behavioral indicators of abuse. Like physical signs, behavioral signs are helpful but not conclusive. After all, a number of events could be responsible for changes in behavior: illness, a death in the family, separation of parents, and so on. Nonetheless, people who are around children should be aware of the following likely predictors of sexual abuse:

1. Overly compliant behavior
2. Acting-out, aggressive behavior
3. Pseudomature behavior
4. Overly sexual behavior:
   a. Hints about sexual activity
   b. Persistent and inappropriate sexual play with peers, siblings, toys, or themselves
   c. Sexually aggressive behavior with others, especially peers and siblings
   d. Detailed and age-inappropriate understanding of sexual behavior (especially by young children)
   e. Seductive behavior with adults (especially by girls with men, in cases of a male perpetrator and female victim)
5. Changes in school behavior:
   a. Arriving early at school and leaving late with few, if any, absences or a sudden increase in or pattern of absences
   b. Refusal to participate in school and social activities
   c. Inability to concentrate on work
   d. Sudden drop in performance
   e. Refusal to undress for physical education or excuses to avoid participating (which would mean undressing)
6. Relationship problems:
   a. Poor peer relationships or inability to make friends
   b. Lack of trust, particularly of significant others
   c. Extraordinary fear of adults (especially resisting being touched by or being alone with them)
   d. Running away from home
   e. Withdrawal and isolation
7. Sleeping and eating disturbances

8. Regressive behavior
9. Clinical depression or paranoia
10. Talk of or attempts at suicide
11. Substance abuse

Family Signs

Professionals who are in situations with the family should also be aware of signs of abuse. Family dynamics, including the following, are strong indicators of child sexual abuse.

1. The parents show extreme overprotectiveness toward the child.
2. The family is characterized by clear paternal dominance.
3. The mother and daughter demonstrate role reversal.
4. The family strongly overreacts to the child receiving formalized sex education in school.
5. The family is socially isolated from the community and attempts to prohibit the child's social activities.
6. The child is exposed to several men who are in relationships with the mother.
7. The child is generally unsupervised and neglected.
8. The family unit is unstable.
9. The family has strict, fundamentalist religious beliefs that condemn sexual expression or experimentation.
10. The home atmosphere is generally abusive, physically and otherwise.
11. The family is characterized as being "sex negative" (Goldstein, 1987).

See also Chapter 5 on family dynamics.

Sorting It Out

Again, the idea of sudden change is important, particularly change that cannot be explained by other things happening in the child's life. For instance, a child may suddenly reject his or her friends for no apparent reason and then gradually become more and more isolated and withdrawn. Or a child may begin acting out sexually; teasing or flirtatious behavior may eventually become aggressive and even violent. In both cases, abuse should be considered as a possible cause of the behavior. On the other hand, if a child has always been easily distracted and has trouble completing schoolwork, it shouldn't be assumed that the reason behind these problems is abuse. An attention deficit or learning disability may be a more likely reason.

How much unexplained change should be considered symptomatic of abuse? Some children may display only one of the effects of sexual abuse, while others may display a combination of effects. Some professionals employ what is called "the rule of three," according to which observers look for clusters of symptoms of abuse. One or two symptoms are not necessarily significant, but when a child displays a number of symptoms on a continual basis, something is likely to be wrong. Once more, consider what is normal or typical for the individual child. And keep in mind that a number of things other than sexual abuse may be responsible for the child's behavior. Symptoms are certainly useful in detecting abuse, but they are hardly conclusive.

Documentation

The remainder of this chapter addresses *you*, the reporter, as we continue with direct instruction in how to be a proactive reporter.

To begin, we want to emphasize that a reporter is not expected to investigate or assess the situation before making a report; nothing needs to be proven at this point. Instead, you must have *reason to believe* that a child is being abused. The best advice is to rely on your instincts. If you think that something is wrong, make a report.

Sepler (1988) recommends going with "gut feelings" but stresses the need for careful documentation. Keeping everything in your head doesn't work, no matter how good you think your memory is. Besides, in order to share information, it will eventually have to be recorded. Written documentation is the best means of recording the information necessary to make a report that will hold up under scrutiny.

In addition to serving as a record, maintaining written documentation will help you decide if and when you should report. If you begin with your first suspicion and continue to record over a period of time, you will see a development, a pattern, a succession of events. And with this written record before you, you will *know* when to report. It will be obvious that something is wrong.

Keep some type of journal or record, whatever is appropriate for your profession. Begin with some background information to establish your assumptions and values: how you know the child, how long you've known the child, and what the child is usually like (e.g., "normally very active" or "frequently ill"). Also include what in particular has aroused your suspicion and prompted your recording. This information will portray your mind-set as you begin your record.

After establishing this background, proceed with the actual documentation. Observe on a regular, ongoing basis. Make each entry while you're observing or as soon thereafter as possible; don't wait several days and rely on your memory. And provide enough detail that you will be able to share the information with others. The quality of your documentation is critical to the credibility of the report.

The language you use is very important. Record physical and behavioral evidence in graphic and specific terms. Avoid professional jargon and labels and descriptions commonly found on scales and checklists, including those on our lists of symptoms above. For instance, exactly what does "displays excessive masturbatory behavior" mean? Stated in those terms, nothing. To have meaning, you must describe specific actions: Where did he touch himself? What did he touch himself with? How did he touch himself? How long did he do it? How many times did he do it?

To be even more specific, employ all of your senses as you observe. Too often, we limit ourselves to describing visual or auditory elements. The senses of touch and smell are also needed to paint a complete picture. This is especially important if you are documenting an atmosphere or environment. How did it smell? How did it feel?

You must also avoid drawing conclusions or making assessments; doing so goes beyond merely observing. For instance, based on what you've observed, you may have come to the conclusion that a young girl is afraid of men. However, the statement "She is afraid of men" presents a conclusion—a judgment—not an observation. Go back to what you have based this statement on, your observations: "She cries hysterically when an adult male touches her" or "She turned and ran when she saw two men coming down the hall." Record what you observe, not what you think it means. Stick to the details.

Finally, it's important that your documentation establishes the chronology of your observations, in particular, how the child has changed over time.

1. *Sequence*—Show a pattern or development of behavior over time. When did you first notice something, and how did it progress?
2. *Frequency*—Show that the behavior is recurring and predominant and that it can't be explained by something else. Something that happens only once may be attributed to other factors, including the child having a bad day.
3. *Disruptiveness*—Show that the behavior is disruptive to the child's life, as well as others'—namely, that something needs to be done. What problems is the child or the class having as a result of this?

When the Child Comes to You

When a child decides to disclose sexual abuse, he or she often seeks out a trusted adult, such as a teacher or group leader. Although you shouldn't wait for this to happen—that is, you don't need the child to confirm your suspicions before reporting—you should be prepared for such an encounter.

Suzanne Sgroi (Sgroi, Porter, & Blick, 1982) stresses that this initial interview is critical to the child's ability to deal with his or her abuse. After all, disclosure by itself has to be traumatic. The child is taking an incredible risk. Thus, the primary goal should be to make the interview as therapeutic as possible. If handled correctly, this first interview can begin the healing process.

1. Try to talk to the child in a neutral, comfortable setting, such as the schoolyard, a classroom, a park, or a friend's house. Do not talk to the child in his or her own home, not only for obvious confidentiality reasons but because of the pressure being in that environment will create. Be sure that you will have privacy and will not be interrupted.

2. Talk to the child alone, one on one, or with another supportive adult ally present, if the child wants someone there. If another adult is present, he or she should remain quiet and let the child talk without interruption.

3. Explain to the child that you have talked to others in the same situation and that help is available. This will enhance your credibility in dealing with this matter, as well as reduce the child's feelings of isolation and freakishness. Also assure the child that you believe him or her and that, although you must report the abuse to authorities, you will otherwise keep whatever he or she tells you confidential.

4. Maintain self-control throughout the interview, avoiding any reactions of disgust, embarrassment, or anger. Also avoid a tone of voice or manner that seems to be accusing or disbelieving. Be calm and supportive throughout.

5. Talk to the child at his or her level. Use the child's terminology for body parts or actions to clarify and translate what actually happened. Don't correct the child or insist on using technical vocabulary that he or she won't know or understand. And don't assume that even older children will have accurate or complete knowledge to describe or understand what happened. Let the child tell the story, literally, in his or her own words.

6. Use tangible objects or props to help the child describe what happened. Have the child draw pictures or refer to photos of body parts or activities. Also encourage the child to point to his or her body parts or to yours to illustrate. If he or she is hesitant, you should do it and encourage imitation. (This will require self-control to avoid embarrassment.) Be careful not to lead the child, however.

7. Keep questions simple and to the point; you want to elicit factual information only. In particular, you want to establish the general details of the abuse, including who the offender is, what he or she did, when it happened, where it happened, and whether anyone else was ever around or perhaps knew of the abuse.

To clarify and confirm the information, repeat what the child said and lead into another question. Be careful, though, not to draw this out for too long. You are not an investigator. Even if you don't have *complete* information, if you have *enough* to warrant a report, make it immediately (Sgroi, Porter, & Blick, 1982).

Your report should include all of the details the child has revealed; refer to the recommendations for documentation. You should also document *exactly* what you said to the child, especially any advice on what he or she should do or what you or others will do to help. This is important because whoever picks up the case must know what the child will expect; it is also important for your own protection. Be careful not to overstep your bounds here.

Again, we reiterate, don't try to prove the allegation of abuse. Instead, your goals should be twofold:

1. to gain the trust and confidence of the child, reassuring him or her that coming forth was the right thing to do and that you are going to help him or her through this; and
2. to make up your mind about whether you have reason to believe abuse happened.

Credibility

The issue of children's credibility is controversial. It is not uncommon for a child to recant at some point, particularly if the family and/or the offender are placing pressure on him or her. Moreover, most children are confused or torn about telling what happened, and they may become frustrated after repeated interviews and examinations. Such anxiety should be expected, but it should not be construed to mean that the child is lying.

Researchers have established that more false reports are made by adults than by children. One study found that, in cases where a false report was made deliberately, nearly three-fourths were made by adults, not children (Jones, McGraw, & Melbourne, 1987). Nonetheless, the issue of credibility remains controversial. The essence of the controversy is summed up in this opinion from Robert Emans, Dean of the School of Education at South Dakota State University:

> *People who maintain that children never fabricate with regard to sexual experiences are deluding themselves. Vengeful or disturbed adults can manipulate children into believing that they have been sexually abused when that has not been the case. Questioning by adults whom they fear and wish to please can induce children to "lie." Having done so, the children come to believe what they have said. After prolonged questioning by investigators, children often confuse fact and fantasy. When adults already (and often too willingly) believe that sexual abuse has occurred, they often deal with the alleged victims in ways that heighten the suggestibility of these children. (Emans, 1987, p. 741)*

Statistics on substantiation are often used to support this view. Increasingly, critics of reporting laws and intervention policies point to the disturbingly large number of reports (about half) that cannot be substantiated. In fact, though, the use of substantiation statistics is somewhat of a "red herring." Credibility is not the sole determinant in substantiating child sexual abuse. Lack of evidence, including corroboration from others, is more often the reason for not substantiating abuse. Also keep in mind that the term *unsubstantiated* does not necessarily mean *false* or even *unfounded*. It simply means that nothing was proven.

Still, the issue of children lying remains at the heart of the controversy, and the rhetoric follows the reasoning of Emans, as given above. To discount this rhetoric, consider the following responses to Emans' comments (in MacFarlane & Waterman, 1986):

1. *Vengeful or disturbed adults can manipulate children into believing that they have been sexually abused when that has not been the case.* Allegations like this are often made during divorce or custody proceedings: An angry woman turns her daughter against her husband, the child's father, citing sexual abuse out of vengeance or to ensure custody. Given the turmoil that surrounds divorce, it is difficult to sort out allegations of abuse. Parents may be on edge and overanxious, which may lead to overreacting to something the child says. And the child may go along with things because of the increased attention he or she has received, which will be crucial during this time of separation.

On the other hand, regarding divorce, specifically, recent research has found that young children are more at risk for abuse during separation or divorce proceedings. And children are more likely to report during this time, perhaps because the offender has been removed from the home or because the turmoil has brought the mother and child closer together. Be aware, though, that reports of abuse made during divorce or custody proceedings are frequently thrown out without any consideration.

2. *Questioning by adults whom they fear and wish to please can induce children to "lie." Having done so, the children come to believe what they have said.* We would be naive to overlook the possibility that a child would lie about being sexually abused. Older children, especially, may have the knowledge to fabricate a story and the manipulative ability to make it believable. Children may also go along with a lie because they think they are pleasing adults and be-

cause they enjoy the attention this brings. Nonetheless, even carefully contrived lies lack depth and plausibility, which will be apparent upon specific questioning.

3. *After prolonged questioning by investigators, children often confuse fact and fantasy.* Gail Goodman, of the University of Denver, has shown that children as young as 3 years old can remember events and give clear verbal recollections of them, even after some time has passed. And other researchers have discounted the notion of children's fantasizing about sex. Young children (i.e., less than 7) do not have the mental ability for abstract thought, which means that they must depend on actual experiences to produce images of fantasy. Therefore, children would not fantasize about sexual relationships with adults unless they had some experience in that area.

4. *When adults already (and often too willingly) believe that sexual abuse has occurred, they often deal with the alleged victims in ways that heighten the suggestibility of these children.* Again, work by Goodman with young children refutes this argument. Five-year-old children were shown videotapes; some weeks later, adults discussed the videos with the children and tried to mislead them about what they'd seen. None of the adults was successful; the children maintained their accounts of the videos 100% of the time.

Establishing Credibility

The evidence discounting Emans' views of children lying is convincing. And although we cannot say that children never lie, at least we can conclude that most claims of conniving and vengeful children are exaggerated. Nonetheless, before making a report of child sexual abuse, you should consider the child's credibility. Not to do so would be to overlook a significant step of the documentation process.

If a child is lying, you can usually tell by the nature of the story and how it's told. The following characteristics enhance credibility:

1. The abuse has been ongoing for some period of time, and the nature of the sexual activity has progressed.
2. The child's scenarios include elements of secrecy and collusion between him or her and the offender and perhaps between other family members, as well.

3. Pressure and/or coercion were employed to ensure the child's participation and perhaps the silence or collusion of others.
4. The child is able to provide explicit details of his or her molestation, including specific information about anatomy and behavior (Sgroi, Porter, & Blick, 1982).

On the other hand, there is some reason to doubt the child's story if it may be characterized as follows:

1. The account lacks descriptions and details.
2. The account lacks variation (i.e., sounds memorized upon repeated retellings).
3. The child is unemotional about the incident.
4. The child uses adult words, language, or rationales to describe what happened.
5. The child's account of the abuse is out of character with his or her developmental level and normal pattern of self-expression.
6. The account generally lacks authenticity or plausibility.
7. The child's statements don't fit with other data about the offender or the situation.
8. The account lacks convincing detail (MacFarlane & Waterman, 1986).

The child's credibility is not simply a matter of telling the truth. Instead, it concerns how believable the child is and thus how believable your report will be. If the account is questionable and the child is unclear or inconsistent, it is unlikely that your report will be acted upon.

See also the discussion of child development in Chapter 4.

Packaging Your Report

Perhaps the ultimate frustration for reporters of child abuse or neglect is the fear that their report will be tossed out, for any of a number of reasons. Certainly, knowing the procedures, what to look for, how to document, and so on will increase the likelihood that your report will be addressed. But you should go one step further to improve your chances by "packaging" your report.

The term *packaging* has strong commercial, marketing-oriented connotations. It means presenting something in the best way possible to a given audience in an attempt to persuade them to a particular point of view. It requires knowing that audience well. What will it take to sell them your package?

In the context of reporting child sexual abuse, *packaging* means presenting your information in a way that is sure to receive the attention of local law enforcement or CPS workers. To be sure, this does not mean altering the facts in any way by distorting or eliminating information; that would be unscrupulous and illegal. Instead, packaging means knowing who you're reporting to and what they need to have before they can assess or investigate.

Sepler (1988) offers these guidelines for packaging your report:

1. *Take responsibility for knowing the intake process.* Prepare for making a report before you ever have to. Get the form and guidelines for reporting, go over them, and ask questions. In the process, get to know the people you'd report to. Then, should you make a report, it will be easier for you to approach them, and they will be likely to receive you better if they know who you are.

2. *Know the law and any local interpretations of it.* First of all, be familiar with the abuse and neglect statutes. If you can discuss the law accurately and in detail, your credibility will be established. Second, although the law is set down by the state, local agencies may have slightly different standards for enforcing it. Semantics is important. How you describe a bruise (i.e., size, color, duration) may be significant in establishing the merit of your report. Know the law and the language of your local agency, and prepare your report according to its terms.

3. *Know the priorities and operation of your local agencies.* You must be willing to accept that there is a hierarchy of cases. Understandably, some are considered more high risk than others, which means they will be addressed first. And still other cases (e.g., involving divorce or custody) may be rejected immediately because they have been proven difficult to substantiate. Once you understand these priorities, you will know how your report will be received.

4. *Begin with your bottom line.* In making your report, be direct. Don't apologize, and don't beat around the bush. To do so will destroy your credibility. Begin the conversation by telling the worker that you have reason to believe a child has been sexually abused and that he or she needs help immediately.

5. *Justify your allegation promptly.* Once you've stated your bottom line, follow up with your reasoning. Go through your documentation specifically, mentioning dates and details. This is much more convincing than giving a vague summary based on memory. Again, establish your credibility.

We want to stress the importance of knowing your local CPS and law enforcement personnel. They have a good deal of discretion in following up reports of abuse. If you know what they need, you can make their job easier. In the process, you will gain credibility, and they will appreciate your efforts. Moreover, you can have a positive impact on the status of the case you report.

Disclosure

Researchers are at odds over the effects that disclosure of sexual abuse has on the victim. Some stress that disclosure by itself creates trauma and that, depending on the circumstances, it may be even more traumatic than the abuse itself. Even the child who does not originally feel guilty for compliance or for breaking up the family can be made to feel guilty by hysterical or judgmental adults. Negative reactions by adults can bring on all kinds of emotions in children, producing both immediate and long-term effects (Finkelhor, 1979).

It is difficult to verify the effects of disclosure per se since we cannot gather data about children who do not disclose their abuse. Studies of adults who report that they were victimized as children yet never disclosed their abuse until being interviewed provide some information about the trauma of disclosure but not enough to be conclusive.

Sgroi included disclosure as the fourth phase in her five-phase model of sexual abuse (see Chapter 5) (Sgroi, Blick, & Porter, 1982). To recap, disclosure may be accidental (e.g., observation by a third party of activity, behavioral changes, or resultant injuries to the child) or purposeful (e.g., one of the participants, usually the child, reports).

Accidental disclosure is followed by crisis intervention, which is highly traumatic. No one will be prepared, from the victim to the family to the professionals who must intervene. The scene will be chaotic, and emotions will run high. The professionals involved should try to diffuse the anxiety, reinforce the reality of the situation, and attend to gathering information and planning intervention.

Purposeful disclosure is followed by planned intervention, which is much more orderly. The typical scenario is that the child will tell someone about the abuse, and that person will make a report to a child protective or law enforcement agency. The particular advantage here is that the child can be engaged in a calm, supportive manner, reducing some of the trauma that is inevitable. Information can be gathered, an assessment can be made, and plans can be formulated in a reasonable and workable manner.

Suppression

Again, referring to Sgroi's model,[5] disclosure is always followed by suppression. No one wants to admit what has happened, and everyone would like to avoid the publicity and stigma that are sure to follow disclosure. "All family members can be expected to react to disclosure of child sexual abuse within the framework of a response to the question, 'How will this affect me?' " (Sgroi, Blick, & Porter, 1982, p. 24).

The perpetrator will be alarmed, in most cases, since the disclosure will be a surprise to him or her. He or she will fear the legal and social sanctions that are to come and will be defensive and self-protective. The offender will be hostile toward the child and anyone else—family and intervening professionals—who is believed to be cooperating with the authorities. In cases of incest by fathers, especially, the offender will try to assert his power and control the child and the family, preventing successful intervention.

The parents of a victim usually react with feelings of protection for their child. They are also likely to feel guilty at some point, condemning themselves for not protecting their child or knowing what was going on. This guilt may lead to denial about what happened and the role they played in it. To end the ordeal, parents may refuse to cooperate with intervention and may even refuse to prosecute the perpetrator. The desire to forget and be left alone may be controlling.

In cases of incest, mothers may have difficulty maintaining their concern for the child. Many of these women are not very strong and independent to begin with, and many come from dysfunctional families themselves. Considering the conflicting loyalties involved, it is not surprising that some mothers are unable to protect their children from further abuse. Some may completely collapse, withdrawing their support from the child and abandoning all responsibility. Clearly, mothers in such situations need a good deal of support and understanding.

The reactions of siblings should not be overlooked. Like their parents, children are likely to be concerned and protective at first but may eventually have more selfish interests. They may be angry at their brother or sister for bringing this problem onto the family, and they will blame him or her for whatever happens. The fear of separation and destruction of the family will be especially great. If other siblings were also victims, they may feel guilty about not having disclosed themselves (thus preventing further abuse of other children in the family), or they may be relieved that the abuse was finally discovered.

Other family members and friends are likely to pressure those involved to keep the abuse a secret. Most are afraid of the social reaction that will follow and feel the best means of handling the problem is within the family, without outside help. Thus, family members and friends are often unwilling to cooperate in the assessment and intervention planning.

Certainly, it takes a good deal of individual strength and security to respond to the disclosure of sexual abuse in an unselfish, caring, supportive manner. It is difficult for most people to do so unflinchingly, which is understandable. Not only the victim but the entire family need support and encouragement to sustain them through this ordeal.

Summary

The concept of mandated reporting is relatively new, originating in the United States in the early 1960s. Minnesota first enacted legislation in 1963, mandating reporting of child abuse and neglect by certain professionals. This statute, Minnesota 626.556, the Reporting of Maltreatment to Minors Act, has been revised and made more specific over the last 25 years.

In Minnesota, mandated reporters include those in the healing arts, education, child care, clergy, social services, and law enforcement. The condition for reporting is to know or have reason to believe that abuse is occurring or has occurred within the last three years. Nonmandated reporters should report if they know, have reason to believe, or suspect that abuse is occurring or has occurred within the last three years.

Both mandated and voluntary/nonmandated reporters make their reports to either a local CPS or law enforcement agency. A mandated reporter must follow up with a written report within 72 hours, identifying the child, the offender (if known), the nature and extent of the abuse, and his or her own name and address. The mandated reporter should also include any documentation he or she has with the written report. Reports of child sexual abuse remain confidential (except when the reporter is called as a witness), and all reporters are protected from any civil or criminal liability and other types of retaliation.

To be an effective reporter, you must be proactive. This means being aware and observant, looking out for children on an ongoing basis, using both covert and overt means of observation. The key in identification is to look for change that is sudden and then progressive and cannot be explained by something else in the child's life. Consider what is normal for the child.

Maintaining documentation is vital to an effective report and will also help you know when it's time to make a report. Your documentation should be specific and graphic; avoid making assessments or drawing conclusions. Establish the details, especially how the child has changed and how what you've observed has progressed over time. You should not assume the role of CPS worker or investigator, but you should be aware of basic interviewing skills and means of assessing credibility.

Packaging the report is the final responsibility of the proactive reporter. Get to know local CPS and law enforcement personnel, the people you will report to. Find out what they need to proceed with an assessment or investigation. Establish yourself as a competent and caring professional, someone who wants to help and knows what he or she is doing. Doing so will not only improve the chances that your report will be acted upon but will perhaps reduce some of the frustration that reporters often feel.

Finally, after the abuse has been disclosed, you should know what to expect from everyone involved. Consider that everyone will ask the question, How will this affect me? Although family members may initially respond with feelings of care and protection, they may give in to their own needs or interests over time. Everyone needs a good deal of support and understanding to get through the ordeal.

Notes

1. The information in this section on mandated reporting is based on Minnesota statutes, section 626.556, the Reporting of Maltreatment to Minors Act, as well as seminars conducted by Jean Swanson Broberg, Michael Clancy, and Fern Sepler through Project IMPACT.

2. The word *suspect* was recently eliminated from the statute as sufficient requirement for mandated reporters and was replaced with *having reason to believe*. Note, however, that *suspicion* is included as sufficient level of certainty for nonmandated/voluntary reporters.

3. Social service personnel conduct an *assessment*, while law enforcement personnel conduct an *investigation*.

4. Physical and behavioral signs checklists are based on material from the following: Goldstein, 1987; James and Nasjleti, 1983; MacFarlane and Waterman, 1986; and Sgroi, Blick, and Porter, 1982.

5. See Chapter 5, "A Model of Child Sexual Abuse," for a complete review of Sgroi's model. The information in this section is from Sgroi, Blick, and Porter, 1982.

Chapter Seven

Introduction to Systems Theory

During the past 10 years, there has been an explosion of research about organizations: how they are structured, how they operate, what makes them successful or unsuccessful, and so on. Some of this research has examined organizations in general, and some has examined specific types of businesses and systems. In this chapter, we will review some of both: general information about how organizations are structured and more specific information about public service systems.

This chapter serves as an introduction to Chapters 8, "The System at Large," and 9, "Making the System Work." In this chapter, we will examine systems theory in an overview of how organizations are structured and how they work. Our emphasis will be on what makes a system functional versus dysfunctional and how systems must adapt to changing conditions to remain viable. Hopefully, this discussion will establish a foundation upon which to build the concepts in Chapters 8 and 9.

Defining the System

To begin, several definitions are in order. Some literature uses the term *system* to denote the topic under study. Webster's defines a *system* as "a set or arrangement of things so related or connected as to form a unit or organic whole." When applied to a business or similar enterprise, a working definition of *system* is "the interaction of a set of forces that produces a distinguishable result" (Mercer & Koester, 1978, p. 7).

Other literature uses the term *organization*, which is defined as "an administrative and functional structure." An organization is therefore a type of system, one with a specific purpose. Note that this is very similar to the working definition of *system*, given above, in that it specifies what is to be accomplished. We will use the terms *organization* and *system* interchangeably to mean "a structure that coordinates resources and activities to accomplish a selected purpose."

Resources

Every system has two types of resources, human and nonhuman. *Human* resources include the people that perform various tasks within the organization—from CEO to maintenance worker—and their social system, or group behavior. *Nonhuman* resources include the technology, machines, and materials needed to make the product or provide the service. Together, these two types of resources create a sociotechnical subsystem within the larger system. This subsystem is unique for each given organization. To optimize performance, the organization must achieve a balance between social and technical needs (Kerzner, 1984).

Structure

All systems are hierarchies of some type. The subordination may occur internally, with the organization being divided into smaller units, or the organization may be part of a larger system, as is the case with all government agencies. Regardless, to function, each system must be considered separate and finite. It must have a purpose and a mode of operation that enables it to do what it is supposed to do.

But no system functions in a vacuum. The purpose and operation of any system are constantly being affected by the environment in which the system functions. Consider the influences that auto manufacturers have faced in recent years: increased oil prices, government safety regulations, public needs and tastes, foreign competition, and so on. The industry has responded to each of these influences by adapting its operation, that is, changing its product. And to stay in business, the auto industry will have to continue to adapt to what's happening in the world.

In comparison to private systems, some would argue that public systems are even more subject to environmental influences. After all, their primary purpose is to serve the public. In theory, these systems should receive input from the public and respond accordingly, continually adapting their policies and operations. Clearly, this gives the public a good deal of the decision-making authority for the system. But in practice, this degree of accountability renders the system ineffective, if not inoperable. There will be too much input, too much change, and too little control (Mercer & Koester, 1978).

System Dynamics

Much of the research on organizations has addressed this issue of change and adaptability. The consensus is that systems must be dynamic in order to survive. In other words, a system must be able to adapt to change—whether it comes from external or internal forces—and do so quickly and efficiently to continue functioning effectively.

You may notice that this theory of organizational dynamics is very similar to that of family dynamics, which we discussed in Chapter 5. Two points are significant: (1) A system must be examined within the context of its environment for us to understand how it works; and (2) a system, like a living organism, must continually adapt to its changing environment in order to survive. In short, how the system works within its environment is the key to its functioning.

Closed versus Open Systems

Theories about closed and open systems grew out of the physical sciences research of Ludwig von Bertalanffy in the 1950s and have been adapted extensively by social scientists to explain the operation of social systems, as well. When applied specifically to organizational dynamics, these theories describe how systems tend to move to homogeneity (sameness, stagnation) and homeostasis (rigidity).[1]

- A *closed* system is reactive, defensive, and resistant to change.
- An *open* system is continually evolving and struggling for growth and change; there is no status quo.

The most definitive factor in assessing whether a system is open or closed is its boundaries: What distinguishes the system from its environment and its members from nonmembers and one another? That is, how permeable are the boundaries?

A closed system has very rigid boundaries, or low permeability. Interaction between the system and its environment and between members and nonmembers is restricted. Some theorists describe such a system as *centralized*, one that is held under tight control. Conversely, an open system has highly permeable boundaries, allowing easy access and free interaction. This system is *decentralized*, allowing autonomy and diversity (Aldrich, 1981; White, 1986).

Systems may be characterized according to boundary permeability, or how closed or open (centralized or decentralized) they are. Figure 7-1 presents a continuum of permeability, ranging from low to high, that designates three types of systems: enmeshed (far left), disengaged (far right), and self-regulated (center).

1. The *enmeshed* system has the lowest boundary permeability and is thus the most closed. It is characterized by:
    - Extreme demands for time and emotional commitment to the organization
    - Strong focus on the group and not on individual activities and accomplishments
    - Minimal internal boundaries providing private space
    - Tyrannical, authoritarian, and manipulative leadership
    - Harsh response to nonstandard behavior
    - Implicit rather than explicit organizational rules

Figure 7-1 *System Types according to Boundary Permeability*

Enmeshed	Self-regulated	Disengaged
Low		High

Source: Adapted from White, 1986.

Small and simple types of systems are often enmeshed. Because of the high stress and negative experiences involved, law enforcement and social services systems are frequently enmeshed, as well.

2. The *disengaged* system is the most permeable and thus the most open. In fact, it is too open, perhaps even without boundaries. As a result, there is little cohesion and stability. The disengaged system is characterized by:
- Low expectations of loyalty and commitment to the organization
- Lack of common purpose and goals
- Low level of organizational identity or unity
- Compartmentalized division of tasks and responsibilities, involving little interaction and interdependence
- Leadership that is rarely present or involved only erratically in work
- Individuals who are "retired on the job" (i.e., invisible or "deadwood" workers)
- Explicitly defined norms and rules

The prototype of the disengaged system is the large government agency and similar complex bureaucracies.

3. The *self-regulated* system is able to strike a balance between low and high boundary permeability by being flexible. Note that the other two systems are both rigid and fixed in some way; they are locked into a single mode of operation. The self-regulated system moves along the continuum of permeability, higher or lower, in response to changing conditions. It is like a living organism that adapts to its changing environment to survive. The self-regulated system is characterized by:
- Changing but controlled degree of boundary permeability
- Awareness of environmental trends and changes
- Balanced climate, one that is not too intimate yet not too impersonal
- Decentralization of power and authority
- Organizational values and rules are stated explicitly yet open to negotiation as needs and conditions change

The most important of these factors is the first, the changing boundary permeability. Leadership continually monitors the environment and makes conscious decisions about changing boundaries. The system does not float along the continuum undirected; rather, it is monitored and evaluated regularly. This flexibility is the key to self-regulation.

It is possible for a system to be *mixed*, or both enmeshed and disengaged at the same time. Also, certain subsystems within a larger system may be one or the other—enmeshed or disengaged—which would also produce a mixed system. Whatever the case, the central issue is the polarity on the continuum of permeability, either high or low. The lack of flexibility and thus the inability to adapt to a changing environment is the problem (White, 1986).

Organizational Incest and Closure

Consider how boundary permeability affects the flow of ideas and the interaction of people within and among systems. Clearly, the closed system is prohibitive. As a result, people are forced to look within the system for the satisfaction of all of their needs—personal, professional, social, and sexual. Some call this phenomenon *organizational incest,* for obvious reasons (White, 1986).

Closure is not unusual if a system is being organized, reorganized, or facing some type of crisis. It is natural to try to shut out the world while getting established or sorting out problems; in fact, sometimes it's healthy. The problem, however, is that once a system closes, it becomes enmeshed and rigid and is usually unable to open up again. In this case, the system becomes like an overprotective parent who wants to provide everything and ensures gratitude by portraying the outside world as hostile and threatening.

Closure follows a predictable pattern, one that is usually slow and subtle. Initially, the organization demands loyalty and commitment from all members. Leaders take on a spiritual role, serving as motivators and crusaders, not managers. Individuals begin to lose their identities, and the group becomes homogeneous. Commitment becomes more important than ingenuity and competence. People become workaholics. They have little outside contact and begin to have personal problems. Internal problems, such as competition and boredom, also begin to emerge. People feel trapped and become paranoid. Power plays and other political issues lead to unrest. The administration may try to take control, distancing themselves from the workers. Leaders may lose their jobs, and the organization may break apart.

Identifying Problems

In discussing "Human Aspects of Teamwork," Schmitt and Carroll (1978) assert that the ability to participate on a child protective team requires more than just competence in one's discipline. A helpful, positive attitude is also important, including:

1. the desire to do a good job and apply your ability toward a common goal;
2. the willingness to participate in performance evaluation of yourself and others, sharing problems and exposing weaknesses;
3. the maturity to acknowledge your mistakes;
4. the perspective to accept setbacks or problems without feeling defeated; and
5. the understanding that mutual support is needed within the team, since gratification is unlikely to come from external sources (Schmitt & Carroll, 1978).

Attitudes that are destructive to teamwork may be described as follows:

1. *Impractical*—Being inexperienced, overly optimistic, and unrealistic about what you can accomplish
2. *Rigid*—Denying other people's views and professional knowledge
3. *Distrustful*—Feeling suspicious of co-workers
4. *Critical*—Leveling unnecessarily harsh or judgmental attacks against co-workers
5. *Controlling*—Struggling for power, trying to fulfill personal agendas, guarding territorial lines
6. *Indecisive*—Stalling due to disagreement or inability to be authoritative, "decision by indecision" (Schmitt & Carroll, 1978).

Although worker attitudes contribute greatly to an organization's effective operation, they are usually a sign of underlying issues. That is, worker attitudes are most likely an effect, not a cause.

Unfortunately, when there are problems within an organization, management often looks at effects without diagnosing what is really the cause of the problem. Thus, a typical response is to look outside the system for the solution. For instance, management may think that the answer to low productivity is to bring in a new manager. But to do so ignores what is more likely the problem: the work situation itself. Internal problems involving policy are more often to blame (Kerzner, 1984).

What Works Best?

In public systems, there has always been a conflict between those who favor a closed/centralized versus an open/decentralized structure. Because this is a historical problem, public systems have always dealt with internal chaos and instability to the point that the conflict has become intrinsic to public systems. Bureaucrats and administrators favor centralization, arguing that it provides better coordination of resources and eliminates duplication of efforts. Clients and the public, on the other hand, favor decentralization, arguing that it allows better and more personal access to the system (Aldrich, 1981).

There is no one best structure that will work for all systems, not even all public systems. In fact, "there is no such thing as a good or bad organizational structure; there are only appropriate or inappropriate ones" (Kerzner, 1984, p. 93). An appropriate structure is one that balances social and technical requirements to optimize organizational performance. Thus, issues such as productivity and resource costs must be weighed against human needs and interests. "Since the relative influence of these factors changes from situation to situation, there can be no such thing as an ideal structure making for effectiveness in organizations of all kinds, or even appropriate to a single type of organization at different stages in its development" (Sadler, 1971, in Kerzner, 1984, p. 92).

Summary

A *system* is "a structure that coordinates resources and activities to accomplish a selected purpose." Human and nonhuman resources are used and must be balanced in order to achieve optimum performance.

Every system is a hierarchy. The focus may be on the larger system, which is divided into a number of subordinate units, or on one of these units. Regardless, each system must exist as an individual entity, with its own purpose, in order to function. It is naive, however, to ignore the effects of environment on the system. An analogy can be made to a living organism, which must continually adapt to its changing environment in order to survive.

System adaptability is characterized by how open or closed the system is. A closed system is tightly controlled, or centralized; it is reactive and resistant to change. An open system is autonomous, or decentralized; it is continually evolving and struggling for change. A system that is completely closed will be enmeshed; a system that is completely open will be disengaged. The ideal is self-regulation, in which the system achieves a balance between being closed and open. This is accomplished through continual self-monitoring and self-correction.

In public systems, there has always been a conflict between those who favor a closed/centralized versus an open/decentralized structure. Thus, public systems have always dealt with internal chaos and instability to the point that the conflict has become intrinsic.

There is no one best structure that will work for all systems, not even all public systems. In fact, a given organizational structure cannot be characterized as good or bad; instead, it must be characterized as appropriate or inappropriate.

Note

1. These terms are not opposites or the polar dimensions on a continuum. In fact, homeostasis and homogeneity frequently occur simultaneously in both open and closed systems. Do not misinterpret *homeostasis* to mean "closed"; rather, it means "rigid" and "inflexible," which describes both open and closed systems.

Chapter Eight

The System at Large

Chapter 7, "Introduction to Systems Theory," presented basic information about organizational theory, namely, how a system functions and what factors may be responsible for dysfunction. In this chapter, we will look more closely at the structure and operation of a specific system: the system that responds to child sexual abuse.

In our review of the system at large, we will examine each of its individual components, including the responsibilities each has for the victim and the offender. This review is not intended to be exhaustive, identifying every exception to every policy or procedure. Rather, the purpose is to demonstrate how a case is processed through the system and how individual agencies work together and separately at various stages.

Overview

The complete system is a large organization, one made up of many other organizations from different disciplines. Although the system as a whole shares a common goal, the protection of children, each organization is a separate entity that operates according to its own procedures and policies. Perhaps the best illustration of the size and diversity of the system is the group that comprises mandated reporters, which includes individuals from literally every profession that encounters children.

The system at large can be envisioned as a wheel, containing a hub from which spokes extend to outer divisions (see Figure 8-1). At the hub, or center, is Child Protective Services (CPS), which is a specialized function of the local county welfare and social services agencies charged with the primary responsibility for safeguarding

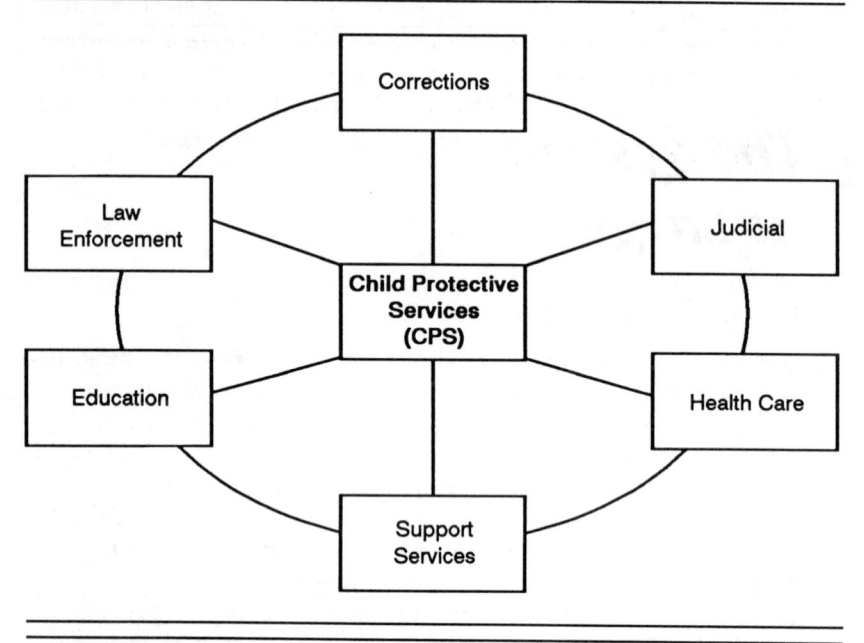

Figure 8-1 *Components of the Child Protection System*

```
                    ┌──────────────┐
                    │  Corrections │
                    └──────────────┘

┌──────────────┐                          ┌──────────────┐
│     Law      │                          │   Judicial   │
│ Enforcement  │      ┌─────────────┐     │              │
└──────────────┘      │   Child     │     └──────────────┘
                      │ Protective  │
                      │  Services   │
                      │   (CPS)     │
┌──────────────┐      └─────────────┘     ┌──────────────┐
│  Education   │                          │ Health Care  │
└──────────────┘                          └──────────────┘

                    ┌──────────────┐
                    │   Support    │
                    │   Services   │
                    └──────────────┘
```

Minnesota's children.[1] To do so, CPS is empowered to employ other state and private agencies as needed to offer protection and support. The following agencies comprise the "spokes" of the wheel:

1. *law enforcement*—both county sheriff's offices and community police departments;
2. *judicial*—judges, county attorneys, public defenders, and private attorneys;
3. *corrections*—municipal-, county-, and state-level correctional agents and facilities;
4. *health care*—public and private organizations, including physicians, nurses, and staff in physical and mental health fields;
5. *education*—public and private schools, including administrators, teachers, and staff, as well as school nurses, psychologists, and so on; and
6. *support services*—including therapy and advocacy programs, as well as the clergy.

Each of these agencies plays a vital role in the system, working with CPS and one another to protect neglected and abused children. Rather than discuss each agency and the role it plays in isolation, we will present an overview of the process followed once a case of child sexual abuse has been reported (see Figure 8-2). Our concern is the system at large.

Working through the System

Reporting

The first step is the report. In Minnesota, mandated and nonmandated reporters make about the same number of reports to child protective agencies (43% versus 48%), and there is some overlap, such that some cases are reported by both (9%). To review, reports of suspected abuse are made to either local CPS (i.e., county child protection) or law enforcement agencies (i.e., sheriff or police). An oral report is usually made first; a mandated reporter must file a written report to the agency within 72 hours of his or her oral report.

Intervention

Intervention, whether planned or in immediate response to a crisis, is always traumatic for the individuals involved. In fact, the nature of the initial intervention has been tied to the severity of the effects experienced by the victim and to treatment success. One of the most important goals of intervention, therefore, should be to lessen the trauma as much as possible, given the circumstances of the case (Sgroi, 1982).

Law Enforcement

Recall from Chapter 1 that most of the people in Finkelhor's Boston survey said they would report child sexual abuse to the police, in part, because they were unaware of which social agency to contact (Finkelhor, 1979). Other research has shown that law enforcement agencies (i.e., police, sheriff's office) are most likely to get reports of

Figure 8-2 *Processing of Child Sexual Abuse by the System*

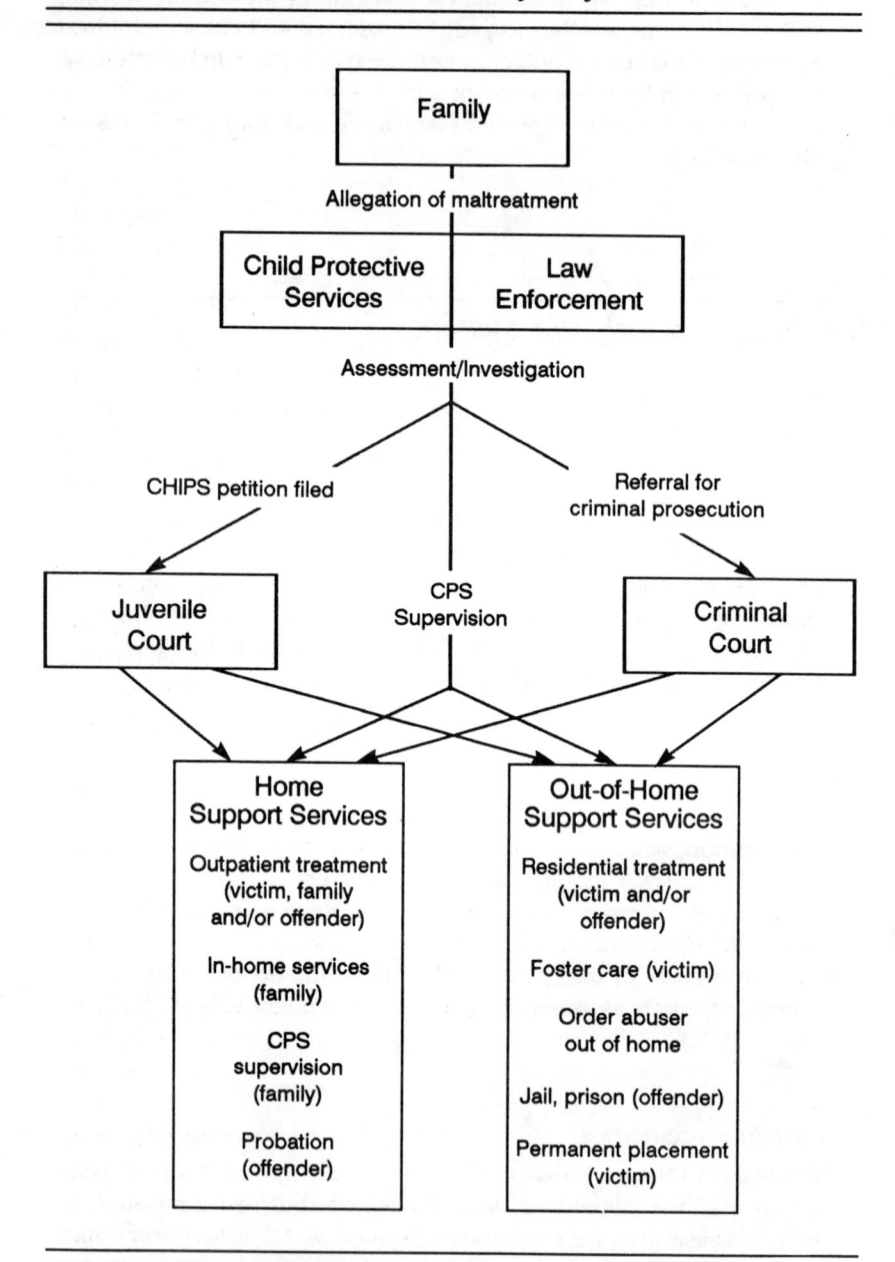

```
                        ┌─────────────┐
                        │   Family    │
                        └──────┬──────┘
                     Allegation of maltreatment
              ┌────────────────┴────────────────┐
              │ Child Protective │     Law       │
              │    Services     │ Enforcement   │
              └────────────────┬────────────────┘
                      Assessment/Investigation
         ┌──────────────────────┼──────────────────────┐
   CHIPS petition filed      CPS                Referral for
                          Supervision       criminal prosecution
         ↓                     │                     ↓
   ┌──────────┐                │              ┌──────────┐
   │ Juvenile │                │              │ Criminal │
   │  Court   │                │              │  Court   │
   └──────────┘                │              └──────────┘
```

Home Support Services	Out-of-Home Support Services
Outpatient treatment (victim, family and/or offender)	Residential treatment (victim and/or offender)
In-home services (family)	Foster care (victim)
CPS supervision (family)	Order abuser out of home
Probation (offender)	Jail, prison (offender)
	Permanent placement (victim)

Source: Minnesota House of Representatives Research Department

the most severe cases of abuse, often extrafamilial abuse by a stranger or cases in which the child has been injured or perhaps physically abused (Finkelhor, 1984). Clearly then, the police are often called to intervene in emergency situations.

If the police believe that the child is in a situation that endangers his or her health or welfare, they can immediately remove the child from the home, without a court order, and place him or her in a hospital, shelter, or foster home. Such placement is temporary, however, and cannot exceed 72 hours (excluding weekends and holidays), by which time a hearing must be held.

In addition, the police are responsible for determining if the child has been injured and requires medical aid. In order to gather evidence, the police may request that the child receive a medical examination; likewise, they may authorize that photographs be taken, and they may obtain a search warrant to return to the child's home or other specified location.

Within 24 hours of receiving the report, the police must contact the local CPS agency, both orally and in writing. The police may then proceed with a criminal investigation or participate with CPS in a joint investigation to substantiate the abuse and gather evidence of criminal sexual conduct (also see the following discussion). The police are authorized to interview the child and other children who have lived with or who are currently living with him or her; parental permission is not required. The alleged offender, caretakers, and anyone else who may provide relevant information about the case may also be interviewed. At this point, the police are conducting a fact-finding procedure that is preliminary to possible criminal proceedings against the offender (see "Legal Proceedings," later in this chapter).

Child Protective Services

CPS and law enforcement each receive referrals from individuals involved in the abuse (i.e., offender, victim, or family) and also from reporters in other agencies. Again, the agency that receives the report must pass on the information to the other.

CPS and law enforcement are required to coordinate their efforts in assessing/investigating[2] the case when circumstances indicate a possible violation of criminal statutes involving physical or sexual abuse. CPS frequently conducts assessments without law enforcement participation in cases of neglect. CPS and law enforcement must prepare separate reports of their assessment or investigation, respectively (see also "Interviewing").

Child protective services will likely seek participation from law enforcement personnel for several reasons:

1. A preliminary assessment indicates that the child may need to be removed from the home immediately and placed in protective custody.
2. There is an allegation of sexual abuse.
3. A search warrant is needed to gather physical evidence.
4. The CPS worker may be in personal danger due to the nature of the case.

In addition, law enforcement assistance is available 24 hours a day, which is critical in responding to an emergency situation, and officers have experience in gathering evidence that may assist the caseworker.

Whether or not both CPS and law enforcement become involved in assessing/investigating the same case is largely a matter of judgment by both agencies. The caseworker and officer assigned to the case should confer regarding the best manner in which to proceed. Neither should turn down a request to aid the other (Child Protective Services Practice Guide, 1983).

Upon receiving a report, CPS will commence an assessment to evaluate the child's short- and long-term welfare, determine whether abuse or neglect occurred, and formulate an intervention plan. In short, CPS assumes responsibility for the personal safety of the child.

In conducting the assessment, the CPS caseworker has the authority to interview the child and other children who have lived with or are currently living with him or her; parental permission is not required. The alleged offender, caretakers, and other relevant individuals may be interviewed, as well. If the child is believed to be in imminent danger, the caseworker may make an immediate onsite visit to determine if the danger is real and to recommend action to protect the child or other children in the home. The caseworker must give the parents the option of voluntarily fulfilling his or her protection recommendations. Regardless of whether the parents comply, the caseworker can petition the juvenile court for immediate custody of the child.

Minnesota law gives CPS agencies several options in dealing with families in which child sexual abuse has been alleged.[3] If the danger of being abused is immediate and present, CPS may act on behalf of the child and seek a temporary order from the juvenile court, requesting the removal of either the child or the offender from the home. (Removing the offender is the preferred course of action, since doing so maintains the family unit as much as possible and makes it clear that the offender, not the child, has committed the wrongdoing. However, it must be clear that this course is both feasible and realistic.) Child protective services may also request that the juvenile court issue an order barring the alleged offender from any contact with the child and/or the family.

In turn, the juvenile court will require that CPS be prepared to provide the aid required for the child and/or family; a plan for such provisions must be developed and filed with the court. And once a temporary order for protection has been issued by the court, CPS, through the county attorney, must file a CHIPS (Child In Need of Protection or Services)[4] petition within five days.

Custody Provisions

If the child is removed from the home by law enforcement, they must present to the court and to the supervisor of the facility in which the child is placed (i.e., a shelter or foster home) a signed report describing the details of the custody; the facility must return a report acknowledging receipt of the child.

Part of the law enforcement report is a statement of notification directed to the child and his or her parents. If law enforcement or the juvenile court deems that notifying the parents (or guardians) of where the child has been placed may endanger him or her, the notification may be withheld. If this decision is made, the facility must be informed of it and any other special conditions of the child's custody.

While the child is in emergency foster care, he or she cannot begin mental health treatment specifically for the effects of alleged abuse unless the juvenile court decides that there is probable cause to believe the abuse occurred. Treatment may be provided during custody if the parents agree to it in writing, as well.

Interviewing

Although both law enforcement and CPS have the right to interview the child as part of their investigation/assessment, they are expected to coordinate their efforts to avoid duplicative interviews. State law discourages interviews that "are unnecessary, duplicative, or otherwise not in the best interests of the child."[5]

The caseworker will often recommend the best time and place for the interview, given the child's situation. CPS and law enforcement have the exclusive authority to decide who will attend. The child's parents need not be informed of the time or place of the interview in advance. In fact, by law, both CPS and law enforcement are required to inform the parents of the interview no later than the conclusion of their assessment/investigation; they may choose to notify the parents earlier, however. Once again, such notification may be withheld if CPS petitions the juvenile court and it rules that there is reasonable cause to do so.

Neither law enforcement nor CPS is required to audiotape or videotape interviews with victims, but in the interest of preventing duplicative interviews, the Department of Human Services recommends videotaping victim interviews. County attorneys are required to develop guidelines on how to make audio or video recordings when they are believed to be necessary. For example, the Hennepin County attorney's office recommends that police and CPS personnel conduct joint interviews whenever possible and prepare a tape-recorded interview immediately or as soon as is practical. In addition, the county attorney's office recommends the use of discretion in deciding whether recording an interview will be traumatic for the child, in which case no recording should be made.

Minnesota statutes require that any record of an interview with a victim, written or otherwise, must contain the date, time, place, and duration of the interview; the identities of all people present; and, if the record is written, a summary of the information obtained.[6]

Determination

Some conclusion about a case of child sexual abuse must be reached by CPS within 90 days of receiving the initial report. Law enforcement and CPS may arrive at separate conclusions. Law enforcement's primary role is to determine whether there is sufficient evidence to charge a crime, which will eventually require either an admission of guilt or proof "beyond a reasonable doubt" for criminal court action. CPS, on the other hand, is concerned primarily with whether services are needed to protect a child, which requires "credible" or believable evidence for a determination of maltreatment and "clear and convincing" evidence for juvenile court action.

Upon the conclusion of the assessment, CPS is required to make two determinations: (1) whether maltreatment occurred and (2) whether child protective services are needed. The first determination requires that credible evidence (or believable facts) be provided to support an affirmative statement that maltreatment—sexual abuse, physical abuse, or neglect—did occur. If such convincing evidence cannot be provided, CPS cannot make a determination of maltreatment. The omission of the "inconclusive" category of determination (August 1, 1988) means that CPS can conclude only that maltreatment did or did not occur.

The second determination, whether services are needed, requires that a variety of factors influencing the risk to the child be assessed. CPS must document that there is a *significant* risk to the child if protective services are not provided and that the persons responsible have not taken and/or are unlikely to take actions to protect the child from maltreatment or continued risk of maltreatment.[7] Once again, this is a "yes or no" determination; there is no "inconclusive" outcome.

While criminal prosecution of an offender can be pursued only if law enforcement has concluded that there is enough evidence to charge a crime, CPS has a variety of options available, regardless of law enforcement's conclusion or the CPS determinations. When CPS can make neither a determination of maltreatment nor a determination of need for protective services, they can still offer services to the child and/or family. In such a case, the parents are free to accept or reject the offer of any or all services.

The key determination for CPS, in contrast to law enforcement, is whether child protective services are needed. Thus, even if CPS cannot make a determination of maltreatment, they may find significant risk to a child. In some cases, parents may be willing to accept services without any legal intervention. When parents are unwilling to accept services voluntarily, CPS may initiate a CHIPS petition to try to gain authority to provide services against the parents' wishes. Since the juvenile court has authority over a variety of circumstances presenting harm or risk to children, it may not be necessary to prove abuse in order for the CHIPS petition to prevail. Some other kind of risk to the child must still be proven, however.

Also, since a CHIPS petition to the juvenile court is a civil proceeding, the burden of proof of abuse is less than in a criminal proceeding. Juvenile court action can be used to remove the child from the home, even temporarily; to provide other measures of social services or protection for the child; and/or, in extreme cases, to terminate the parental rights of abusive parents.[8]

Law enforcement agencies are most often responsible for bringing criminal prosecution, but they may be influenced by the recommendations of the CPS worker. Criminal prosecution may be pursued for several purposes: again, to protect the child; to punish the offender; or to compel the offender to attend treatment. The decision to prosecute the offender is often based on the amount of corroborating physical evidence available and the extent to which the victim's statements can be corroborated or supported by other evidence or information. Again, the burden of proof in criminal proceedings is substantial. Should sufficient evidence exist, criminal prosecution can be brought under the criminal sexual conduct laws.[9] Should the offender be convicted, he or she may be (1) put on probation that requires jail time and/or treatment or (2) sent to prison and receive treatment or be released on supervision and/or receive more treatment. (See "Corrections" and "Support Services," later in this chapter.)

Legal Proceedings

More and more cases of child sexual abuse are being brought into U.S. courts. A 1984 study by the American Humane Association found that 40% of sexually abusive families were referred to court, compared with just 18% of families accused of other forms of abuse and neglect (AHA, 1984).

In Minnesota, child sexual abuse is addressed in two courts: criminal court and juvenile court.[10] Essentially, the role of the juvenile court is to protect the child and preserve his or her ties with the family. (The exception is cases of juvenile delinquency, which are heard in the juvenile court.) In contrast, the role of the criminal court is to prosecute alleged perpetrators of child sexual abuse. Again, the juvenile court is a civil proceeding, whereas the criminal court is a criminal proceeding. A final contrast is that juvenile court proceedings are usually closed to the public, and criminal court proceedings are usually open.

Criminal Court

Many of the cases referred to the criminal court originate with a report to the police or other law enforcement personnel. Thus, many involve extrafamilial offenders who have committed rape or other major contact offenses; a number of noncontact cases of exhibitionism and the like are heard, as well. Cases of intrafamilial abuse also come before the criminal court, but it is still believed that people are hesitant to prosecute family members, for various reasons.

After substantiating the report through an investigation, the police give their information to the county attorney, who then decides whether someone should be charged with a crime. In effect, the county attorney represents the victim's and the state's interests in court.

The county attorney has a great deal of discretion in deciding how to proceed. Obviously, he or she must consider whether there is sufficient evidence to bring charges against and successfully prosecute the offender. The burden of proof for criminal sexual misconduct is very high, since guilt must be proven beyond a reasonable doubt; thus, the initial decision to charge is a major one.

The reasons most often cited for choosing not to prosecute an alleged offender include:

1. lack of evidence;
2. the decision is made to handle the case informally, for instance, recommending treatment;
3. the family or spouse refuse to press charges;
4. the victim will not cooperate;
5. the victim will not be a reliable witness; and
6. the alleged offender's criminal intent cannot be proven sufficiently (Chein, 1981).

The failure of CPS or law enforcement to respond immediately to a report may be responsible for any of these factors.

Once a charge has been made, the county attorney can file a criminal complaint, convene a grand jury, bring the case to trial, subpoena witnesses (including subject experts), negotiate a plea with the defense, and recommend sentencing.

Very few of those cases prosecuted ever go to trial. Chein (1981) reported that nearly 80% of the offenders obtained a plea bargain and/or pleaded guilty to the charge against them. (See also "Plea Bargaining," later in this chapter.)

In the criminal court, the judge has jurisdiction over the defendant (the alleged offender), safeguarding everyone's interests by ensuring that all proceedings are conducted within the law. The judge can issue a variety of orders, including search warrants, and controls what evidence will be admissible in court. The judge also controls sentencing and may impose more or less severe terms than are standard, depending on his or her evaluation of the offender and the crime (see also "Sentencing Guidelines"). What's more, the judge can change the terms of the sentence if he or she feels it's warranted, perhaps revoking an offender's probation or changing its conditions.

The alleged offender, as the defendant, is also entitled to legal counsel. He or she may hire a private attorney or, if eligible, be assigned a public defender or court-appointed attorney. The defense attorney may gather evidence, call witnesses (including expert witnesses), enter into plea negotiations with prosecutors, and make recommendations for sentencing.

An offender is more likely to be convicted of child sexual abuse if he or she has abused more than one child. The victim's willingness and ability to testify also increase the likelihood of conviction, as does the nonoffending parent's support of the child victim, the use of corroborating or expert testimony, and the presence of physical evidence (Chein, 1981).

Juvenile Court

The juvenile court hears cases of delinquency, involving juvenile offenders, as well as cases of dependency and neglect (now referred to as CHIPS), involving primarily victims but sometimes offenders, too. Most of the discussion in this section will be about dependency/neglect cases. Juvenile offenders and delinquency will be discussed at the end.

Most of the cases in juvenile court involve intrafamilial abuse that are referred by CPS. As discussed earlier in this chapter, the juvenile court and CPS work closely together throughout the process to ensure the child's welfare. Nonetheless, the court is a separate entity that considers the information presented and makes an independent decision.

According to state law, any reputable person who has knowledge of a situation of dependency or neglect (CHIPS) may file a petition. Usually, the county attorney, acting as attorney for CPS, drafts and files the CHIPS petition with the juvenile court. The petition states that the child's physical or emotional needs are not being met because the parents are unable or unwilling to provide minimum care. The court may consider the actions of the offending parent as well as the inaction of the nonoffending parent. Whereas the burden of proof for criminal charges is significant (beyond a reasonable doubt), petitions alleging dependency and neglect need only be proven by clear and convincing evidence.

The juvenile court judge has various degrees of authority over the parents, but it is not absolute. For instance, if they refuse to comply with a CPS intervention plan, the judge may find them in contempt. The judge may also decide to remove the child from the home, regardless of whether the parents appear willing to comply, if he or she feels this is in the child's best interests. Because the court's concern is for the child, parental rights may be terminated completely if the county attorney petitions for such extraordinary action and the judge agrees that to do so is appropriate under the circumstances. The judge may order placement in a specific setting for a determined period of time. Criminal charges against the parents for alleged abuse or neglect are filed in the criminal court.

Once a CHIPS petition has been filed, the juvenile court has several responsibilities. Two primary functions are to protect the rights of all parties involved and to determine the legality of the action. In addition, the court is to order and monitor a disposition of the case. This involves reviewing and selecting an intervention plan, which is usually developed and submitted by CPS. The court may also consider other plans or propose its own.

Once the plan has been approved, the court must monitor its implementation. This is usually done through the CPS caseworker, who is responsible to the court for ensuring the child's supervision and protection. Anytime the child's welfare is endangered, perhaps due to changed living conditions, the caseworker must inform the court immediately. The court can then revise provisions made earlier, even removing the child, if necessary.

The general policy is to seek the parents' cooperation with intervention and treatment, allowing them to maintain responsibility for the child. When they are unable or unwilling to handle this responsibility, the court may order that CPS step in.

Both parents, individually or together, and the child have a right to legal representation in the juvenile court. The parents may hire private counsel or be assigned a public defender or court-appointed attorney, if they are eligible.

Regardless of whether the parents have counsel, the child will have separate counsel, either private or court appointed. In most cases, the court will appoint a *guardian ad litem*[11] to protect the child's interests; this is usually done if the child has no parents or if they are incompetent or indifferent or hostile to the child. The court must appoint a *guardian ad litem* in every proceeding in which neglect, dependency, or domestic child abuse is alleged (i.e., a CHIPS petition has been filed). The *guardian ad litem* may or may not be an attorney, but he or she is granted access to all of the records of the case, along with any other relevant information.

Finally, the juvenile court may involve other professionals to assist in the resolution of the case. In short, the judge may determine what services are needed not only for the child but for his or her family, as well. For instance, the judge may order therapy for the child and appoint a therapist. School personnel, such as the school psychologist, may be brought in, as may medical or public health personnel. Various law enforcement personnel may participate, too, depending on the circumstances.

The Juvenile Offender

According to Minnesota statutes, a child less than 10 years old is usually not charged as a delinquent. Instead, such a youth will be handled much like a child victim in need of protective services. A CHIPS petition will be filed in the juvenile court to provide such services for the child as well as any others involved.

A delinquency petition may be filed in the juvenile court against a youth older than 10 but less than 14. In most cases, however, the CHIPS procedure is followed once again, especially if the circumstances indicate problems at home such as neglect.

A delinquency petition will likely be filed against an offender who is older than 14, particularly if the offense committed is a felony. The procedure followed is much like that of CHIPS, since the offender will appear in the juvenile court. If the offender's previous criminal history is extensive or circumstances of the abuse are especially severe, the youth may be referred to the criminal court and tried as an adult. This occurs only in the most severe cases, since it is difficult to get such a referral.

The purpose of the juvenile court is to provide a less public arena to resolve what is considered a family matter. Historically, the juvenile offender has been treated as a victim of circumstances, not as a perpetrator of crime. Today, the intent is to help a troubled youth recover through treatment and other services that usually include his or her family yet still hold him or her accountable and promote public safety.

The procedure followed in handling a juvenile offender will vary considerably, depending on the jurisdiction and the individuals involved. Legal complications—such as questions over the juvenile offender's right to due process—have brought a criminal connotation to some juvenile delinquency proceedings. In order to avoid this problem, some social workers and county attorneys will not file a delinquency petition; instead, they file a CHIPS petition and recommend treatment (Swanson Broberg, 1989).

Corrections

The courts have a lot of latitude in sentencing sexual offenders, perhaps more so than in sentencing any other type of offender. Input is received from several sources, and a number of factors are considered in deciding the sentence.

A major consideration in sentencing is the information provided by the presentence investigation, which is conducted by a court-services worker and includes input from the victim and his or her family. A report must be filed with the court prior to sentencing, characterizing the offender in terms of his or her nature, needs, criminal history, social history, and potential and summarizing the circumstances of the crime and the financial cost and other damage or harm inflicted on others and the community. The report must also include a victim impact statement, which describes the trauma the victim has experienced as a result of the abuse, the damage or cost suffered by him or her and his or her family, the disposition he or she feels is just, and his or her reaction to the proposed disposition and plea agreement of the case. The victim also has the option of making a personal impact statement to the court, either verbally or in writing (Klumpp, 1989).

Sentencing Guidelines

Using information gathered about the offender, a sentencing guidelines worksheet is completed and submitted to the court. This worksheet is a two-level grid (see Figure 8-3, parts A and B[12]). On the vertical scale, types of felony crime are classified according to severity, forming levels 1 through 10 (10 is the most severe). On the horizontal scale, the offender's criminal history is scored from zero history up, considering a composite of factors (i.e., individual's age, prior

Figure 8-3 *Sentencing Guidelines Worksheets: part A, recommended sentences for offenses committed before August 1, 1989; part B, recommended sentences for offenses committed after August 1, 1989*

Presumptive Sentence Lengths in Months

Italicized numbers within the grid denote the range within which a judge may sentence without the sentence being deemed a departure.

Offenders with nonimprisonment felony sentences are subject to jail time according to law.

CRIMINAL HISTORY SCORE

SEVERITY LEVELS OF CONVICTION OFFENSE		0	1	2	3	4	5	6 or more
Unauthorized Use of Motor Vehicle Possession of Marijuana	I	12*	12*	12*	13	15	17	19 *18-20*
Theft Related Crimes ($2500 or less) Check Forgery ($200-$2500)	II	12*	12*	13	15	17	19	21 *20-22*
Theft Crimes ($2500 or less)	III	12*	13	15	17	19 *18-20*	22 *21-23*	25 *24-26*
Nonresidential Burglary Theft Crimes (over $2500)	IV	12*	15	18	21	25 *24-26*	32 *30-34*	41 *37-45*
Residential Burglary Simple Robbery	V	18	23	27	30 *29-31*	38 *36-40*	46 *43-49*	54 *50-58*
Criminal Sexual Conduct, 2nd Degree (a) & (b)	VI	21	26	30	34 *33-35*	44 *42-46*	54 *50-58*	65 *60-70*
Aggravated Robbery	VII	24 *23-25*	32 *30-34*	41 *38-44*	49 *45-53*	65 *60-70*	81 *75-87*	97 *90-104*
Criminal Sexual Conduct 1st Degree Assault, 1st Degree	VIII	43 *41-45*	54 *50-58*	65 *60-70*	76 *71-81*	95 *89-101*	113 *106-120*	132 *124-140*
Murder, 3rd Degree Murder, 2nd Degree (felony murder)	IX	105 *102-108*	119 *116-122*	127 *124-130*	149 *143-155*	176 *168-184*	205 *195-215*	230 *218-242*
Murder, 2nd Degree (with intent)	X	216 *212-220*	236 *231-241*	256 *250-262*	276 *269-283*	296 *288-304*	316 *307-325*	336 *326-346*

1st Degree Murder is excluded from the guidelines by law and continues to have a mandatory life sentence.

■ At the discretion of the judge, up to a year in jail and/or other non-jail sanctions can be imposed as conditions of probation.

☐ Presumptive commitment to state imprisonment.

*one year and one day

Presumptive Sentence Lengths in Months

Italicized numbers within the grid denote the range within which a judge may sentence without the sentence being deemed a departure.

Offenders with nonimprisonment felony sentences are subject to jail time according to law.

SEVERITY LEVELS OF CONVICTION OFFENSE		CRIMINAL HISTORY SCORE						
		0	1	2	3	4	5	6 or more
Sale of a Simulated Controlled Substance	I	12*	12*	12*	13	15	17	19 *18-20*
Theft Related Crimes ($2500 or less) Check Forgery ($200-$2500)	II	12*	12*	13	15	17	19	21 *20-22*
Theft Crimes ($2500 or less)	III	12*	13	15	17	19 *18-20*	22 *21-23*	25 *24-26*
Nonresidential Burglary Theft Crimes (over $2500)	IV	12*	15	18	21	25 *24-26*	32 *30-34*	41 *37-45*
Residential Burglary Simple Robbery	V	18	23	27	30 *29-31*	38 *36-40*	46 *43-49*	54 *50-58*
Criminal Sexual Conduct 2nd Degree (a) & (b)	VI	21	26	30	34 *33-35*	44 *42-46*	54 *50-58*	65 *60-70*
Aggravated Robbery	VII	48 *44-52*	58 *54-62*	68 *64-72*	78 *74-82*	88 *84-92*	98 *94-102*	108 *104-112*
Criminal Sexual Conduct, 1st Degree Assault, 1st Degree	VIII	86 *81-91*	98 *93-103*	110 *105-115*	122 *117-127*	134 *129-139*	146 *141-151*	158 *153-163*
Murder, 3rd Degree Murder, 2nd Degree (felony murder)	IX	150 *144-156*	165 *159-171*	180 *174-186*	195 *189-201*	210 *204-216*	225 *219-231*	240 *234-246*
Murder, 2nd Degree (with intent)	X	306 *299-313*	326 *319-333*	346 *339-353*	366 *359-373*	386 *379-393*	406 *399-413*	426 *419-433*

1st Degree Murder is excluded from the guidelines by law and continues to have a mandatory life sentence. See section **II.E. Mandatory Sentences** for policy regarding those sentences controlled by law.

■ At the discretion of the judge, up to a year in jail and/or other non-jail sanctions can be imposed as conditions of probation.

☐ Presumptive commitment to state imprisonment.   * one year and one day criminal activity, prior treatment and/or incarceration, whether the offender was on probation or parole when the current offense was committed, etc.). The recommended sentence for each combination of level of offense and individual history score is provided at the intersection of the two values. For instance, the recommended sentence for someone convicted of a level-8 offense with zero criminal history is 43 months for offenses committed before August 1, 1989, and 86 months for those committed after. (Note that this grid is used for all types of offenses, not just criminal sexual conduct.)

A diagonal line, called the *dispositional line*, cuts across the grid and divides it in half. The presumptive, or recommended, sentence for those offense level/criminal history pairings that fall above the disposition line is nonimprisonment and a stayed sentence. The presumptive sentence for those pairings that fall below the line is imprisonment. Thus, imprisonment would be recommended for someone with zero criminal history convicted of a level-8 offense.

The Minnesota sentencing guidelines are based on a "just deserts" philosophy: the most harsh sanctions are recommended for those offenders who are convicted of the most serious crimes against people, even for offenders who have no criminal history (Minnesota Sentencing Guidelines Commission [MSGC], 1988).

The first four degrees of criminal sexual conduct, against children or adults, are felonies and are placed at levels 4 through 8. Fifth-degree criminal conduct is a gross misdemeanor. The following sentences are recommended for these various degrees of criminal sexual conduct:

First degree—"penetration with force or coercion where the victim feared great bodily harm, or the offender caused personal injury to the victim, or the offender was armed with a dangerous weapon, or the offender was aided or abetted by an accomplice(s)" (MSGC, 1988). First-degree criminal sexual misconduct is always a level-8 offense, which carries a presumptive imprisonment sentence of 43 months (86 months after August 1, 1989) at zero criminal history.

Second degree—the same circumstances as first degree except that no penetration occurred (MSGC, 1988); that is, contact with intimate parts of the body, clothed or not, plus circumstances that intensify severity. Second-degree criminal sexual conduct is a level-7 or level-6 offense, depending on the severity of the circumstances. A level-7 offense, which usually involves use of force or the commission of several acts, carries a presumptive prison sentence of 24 months for an offender with zero criminal history (48 months after August 1, 1989). A level-6 offense carries a presumptive stayed sentence at zero criminal history.

Third degree—"penetration with force but not to the degree of violence to define the offense as first degree" (MSGC, 1988). Third-degree criminal sexual conduct is a level-7 or level-5 offense, again, depending on the severity of the circumstances. A level-7 offense, which usually involves use of force, multiple acts, injury to victim, and a significant victim/offender relationship, carries a presumptive prison sentence of 24 months for an offender with zero criminal history (48 months after August 1, 1989). A level-5 offense carries a presumptive stayed sentence at zero criminal history.

Fourth degree—contact with intimate parts of the body with less severe circumstances than second degree. Fourth-degree criminal sexual conduct is a level-6 or level-4 offense, again, depending on the circumstances. Both levels carry a presumptive stayed sentence for an offender with zero criminal history.

Fifth degree—contact with intimate parts of the body with less severe circumstances than second or fourth degrees. Fifth-degree criminal sexual conduct is a gross misdemeanor offense, for which the recommended sentence is a 1-year imprisonment and/or a $3,000 fine.

After considering the presentence investigation report, the victim impact statement, and the sentencing guidelines worksheet, the judge is to decide on the appropriate sentence for the convicted offender. Although presumptive sentences are established for all criminal sexual conduct offenses, the judge may choose to depart from these recommendations. Departure is actually very common, since most sexual offenders of children are being convicted for the first time and many of the cases involve intrafamilial abuse.

Dispositional Departure

A 1988 paper by the Minnesota Sentencing Guidelines Commission (MSGC) reported that, in 1987, the mitigated dispositional departure rate for level-8 child sexual abuse offenses was 52.6%, which is clearly the highest rate of the five level-7 and level-8 offenses studied.[13] The number of cases of level-8 child sexual abuse increased dramatically from 1981-1987, but the departure rate from sentencing guidelines increased, as well, from 30.8% in 1981 to 52.6% in 1987.

During the 1981-1987 period, in over half the cases, the reason given for departing from the recommended guidelines was that the offender appeared to be in need of and amenable to treatment. The second most common reason for departure was consideration of the victim. In some cases, victims recommended or concurred with the sentence or were unwilling or unable to testify. In child sexual abuse cases, consideration of the family's welfare was often used to justify departure (MSGC, 1988).

In 1987, only 30.7% of those offenders convicted of a level-8 sexual offense against children had some criminal history, compared with 49.5% of the overall offender population. Only 7% of the child sexual abuse offenders had a criminal history of 4 or more, and only 14% had committed a previous sex offense (MSGC, 1988). These averages are not completely representative, however, since the departure rate for a level-8 offender with zero criminal history is about 90% (Klumpp, 1989).

Imprisonment Rates

The same MSGC study (1988) reported that imprisonment rates decreased in 1987 for level-8 criminal sexual conduct cases involving children, which goes against the overall trend for increased imprisonment rates for crimes against people. In fact, the imprisonment rate for level-8 child sexual abuse cases dropped from a high of 69.2% in 1981 to 47.4% in 1987. This was the lowest imprisonment rate reported in the study, which examined five level-7 or level-8 offenses.

The average pronounced prison sentence for sexual offenders of children increased from 1984 to 1987, from 55.9 months to 64.2 months. However, the 1987 average was still lower than the 1981 average, which was 86 months (MSGC, 1988). Nearly half (47.4%) of those convicted of level-8 child sexual abuse did serve some time in a local jail or workhouse as a condition of their stayed sentence. The average duration of incarceration was 301 days (MSGC, 1988).

Plea Bargaining

This discussion of sentencing would be incomplete without acknowledging the role of the prosecutor, who decides the level of offense with which to charge the offender. Clearly, if a charge is reduced to a lesser offense, for whatever reason, the severity level of the sentence will be reduced correspondingly. The MSGC study (1988) found a drop in the number of level-8 child sexual abuse cases in which charges were reduced, from nearly 80% in 1981 to 36.1% in 1987. The MSGC postulated that this drop may reflect a change in plea bargaining practices, improved evidence gathering and case preparation, increased victim and witness cooperation, or less overcharging.

Probation

Probation is the most common sentence given convicted sexual offenders. The MSGC study (1988) reported that just over half (52.6%) those convicted of level-8 child sexual abuse were put on probation.

The offender is under the supervision of a probation officer, who monitors his or her progress as he or she participates in treatment or work programs. The probation officer is responsible to the court and reports any problems or changes in the offender's situation. The court may revoke or change the terms of the offender's probation as deemed appropriate.

Conclusion

The MSGC report concluded that the sentencing of and imprisonment rate for level-8 child sexual abuse offenses were the most inconsistent of the five types of offenses studied. In response to the dramatic increase in this type of offense during the 1980s, the courts have tried to deal with about half these cases by keeping the offenders out of prison, recommending treatment and local jail or workhouse incarceration.

The MSGC (1988) also concluded that this inconsistency raises important questions about what is the appropriate sentence for someone who commits child sexual abuse: prison or community sanctions. Even though reasons are cited to justify departure from presumptive sentencing guidelines—including the offender's amenability to treatment and the victim's and family's concurrence with this recommendation—these reasons are not consistent with the "just deserts" philosophy of the Commission and the guidelines. To resolve this conflict, nonimprisonment sanctions would have to be increased to make them more comparable with levels of prison sanctions.

Health Care Professionals

Certainly, one of the most crucial roles played by health care professionals is that of mandated reporter. In Minnesota, all individuals involved in the healing arts are mandated reporters.

Another vital role is performed in treating sexually abused children and documenting evidence of abuse. Although most cases of sexual abuse are not characterized by observable physical injury, a physical examination should be conducted to look for subtle physical evidence and to test for sexually transmitted diseases and pregnancy. A complete medical history should be prepared, and the results of the examination and all tests should be documented and submitted in a written report to CPS. Since physical evidence is rarely conspicuous, the medical history and interview conducted by the child's physician should be documented, as well, hopefully corroborating the child's statement. The physician's record is clearly a valuable piece of evidence.

Educators

Educators play a unique role in the daily lives of children, which gives them an opportunity not only to discover and report abuse but to maintain contact with the victim throughout the intervention and treatment process. Teachers can be trusted allies to children who may have no other adults to turn to for guidance and support.

To help educators understand their responsibilities as mandated reporters, the Minnesota Department of Education (1984) has developed a model for identifying behaviors that suggest sexual abuse. This model, presented in a manual called *Minimizing Abuses of the Balance of Power,* incorporates what educators must do according to state law and also departmental policy. The teacher is expected to be a "key observer," not an investigator, therapist, or sole service provider.

Support Services

A significant number of support services, for both victims and offenders of child sexual abuse, are available in Minnesota. A survey by the Minnesota House of Representatives Research Department

(1985) identified 195 services, not including government- or school-sponsored services. Overall, these services fall into five categories:

1. *Community mental health centers*—nonprofit treatment centers that offer programs for offenders, victims, and families. Treatment may address specific abuse situations or more general individual and family needs.
2. *Private counseling clinics*—private therapists and clinics that either specialize in child sexual abuse programs for offenders, victims, and families or handle a large proportion of these types of cases as part of their regular caseload.
3. *Community organizations*—programs in prevention, crisis intervention, and support offered to the community at large or targeted to a specific group or neighborhood.
4. *Residential facilities*—comprehensive, live-in programs for adult offenders, adolescent offenders, and adolescent victims. The conditions of the facilities range from homelike to institutional.
5. *Miscellaneous*—specialized programs that focus on unique crisis situations or victim needs (i.e., advocacy programs).

Availability

Most of these types of services are available throughout the state, although there is a concentration of services in the Twin Cities metro area. Private counseling is the most common type of service available, and community mental health centers is the second. The least common type of service is residential facilities designated specifically for abuse victims and offenders. Children who are removed from the home are usually placed in foster homes for protection, rather than treatment. They are placed in residential treatment programs only when they are considered to be emotionally disturbed. There are hundreds of residential programs for children that handle youths with a wide range of emotional problems, but few specialize in sexually abused children.

However, the House of Representatives report stipulated that the number of services available is not necessarily an indication of the quality of services available. The number of staff available to the local population is an important factor. Once again, the metro area enjoys a concentration of services. Perhaps surprisingly, the northwestern and southwestern regions of Minnesota also have higher concentrations of staff than most other regions, reflecting large community health programs in these areas.

Orientation

Most of the services offered in Minnesota are treatment oriented, rather than prevention oriented (86% versus 14%, respectively). Nearly a third of the services (30%) offer specialized programs addressing child sexual abuse; this is believed to be in response to the increased reporting levels of child sexual abuse. The remaining programs respond to both physical and sexual abuse. Most programs offer individual or family counseling for both offenders and victims, and a few metro-area programs offer specialized services for high-risk parents, new parents, adults abused as children, and the like.

Staff Qualifications

The qualifications of staff employed in various treatment and prevention services range considerably, from extended graduate education to little or no training at all. Structured therapy programs, such as private clinics and residential centers, usually employ psychiatrists, psychologists, and social workers. Community-based services often employ workers with bachelor's degrees in psychology, sociology, education, and child development. In addition, some community programs involve volunteers with no specific training in child sexual abuse; they may or may not have experience in this area. Most programs have at least some personnel with background in counseling or human services, although a few rely primarily on untrained personnel.

Program Duration

Treatment programs range in duration from about 2 months to 2 years; the average is between 9 and 18 months. Programs for adult offenders are usually slightly longer than those for child victims; specialized programs that treat offenders and victims separately run considerably longer for the adults than the children. The treatment for families tends to be longer than that for individuals. Understandably, program length may vary substantially, depending on the circumstances of each case.

Prevention programs for child sexual abuse are very short, unfortunately, usually no more than several hours.

Program Cost

The cost to the patient is determined primarily by the type of program he or she enters. Residential programs are the most expensive, which is understandable. The daily cost of care for a juvenile offender or victim is $80, on average. The yearly cost of care for an adult offender is $25,000 to $30,000, based on costs incurred by state correctional facilities and mental hospitals.

For outpatient treatment, private clinics are the most expensive, with fees that range from $20 to $100 per session; the average is $60. Some offer a sliding fee scale to accommodate people of various income levels.

Community programs usually establish a sliding scale, depending on the patient's ability to pay and the type of treatment needed. The cost per session for counseling with a psychologist or social worker ranges from nothing to $65. The cost per session is likely to increase if the therapist is a psychiatrist.

Program Funding

Over half the abuse programs received most of their funding from public sources, namely, the county in which they operate. Approximately 20% of the funding comes from payments made by patients for services received. About 60% of the programs receive some or all of their funding from sources other than individual payments, for instance, from private and government grants. Seventy-five percent of the programs are operated privately. Seventy-eight percent are nonprofit organizations.

Summary

The system that responds to child abuse and neglect may be envisioned as a wheel. At the hub of the wheel is Child Protective Services (CPS), the agency with primary responsibility for protecting the state's children. Spokes extending from the hub represent the agencies, both public and private, that CPS calls on to assist in its work.

A case of child sexual abuse enters the system when a report is made. Reports are made to either local law enforcement or CPS; the agency that receives the report must notify the other within 24 hours, both orally and in writing. Law enforcement often receives reports that involve extrafamilial abuse, frequently responding to emergency situations. CPS often receives reports of intrafamilial abuse.

Most often, CPS will conduct an assessment of the case. CPS will request the involvement of law enforcement, or law enforcement may conduct a separate investigation if there is an allegation of criminal conduct. Although the amount of collaboration is generally left to the discretion of the caseworker and officer involved, law mandates that they cooperate to avoid duplicative interviews of the victim and fact-finding in general.

The primary purpose of the assessment by CPS is to determine the level of risk to the child or children involved; fact-finding is secondary. A conclusion regarding the report must be produced within 90 days. Two determinations are required: whether maltreatment occurred and whether child protective services are needed.

Although reports with no determination of maltreatment will not result in any criminal action, some type of services may be recommended. Reports in which criminal conduct is documented by law enforcement will be passed on to the county attorney, who may charge the offender and bring the case to criminal court. Because this is a criminal proceeding, the burden of proof is substantial.

Another course is that CPS may request that the county attorney file a CHIPS petition with the juvenile court. In addition, CPS must produce an intervention plan, which the juvenile court will evaluate and enforce. This plan may include provisions for support services from professionals in other agencies, such as health care and education. The juvenile court is a civil proceeding, so the burden of proof is less severe.

As described, the system at large may seem to be an efficient operation, one in which the participants are able to adapt their roles and involvement with one another depending on the circumstances of the case. In reality, however, there is a good deal of institutional insularity and disagreement among agencies about how best to solve the problem. The result, at times, is a lack of coordination and collaboration, sometimes in direct defiance of the law. We will address these issues further in Chapter 9.

Notes

1. Although we will use the term *child protective services*, or *CPS*, primarily, *local* or *county welfare* and *social services* will be used as a synonyms at times.
2. Social service personnel conduct an *assessment*, while law enforcement personnel conduct an *investigation*.
3. Minnesota statute 260.133.
4. In 1988, the term CHIPS (Child In Need of Protection or Services) was introduced to describe what previously was called the dependency and neglect petition (Minnesota statute 260.015, subdivision 2(a)). Doing so eliminated the need to assess the situation as involving dependency or neglect, which required different petitions to be filed. Now the same petition may be filed for either.
5. Minnesota statutes 626.566, subdivision 10(a), and 626.561.
6. Minnesota statute 626.561, subdivision 3.
7. Although most CPS workers have used this process for some time, it has only been required by law since August 1, 1988.
8. Minnesota statutes 260.185, .191, .193, and .241.
9. Criminal sexual conduct laws, citing five degrees of sexual misconduct, are Minnesota statutes 609.342-.3451. The incest law, Minnesota statute 609.653 (1978) is rarely invoked because it requires proof of sexual intercourse between blood relatives and carries a lesser penalty than the comparable criminal sexual conduct statutes.
10. On occasion, child sexual abuse is addressed in family court when it becomes an issue in custody or divorce proceedings.
11. A *guardian ad litem* is a guardian appointed by the court to represent the interests of someone unable to represent himself or herself, such as a minor or an incompetent adult.
12. Two grids are presented because the lengths of sentences were increased as of August 1, 1989. The grid in effect when the crime was committed is that used to recommend sentencing.
13. The five offense types examined were level-7/criminal sexual conduct with force, level-7/aggravated robbery, level-8/criminal sexual conduct with force, level-8/criminal sexual conduct with a child, and level-8/first-degree assault. The dispositional departure rates for these five types of offenses were 15.8%, 12.8%, 5.1%, 52.6%, and 10%, respectively. Note that the dispositional departure rate for level-8/criminal sexual conduct with a child is 3 to 10 times higher than those for the other offense types (MSGC, 1988).

Chapter Nine

Making the System Work

It seems as though everyone has heard some story about how the system has failed to protect a child:

- How a child "slipped through the cracks" and was severely injured or even killed, despite several reports of abuse by neighbors and relatives
- How a father lost custody rights during a divorce hearing after he was wrongly accused of molesting his child by a vindictive wife
- How a mother felt compelled to run away with her own children after a judge awarded custody or visitation to an abusive father
- How an offender was arrested and found to have an extensive history of abusing children yet had never received treatment or been incarcerated

Certainly, such cases have received a good deal of attention in the media. We may be especially aware in Minnesota because of the publicity that surrounded the Scott County case and the WCCO I-Team report in the early 1980s. Such controversy has produced or at least enhanced an overwhelming distrust of the system that is supposed to respond to child sexual abuse. From the general public's point of view, that means being afraid of having one's rights violated, especially one's rights as a parent. From the point of view of those in the system, including anyone who is a mandated reporter, that means being afraid to take a stand and being frustrated by trying to do your part in a system that just doesn't work.

In this chapter, we will discuss how well the system works from a number of viewpoints. We will begin with a survey of professionals working in the system, conducted by David Finkelhor. Then we will examine some of the problems experienced, considering several perspectives on why the system doesn't work. We will conclude with an evaluation of what's been done in Minnesota to make the system work, including Project IMPACT as a model multidisciplinary team approach to child sexual abuse.

A Survey of Professionals

How well do professionals working in child protection think the system works? David Finkelhor sought to answer this question in his survey of 790 professionals in the Boston area who were attending a series of meetings about community efforts to address child sexual abuse. Each individual completed a questionnaire prior to attending the meetings, which took place from September 1980 to May 1981 (Finkelhor, Gomes-Schwartz, & Horowitz, 1984).

The respondents were categorized according to membership in one of six types of professional agencies:

1. mental health (14%)—predominantly social workers, psychologists, and psychiatrists;
2. medical (9%)—mainly nurses, with a few physicians and a group of more mental health professionals;
3. social services (25%)—overwhelmingly social workers;
4. criminal justice (9%)—nearly equal proportions of police on special assignment to sex-related crimes, lawyers, and mental health professionals;
5. education (32%)—teachers, counselors, and school nurses; and
6. other (10%)—professionals from private and state agencies other than the primary child protective agency (i.e., welfare workers, advocacy groups).

Experience with Child Sexual Abuse

Before proceeding with the topics of the questionnaire, it is helpful to understand the experience that characterizes workers from each type of agency. The social services workers had the most experience, on average, with both victims and offenders. Educators had the least experience. Criminal justice professionals had seen the greatest proportion of offenders to victims; almost all of the other groups saw more victims than offenders. No agency could be singled out as having no experience with child sexual abuse.

There were similarly characteristic patterns in what types of cases each agency was likely to see. Criminal justice workers dealt with a large percentage (55%) of extrafamilial abuse, whereas social services and mental health workers responded most often to cases of parent/child incest.

Finally, agencies were likely to encounter abuse of different duration at different times. Most of the workers dealt with cases in which the abuse had occurred fairly recently; however, in nearly a third of the cases, the abuse had taken place over a year before and sometimes over five years before referral took place. Delayed-referral cases such as these were most often seen by mental health workers, who discovered a history of abuse during ongoing therapy with an adolescent or adult patient. In contrast, criminal justice workers were most likely to handle emergency cases; in 93% of their cases, the abuse had occurred less than one year before, and in over half (55%), it had occurred within the last month.

Survey Topics

Mandated Reporting

The first question asked in the survey was about the level of compliance with mandated reporting laws.[1] Many of the professionals indicated that they felt mandated reporting compromised their confidential relationships with their clients; others didn't trust the system to handle the case once they'd reported it. As a result, over a third (36%) of the cases that should have been reported were not.

Two groups proved to be least likely to report: criminal justice and mental health professionals. This is an interesting finding, given the diversity of the groups. Mental health professionals were unlikely to report because of conflicts with confidentiality, frustration with the bureaucracy, concern with protecting the child, and a disbelief in punishment for the offender. The reason for criminal justice workers' lack of reporting was their feeling that they could handle the problem within their own jurisdiction, protecting the child and punishing the offender. This feeling of insularity will be demonstrated in other areas, as well.

Professional Collaboration

A second topic in examining practices was agency collaboration. A clear pattern was established for all groups: Agencies tended to function individually, within their own immediate networks, rather than collaborate with others in the larger system.

There are several reasons behind this insularity. For instance, when a case was not referred by the victim, offender, or family, most of the agencies received a good share of their referrals from other agencies within their network. This trend was most dominant in the criminal justice group, which received nearly half of its cases from other criminal justice groups (i.e., police referral to county attorney) and only 6% from non-criminal justice groups. Education and medical groups received a similarly high proportion of their cases from groups within their professional domains. Only the mental health and social services groups (including the "other" category) showed a truly diverse pattern of referrals.

The same sort of pattern was found when respondents described what resources they consulted in handling cases of child sexual abuse. Criminal justice personnel relied heavily on other criminal justice resources; social services personnel were likely to call in mental health resources.

Perhaps the most alarming finding was the general failure of agencies to notify one another about their cases. Nearly half the education and "other" social services workers and 40% of the mental health workers sought no outside assistance. Many didn't even contact the primary child protective agency, which is required by mandated reporting laws.

To explain these patterns, at least in part, Finkelhor pointed out that the various agencies deal with very different types of cases, which will affect their referral patterns. For instance, mental health groups deal with a lot of adults in therapy who report being abused as children; the police deal with cases involving abuse by strangers, often in emergency situations. Clearly, a therapist would not consult the police to investigate the childhood abuse of a patient who is now an adult, nor would the police likely consult a therapist in handling the case of an exhibitionist or similar offender type (i.e., noncontact offense committed, usually a large number of incidents).

Proposed Intervention

To evaluate the level of intervention preferred by workers in various groups, respondents were given a hypothetical situation (i.e., a mother comes to you suspecting stepfather/daughter incest) and asked to recommend an intervention plan. Based on these recommendations, it is clear that different groups of professionals prefer different courses of action.

Most workers felt it was imperative to interview the child, and many wanted to interview the mother again. Most also recommended a physical examination of the child.

Once again, a large proportion of the workers—at least a third—did not include reporting the case to the mandatory social services reporting agency in their strategy, despite the fact that the majority said they would do so. (There is no question that the case was covered by mandatory reporting laws.)

Workers were in less agreement about the remaining intervention steps, showing distinct preferences along professional lines. Social services workers could be characterized by the number of recommendations they made; they advised taking additional steps that other groups felt were unnecessary. For instance, they were the only group that recommended interviewing the offender. Finkelhor attributed this enthusiasm to the responsibility given to social services workers for the disposition of child sexual abuse cases, as well as the experience and resourcefulness that good workers bring to the job.

At the other end of the scale, educators made the fewest recommendations for intervention. In fact, their primary recommendation was to report the case to social services and let them handle it. Educators felt that becoming too involved interfered with their ability to educate, in part, because of the parental conflict that would result.

Criminal justice workers once more demonstrated insularity, choosing interventive actions that kept the case within their own jurisdiction. For instance, they were very inclined to involve the police in the case, and they were somewhat less inclined than other groups to report to social services. What's more, the isolation of the criminal justice group was enhanced because other groups tended to avoid working with them, seeking assistance elsewhere.

Goals of Intervention

Perhaps the two biggest questions in terms of the system's general goals are (1) Should criminal charges be brought against the offender? and (2) Should the child or the offender be removed from the home to prevent intrafamilial abuse?

In Finkelhor's survey, the respondents were asked to consider these issues in the context of the hypothetical incest case discussed earlier. Not surprisingly, workers from all groups were unanimous in their response to the second question: None favored removing the child from his or her family. Beyond that, however, there was little agreement.

Criminal justice workers were especially out of step with other workers; they favored prosecution and were less concerned with maintaining the family. Social services workers responded in an opposite manner; they felt keeping the family together was crucial and were against prosecuting the offender. Given the different professional orientations of these two groups, this polarity is understandable.

Conclusions

Based on these data, Finkelhor drew two conclusions about the management of child sexual abuse:

1. *There is a high degree of institutional insularity. Agencies do not readily cooperate with one another. They tend to rely heavily on other professionals within their own immediate institution. There appear to be some strong barriers to interaction, particularly between criminal justice and child protective professionals, but also to some extent between other agencies as well.*
2. *There exists a high degree of disagreement among agency personnel about the proper approach to handling sexual abuse. Different agencies give priorities to different kinds of interventions and are at odds with one another about basic objectives in the management of cases. (1984, p. 211)*

What implications do these factors have for actual practice?

1. The way in which a given case of sexual abuse is addressed will depend a good deal on which agency discovers it. The unique characteristics of the case will thus be subordinate to the functioning of the agency handling it.
2. Interagency cooperation is unlikely, even in cases where collaboration seems essential to effective intervention.
3. The lack of consensus on systemwide goals will make it difficult, if not impossible, for the community or state to develop a comprehensive and workable plan for child protection.

Characterizing the System

Clearly, the conclusions drawn from Finkelhor's survey point to some real problems with the system that responds to child abuse and neglect. Given the theoretical background established in Chapter 7, how can we characterize the system?

It is clearly hierarchical, subdivided into many diverse groups, both public and private: child protective services, law enforcement, corrections, judicial, education, health care, and various support groups. Each of these agencies operates as a separate entity, charged with a specific function, but within the context of the larger system. The function of the larger system is prescribed by state law: to protect children from abuse and neglect.

In terms of being open or closed, the system is a mixed system. The system at large (and most likely individual subsystems within) is enmeshed (i.e., low boundary permeability) in several ways:

- demands for time and emotional commitment are strong;
- organizational rules are often implicit rather than explicit; and
- individuality is minimized and even repressed.

The system is disengaged (i.e., high boundary permeability) in that it is a bureaucracy; the sense of a clear and common purpose has been lost.

To assess why the system is this way is difficult, certainly, beyond our means and purpose here. But based on the theory we've presented, the issue of adaptability must be examined. Has the system been successful in adapting to its changing environment?

Policy Issues

The child protective system has evolved dramatically; remember that the first legislation concerning child abuse was initiated in 1963, just 26 years ago. The number of people involved in the system, clients and workers, and the level of services offered have expanded rapidly in response to increased reporting. In this sense, the system has adapted to its changing environment.

However, critics will point out that this change has not been controlled and implemented according to sound policy. Although laws have been revised over the years, in most cases, elements have been added (e.g., child neglect, more mandated reporters), increasing the responsibilities of the system. Ironically, laws have not been made more specific; many would argue that they have become more vague and complicated.

The problem is that policy has not been adapted, or at least not sufficiently. The system has taken on more and more responsibility without setting any realistic limits to what it can and should do. Perhaps this has happened because growth has been so dynamic. Whatever the reason, the result is that the serious problems facing the system are rooted in policy. We will examine two major policy problems: professional limits and legal ambiguity.

Professional Limits

As we discussed in Chapter 7, the specificity with which jobs are defined and expected to be performed varies significantly from organization to organization. Within the system at large, it is often difficult for workers to know and adhere to professional limits, for several reasons.

1. The law provides only vague and ambiguous job assignments; the result is a good deal of overlap and even competition.

2. By nature, most of the people in the system are interested in helping others, which may lead to overzealousness and loss of objectivity.
3. Workers may feel the need to justify what they do and go overboard in doing it.
4. Some individuals are reluctant to admit that they don't know or can't do something and take on work beyond their means.
5. Given the hectic pace of everyday work life, it is difficult for workers to stop and assess their professional limits (Goldstein, Freud, Solnit, & Goldstein, 1986).

Personal Involvement

Workers may also have difficulty separating their personal beliefs and values from their professional ones. For instance, the fact that many of these individuals are parents is likely to influence their emotional involvement with and attitude toward the people they serve. On the one hand, this common base of experience may be beneficial, perhaps drawing the worker and client together. On the other hand, personal feelings may cloud professional judgment, especially in an emotional situation, and the worker may offer advice or make decisions that are inappropriate. "Experience-based wisdom is often an integral part of special competence, but professionals must be alert not to use their reputations as experts to assume roles for which they have no special competence in furtherance of their personal values or of the preferences of those who engage their services" (Goldstein et al., 1986, p. 17).

Role Conflict

Another problem in assessing professional limits is that some jobs expect workers to perform dual roles, roles that are often incompatible. For example, a social worker may be brought into a home both to offer support and to act as an investigator or watchdog. It is impossible to perform both functions well, affecting the quality of service offered and also the attitude of the worker toward what he or she does. Others raise some basic ethical and even constitutional questions about such assignments (Goldstein et al., 1986).

Philosophical Differences

Philosophical differences between members of agencies within the system create similar conflicts in purpose. Such differences surfaced in Finkelhor's survey of professionals, discussed earlier in this chapter, which pointed out that different philosophies about how best to treat child sexual abuse resulted in inconsistencies in case management (1984). A 1981 interview conducted by the Minnesota Crime Control Planning Board of county-level professionals working with sexual offenders of children drew a similar conclusion.

One-third of those surveyed felt that child protective services (CPS) and law enforcement workers disagreed about the purpose of their work, namely, whether offenders should be prosecuted or receive therapy. Workers concluded that this disagreement hindered good communication and coordination; individuals with contradictory ideas seemed to question and undermine one another's authority. Police officers believed that social workers didn't report everything they should and that they were not qualified to conduct investigations. Social workers were frustrated by the lack of successful prosecution of offenders and law enforcement's inability or unwillingness to explain it. Both groups cited problems with school and health care employees who did not report or cooperate or who withheld information out of ignorance or reluctance to get involved (Chein, 1981).

Granted, it is impossible to compartmentalize jobs so completely that there is no overlap. In fact, some overlap is beneficial; it allows professionals to share information and learn from one another. This only becomes a problem when individuals presume that the knowledge or experience they gain from others qualifies them to do those people's jobs. For example, a juvenile court judge has probably seen enough abused children to understand how this experience has affected them. Yet a judge is not a psychologist and should not presume that he or she is qualified to evaluate the mental state of an abused child. Instead, a judge is supposed to listen to information given him or her by other professionals and apply the law to the specific situation (Goldstein et al., 1986).

Burnout

A final topic related to individual limits is burnout. Although individuals in many fields experience burnout, those working with abused children are especially prone. Consider the following at-risk characteristics for burnout, as developed by Maslach and Jackson in the Maslach Burnout Inventory (MBI):

- long and irregular work hours,
- extended and continual contact with people,
- paperwork, "red tape," and bureaucratic dealings,
- lack of rapport with co-workers,
- budget problems,
- hostility from clients,
- dangerous, traumatic, and/or seamy atmosphere, and
- personal problems (Maslach, 1982).

These characteristics describe many of the jobs in the system. Is it any wonder, then, that burnout is a serious problem?

Since the term *burnout* is often used loosely, it's important to define what we mean by it. Maslach defines *burnout* as "a syndrome of emotional exhaustion, depersonalization, and reduced personal accomplishment" (1982, p. 3).

1. *Emotional exhaustion* is caused by emotional overload. Workers become too involved, try too hard, care too much, or perhaps their clients, co-workers, or supervisors simply demand more than they can give. Whatever the reason, the solution is to back away and have less contact, eventually operating as a bureaucrat who handles everything completely "by the book."
2. *Depersonalization* follows emotional exhaustion. The worker comes to expect the worst from everyone, clients and co-workers alike. Initial contempt will eventually lead to shutting people out, and with this alienation will come self-doubt and depression.
3. *Reduced personal achievement* results when the worker loses self-confidence and considers himself or herself inadequate for the job. The worker may consider quitting.

What causes burnout? It's easy to blame people: yourself, your co-workers, your clients. This is understandable, given that the structure of the helping relationship itself develops and maintains a negative view of people. Consider the usual scenario: All the people you deal with have problems, most of them serious and many of them the same or at least similar. Your encounters with people are emotionally charged; clients are often angry or confused or hurt, and they may resent your intervention. To be honest, you may not like many of the people you're supposed to help. You receive little positive feedback from anyone. The problem clients need more help or come back more often than do those who are successful; you may never hear from them again. Similarly, you are likely to be criticized or second guessed more often than you are praised by supervisors or co-workers. In the end, you feel that nothing ever changes, no matter what you do, which must mean that you're ineffectual.

Burnout is a response to chronic, everyday stress. It is not simply a reaction to occasional crises, and it is not a temporary state. It develops insidiously until it finally wears you down to the point of dysfunction. Many people respond with self-criticism: "I used to be able to handle this, but I can't anymore. What's wrong with me?" Unfortunately, the administrative response is similar, albeit unfair.

Legal Ambiguity

One of the strongest critics of the system that responds to child abuse and neglect is Douglas Besharov, who was the first director of the National Center on Child Abuse and Neglect (1975-1979). In Besharov's view, the real problem with the system is legal ambiguity, which affects everything from job descriptions to burnout to personal privacy to child welfare. As you read this section, reflect back upon the problems discussed in the "Professional Limits" section. Note that Besharov addresses many of these problems, as well.

At the most basic level, the law is not clear about exactly what constitutes child abuse and neglect. The language is vague, employing phrases like "when the child's environment is injurious to his welfare" or "when the child lacks proper parental care." The language is also tautological, using terms like *sexual abuse* and *neglect* without ever defining them. Semantics is critical; even words like *adequate* and *necessary* merit legal definition.

Unfortunately, efforts to revise laws and develop better standards for intervention have, for the most part, been unsuccessful. Even a major attempt by the Juvenile Justice Standards Project for the Institute of Judicial Administration and the American Bar Association (ABA) to develop standards regarding state intervention in child abuse and neglect was thwarted by opposition and criticism. And although communities, school systems, hospitals, and other professional groups have produced an enormous amount of material about child abuse, little of it is uniform. C. Henry Kempe summed up the situation well when he said, "Child abuse is what the courts say it is" (reported in Besharov, 1985, p. 22).

Some critics take the problem one step back, claiming that laws cannot and will not be revised until the policies prescribing them are clarified. "Existing legal standards . . . are a direct reflection of society's overambitious expectations about the ability of social agencies and courts to identify and protect endangered children" (Besharov, 1985, p. 22). People are unwilling to accept the fact that not all children can be protected from abuse and neglect. It is inevitable that some will be hurt, and some will even die. And frustrating as it is, we cannot predict who will abuse or who will be abused.

Our child protective laws are based on the idealistic notion that all children can be safeguarded. This not only makes the laws impractical, it also places incredible pressure on those expected to enforce them. At one extreme, people are confused and afraid to act for fear of making a wrong decision or incurring personal liability. At the other extreme are those who feel they have the responsibility and authority to intervene at will in people's lives. That is the criticism heard more and more frequently: that reporting of child abuse has become rampant and irresponsible and that the system has assumed too much authority over children and their families.

It is true that reporting of abuse has increased dramatically over the last 25 years. In 1963, no state mandated the reporting of child abuse; nationally, only 150,000 reports of abuse were made in that year. In 1982, however, over 1.3 million children were reported because of suspected abuse—a nearly ninefold increase over 20 years.

But how many of these reports are warranted? Critics point to the number of cases of so-called abuse that involve nothing more than a spanking or the grabbing of an arm. Even more controversial are cases of alleged neglect that simply reflect poor or inappropriate childrearing: children living in dirty homes or keeping late or irregular hours. The National Study of the Incidence and Severity of Child Abuse and Neglect found that more than half of all reports substantiated by child protective agencies involved nothing more than minor problems such as these (reported in Besharov, 1985).

Concern may have been warranted in these cases, but maltreatment did not occur. Nonetheless, before such a determination could be made, an investigation was conducted, involving family, friends, co-workers, neighbors, and a number of people in contact with the child—teachers, coaches, club leaders, and so forth. This is an enormous and embarrassing intrusion on the family, one that is unavoidably traumatic. Furthermore, conducting what appear to be needless investigations is expensive and taxing for the professionals involved.

Correspondingly, intervention by social agencies into family matters has increased dramatically. It's estimated that, even after reported cases are screened and investigated, approximately 400,000 U.S. families are being supervised by child protective agencies at any one time. In 1963, about 75,000 children were placed in foster care because of abuse or neglect. In 1980, more than 300,000 children were in foster care for the same reason; about half had been in foster care for at least two years and about a third for over six years. Yet data collected for the federal government revealed that perhaps up to half of these children were not in any immediate danger and would have been safe in the care of their parents (Besharov, 1985).

Thus, it appears that "protection for abused and neglected children has been purchased at the price of enormous governmental intervention into private family matters" (Besharov, 1985, p. 21). But, you may ask, isn't it better to be "safe than sorry"? In others words, if we're going to err, isn't it better to provide children with too much protection than not enough?

According to Besharov, current laws and intervention standards do not ensure that children are protected from abuse. We know that not all cases of abuse are reported even by professionals in regular contact with the children. A 1979 study estimated that over 50,000 children with observable injuries serious enough to merit hospitalization were not reported. A similar study in Texas found that more than 40% of approximately 270 children who died because of maltreatment had not been reported, despite the fact that they were being supervised by a public or private agency at the time of or within a year of their death.

Nor does reporting guarantee a child's safety. Data from a number of state surveys show that about 25% of all children who die from maltreatment had already been reported to a child protective agency. And a countless number of children continue to be abused even while under protective supervision.

Ironically, increased reporting only seems to make the problem worse, glutting the system with unwarranted cases. More reports bring more parents and children into the system, which means that more services are being provided for an increasing number of people, some of whom don't need or want such help. It's inevitable, then, that legitimate cases of abuse may not receive the attention they deserve.

Again, quoting Besharov, "Unless something is done to break this ironic equation, the continued pursuit of fuller reporting will produce a cruel trade-off—to the community as well as to the children and parents involved" (1985, p. 21).

Resolving the Problems

What can be done to resolve the problems that make the system dysfunctional? Besharov has pointed to problems that are rooted in policy, arguing that the system has not kept pace with the explosive developments that have occurred in the child sexual abuse field within the last 20 to 30 years. Finkelhor and others have examined the system's problems on a more practical level: the day-to-day philosophical and procedural conflicts experienced by workers in the system.

Given the subjectivity that surrounds child sexual abuse, it is likely that policy issues will be debated for some time to come, if not forever. In fact, if the system is to evolve and remain viable, it is inevitable that policy will be continually reexamined and revised. Consider how much policy has changed since the first child abuse legislation was passed in 1963.

At the risk of being simplistic, the answer to both policy and procedural questions is collaboration. The individual components of the system need to understand that, even though they have different philosophies of how to handle the problem of child sexual abuse, this need not preclude their collaboration. After all, their ultimate goal is the same: to protect children from abuse and neglect.

Clearly, the best means of achieving this collaboration is through a multidisciplinary team approach to handling child sexual abuse. Actually, the legal and social groundwork for such an approach has already been laid. Legally, child sexual abuse is a crime in all 50 states, and the criminal justice system has established means to address it. In addition, legislation in many states has made great strides in reducing system-induced trauma for victims and their families. In the social realm, child protective services have become more vigilant and responsive to the protection and treatment needs of victims and their families (Saunders, 1988).

On a national scale, Minnesota is relatively progressive in its response to child sexual abuse. In order for states to receive federal grant monies, they must comply with policy recommendations established by the federal government. For instance, federal policy encourages acknowledging the competence of juvenile witnesses, promoting coordination between social services and law enforcement, and using alternative means of interviewing child witnesses (i.e., closed-circuit TV). When Minnesota received federal funding in 1988, such policies were already in place. Moreover, the attitude in Minnesota about how best to address child sexual abuse is healthy and realistic. Despite (or perhaps as a result of) the sensational accounts of abuse that surfaced in the early 1980s, today Minnesota is prone to neither over- nor underintervention (Swanson Broberg, 1989).

Minnesota has also been progressive in the establishment of multidisciplinary teams to work in child sexual abuse. Project IMPACT was initiated in 1986 when the Governor's Task Force on Criminal Justice Policy allocated state funds received from the Federal Justice Assistance Act for use in multidisciplinary training of workers in the criminal justice system's response to child sexual abuse. The project was administered through the Minnesota State Planning Agency by the Government Training Service and overseen by the Interagency Team on Child Abuse and Neglect, which is composed of individuals from the following state agencies:

- Department of Corrections
- Department of Education
- Department of Human Services
- Department of Public Health
- Department of Public Safety
- Minnesota Supreme Court
- State Office of the Attorney General
- State Office of the Public Defender
- State Planning Agency

Project IMPACT had three primary goals:

1. to build communication and cooperation among professionals;

2. to improve the skills of individuals involved in the detection, intervention, prosecution, defense, adjudication, and treatment of child sexual abuse cases; and
3. to build consistency among counties and agencies statewide to enhance the ability of the criminal justice system to respond effectively to the sexual abuse of children.

An evaluation of Project IMPACT, completed in October 1988, found that the project had been successful in several areas, "most notably in motivating professionals from several disciplines to work together to identify and achieve necessary changes in Minnesota's counties" (Morehouse & Hoaglund, 1988, p. i). Over 3,500 professionals, from different fields and from all over the state, participated in a series of training sessions, conferences, and systems change forums. These activities gave professionals from different fields the opportunity to share a common experience and develop a common basis of understanding.

Systems change forums, which provided activities and strategies aimed at specific concerns in local settings, were especially effective. Nearly 70% of the counties involved in these systems forums implemented new policies and procedures as a result of their participation, addressing issues ranging from public awareness of child sexual abuse to inconsistencies in case management.

Other results achieved by Project IMPACT are more difficult to measure, in part, because insufficient time has elapsed to see results in most areas. Future, long-term evaluation must examine whether new learning has promoted changes in worker attitudes and, more importantly, improved performance. The ultimate goal is obvious: to reduce the incidence of child sexual abuse.

Participants overwhelmingly endorsed the multidisciplinary approach of Project IMPACT. System problems, such as "turf" sensitivities and worker overload, were identified as obstacles to widespread change. But the commitment and dedication of professionals in the system were recognized, as well, which fueled the desire for more information and ongoing support.

The executive summary of the Project IMPACT evaluation (Morehouse & Hoaglund, 1988) concluded by noting the importance of the project as a model of effective multidisciplinary interaction. Although Project IMPACT functioned on a state level, its structure and operation could be adapted to form local teams.

Addressing child sexual abuse at a local level has several definite advantages. Namely, the demographics of the area could be considered in planning intervention and prevention programs and strategies; factors such as race, ethnicity, and socioeconomic status could be addressed, as could differences in urban versus rural environments. The availability of local professionals and the services they offer could be considered in such planning, as well (Lyon & Kouloumpos-Lenares, 1987).

Another significant benefit of local team work is improved education and training of both professionals and citizens. For learning to occur and for practices to change, the problem of sexual abuse, along with the operation of the system and the roles its workers play, must be discussed in a familiar, personal context. The local setting is the best place to establish a realistic understanding of the problem and the system (Lyon & Kouloumpos-Lenares, 1987).

In sum, the multidisciplinary team approach to child sexual abuse is not easily accomplished, nor does it guarantee solutions. It does, however, draw everyone into the forum needed to address the problem. Professionals and citizens must learn to trust and respect one another before they can work together to solve the problem of child sexual abuse.

Conclusion

In the meantime, work goes on. And on an individual level, workers are looking for practical solutions to the everyday problems that hinder the system. Finkelhor advocates a grass-roots approach to resolving these problems, calling on individuals to take the initiative and make things work, even on a very small scale. He points to several communities across the country in which child protective systems have demonstrated that collaboration among agencies has actually helped them achieve their individual goals simultaneously. For example, prosecutors have brought in mental health and social services workers to help them prepare child victims for testimony; the result has been improved conviction rates (Bulkley & Davidson, 1981). And social services workers found they had more success working with offenders when they collaborated beforehand with prosecutors and courts, for instance, using the threat of prosecution or revoked parole to encourage treatment (Giaretto, 1982).

In both these examples, social services and criminal justice agencies were able to fulfill their own goals but not at the expense of one another or of the system at large. And interestingly enough, the initiative to collaborate did not require any elaborate policy decision or bureaucratic involvement. Rather, successful collaborations such as these have been prompted by small groups of workers who have used their own experience and personal contacts to make things work. They were able to acknowledge others' professional abilities and willing to trust in them. In sum:

> *This observation is encouraging. It suggests that the opportunity exists for creative restructuring of service systems by individual workers who are willing to take the initiative. As workers continue to be frustrated over the handling of child sexual abuse, and as models for other modes of cooperation become better known, it is possible that more and more of these efforts will take hold and succeed in communities across the country.* (Finkelhor, 1984, p. 215)

Summary

Finkelhor's survey of professionals working in child sexual abuse considered three primary issues in assessing how well the system works: mandated reporting, professional collaboration, and proposed intervention. The results of the survey demonstrated that there is a high degree of institutional insularity among agencies within the system, as well as a lot of disagreement about the proper approach to handling child sexual abuse.

Finkelhor cited three major implications of these factors on actual practice: (1) the way in which a given case of sexual abuse is addressed will depend a good deal on which agency discovers it; (2) interagency cooperation is unlikely, even in cases where collaboration seems essential to effective intervention; and (3) the lack of consensus on systemwide goals will make it difficult to develop a comprehensive and workable plan for child protection.

The system that responds to child abuse and neglect can be best characterized as mixed, or both engaged and enmeshed in certain respects. Based on the theory presented in Chapter 7, we can conclude that the system has not successfully adapted to its changing environment. The system has grown rapidly, offering more and more services to increasing numbers of people. But this change has not been controlled and implemented according to sound policy. Questions about professional limits and legal ambiguity must be addressed before the system will change.

Improvement will only come about when individuals understand that collaboration can help everyone achieve individual goals simultaneously but not at the expense of one another or the system at large. The approach recommended to achieve collaboration is a multidisciplinary team of professionals working in child sexual abuse. Project IMPACT, which worked successfully over $3\frac{1}{2}$ years, should be viewed as a state-level model of a multidisciplinary team that can and should be adapted at the local level.

Finkelhor concurs with the need for local, grass-roots initiative in making the system work. Although the individual worker seems, at times, to be lost in the system, we must not forget that individuals can and must make a difference.

Note

1. The survey was conducted in Boston, so the mandated reporting laws mentioned here are those of Massachusetts. Nonetheless, state reporting laws are similar enough to extend this discussion to general situations involving workers across the country.

Epilogue

Divergent Issues

Child sexual abuse has developed from an issue of seemingly straightforward facts and appearances to become a remarkably complicated issue characterized by facets that are still subject to analysis and consideration. That complexity, coupled with high visibility, has pushed child sexual abuse into the forefront of the public policy arena. Attempts to cope with the practical and theoretical dilemmas posed by the problem have resulted in ongoing philosophical and policy struggles that serve both to divide and unify professionals and the public alike.

The Rights of the State: Over- and Underintervention

Perhaps some of the most widespread and well-publicized debate has involved the appropriate balance of child protection and familial integrity. There is a strong and constant interchange between the concepts of familial self-determination and respect for cultural, ethnic, and individual differences and the notion of a child's right to live free of abuse. The state is forced to draw a conceptual line where none exists in defining abuse, particularly as it relates to corporal punishment but also as it relates to appropriate and inappropriate physical contact.

After drawing this line and establishing the boundary between acceptable and unacceptable conduct, the state must then enforce its decision, employing a combination of services and consequences for failure to comply. To do so requires literally hundreds of discretionary decisions, each of which may be subject to scrutiny and criticism.

There is continuing discussion as to what is an appropriate level of state intervention and authority. The most conservative view assumes that the state only has a right to intervene upon a prima facie showing of physical harm, imminent endangerment of life and limb, or criminally sexual behavior. Suspicion should not be the basis for government interaction. Essentially, this view holds that government intervention is more harmful than helpful in face of the limited occurrence of actual child abuse. Many who espouse this conservative opinion feel that government has been part of a witchhunt, planting the seeds of abuse in children's minds through repetitive interviews and brainwashing tactics.

At the other end of the spectrum are those who feel that the state has limited its discretionary power without cause and that the system merely "massages" abusive families, allowing them to continue to thrive in a dysfunctional manner until the worst occurs—only then does the state use its interventive powers effectively to remove children from the care of their parents. The child advocates cry out for swifter and more easily implemented methods of child protection, subordinating the focus upon healthy family functioning in deference to the need to focus exclusively upon the physical and emotional safety of children.

In this particular debate, most professionals have found a comfortable range of functioning between the two extremes. However, continued direction by the court and legislature, mandating a strong policy to keep children in their own homes, along with ongoing litigation over cases in which the state intervened without finding abuse or failed to intervene and a child suffered injury, will keep the debate about appropriate intervention in child sexual abuse alive.

The Veracity of Children

Early in the development of professional approaches to suspected child abuse, those involved in investigations were heard to unilaterally declare that "children never lie about child abuse." It made sense, after all, that no child would be able to describe an experience to which he or she had not been exposed. It was particularly important to convey to child care, health, and education professionals that children should be believed when they say they've been abused. In fact, very few false reports could be documented, and research into the ability of children to fabricate allegations seemed fairly conclusive: They should be believed.

Nevertheless, with the emergence of high-visibility cases in which the veracity of allegations or the veracity of the extent of the allegations has been questioned, professionals and laypeople have cause to reconsider the circumstances under which a child might lie about being abused. Growing evidence suggests that older children are, in fact, capable of fabricating allegations of abuse, particularly when they have been exposed to specific sexual stimulus or are the subject of a custody battle between parents desperate enough to coach a child into deceit. (The general reliability of young children remains high.)

Once again, this is an issue about which professionals have widely varying opinions. Therapeutic professionals remain fairly loyal to the notion of children's veracity, while those in the criminal justice system have become increasingly wary of statements made by children where certain factual information exists. As more is learned about children's ability to fabricate or to be coached and as better documentation is available to show the long-term disposition of such children, the debate will take on new colors.

Treatment versus Punishment

Perhaps the topic most volatile in terms of public attention is the appropriate manner in which to treat those who offend against children. In 1986, Minnesota Attorney General Hubert Humphrey convened a state task force to examine the problem of child abuse within the family. The task force held public hearings, took substantial testimony from professionals and laypeople, reviewed records, and ultimately made over 100 recommendations, many of which were enacted to improve the system's response to child abuse. One of those recommendations not enacted was the use of preplea diversion in handling sexual offenders (i.e., offering options other than prosecution before the defendant even enters a plea).

Many professionals working in the system responded negatively to this recommendation, particularly to the specific provision of alternatives to incarceration and diversion from prosecution pending treatment for certain intrafamilial sexual offenders. Diversion, hand in hand with "target charging" (i.e., a pending charge can be activated and tied to a full confession should the perpetrator fail treatment or violate the terms of probation), is a strategy that is becoming widely accepted across the country. Many professionals in the criminal justice system believe that, by sparing the public the expense and the victim the trauma of a trial, society is better served—as long as it can be assured that the public interest and safety will be protected by maintaining a figurative hammer over the head of the offender as he or she receives treatment.

On the other hand, there is a large and knowledgeable segment of the professional community that is strongly committed to aggressive and consistent prosecution and conviction of sexual offenders whenever sufficient evidence allows them. These proponents argue that it is not acceptable to pass a message to society that appears to allow, condone, or excuse egregious violence, which has seemingly been minimized or dismissed rather than accepted as being completely devastating for a person and his or her family. These professionals also argue that a policy of selective diversion will allow the wealthy to escape prosecution, since they can afford adequate psychological treatment and a sophisticated legal defense, while the same alternative is not available to those without the means. They fear this would perpetuate a two-tiered approach to criminal justice, which should not be acceptable in this society.

The practice of diversion continues on a jurisdiction-by-jurisdiction and a case-by-case basis. To some, diversion is a case management tool; to others, a cause celebre. In any case, as the approaches to diversion continue to develop and expand, so does the strong opposition to it.

Ritualistic Abuse

In the past two years, reports of ritualized, satanic, and cult-associated abuse and assault of children have grown in frequency. While their number is hardly significant in terms of the total cases of abuse reported to authorities, some professionals claim that the very nature of ritualistic abuse makes it a phenomenon that is substantially unreported and extremely hard to detect. To complicate matters, some have alleged occasional involvement of professionals in child protection as perpetrators of such assault, thereby making disclosure nearly impossible for victims in such cases.

The occurrence of ritualized sexual assault of children, as part of satanic or other cult worship, is not disputed when the topic is referred to as an oddity or a transient phenomenon worthy of study due to the particularly savage nature of the psychological and physical terror usually inflicted on its victims. The dispute comes from the professional community, who question the nature and severity of the problem. Some professionals describe the virtual hysteria over the issue as an overreaction to a recent spate of education, media, and popular literature treatment of a small number of cases. Others insist that, as strong as the push for public attention has been, the phenomenon is even larger than assumed and that serious and immediate professional attention is imperative.

Few studies have assessed the number of cases of ritualistic assault reported, and practitioners who deal with child victims of such assault are often reluctant to participate in research or evaluation studies. What's more, as already mentioned, there is strong suspicion among some that a professional network is involved in perpetuating and covering up such abuse; strong public involvement with certain cases might, in fact, be dangerous. Still other professionals are frustrated by the seemingly disproportionate amount of attention devoted to this topic and by the use of unscientific information as training material for law enforcement and others who identify and intervene in such cases.

The professional community has much to do in clarifying the status of ritualistic assault and abuse.

The Importance of Conflict

In a complex system with a complex mission, it is nearly impossible for successful work to occur unimpeded by conflict. As actors with varying objectives, directives, authority, and responsibility, dedicated professionals develop individual perspectives on the problem of child sexual abuse. Inevitably, those perspectives are colored by experience, including one's professional training, disciplinary biases, and organizational objectives. In addition, when the system fails to function effectively as a whole, it is easy to become absorbed with the organizational and resource realities affecting one's own profession, losing sight of others' interests, not to mention systemwide interests.

This is especially likely with an issue as volatile and controversial as child sexual abuse. Individuals develop strong opinions and hold essential beliefs about what is at the root of the problem and what is the most successful means of addressing it. Given the depth of commitment and the strength of belief shared by dedicated professionals, it is natural that divergence surfaces in the form of conflict.

Conflict that emerges in this manner provides an opportunity for resolution, allowing a better understanding across professions and agencies and thus more productive working relationships. At times, however, conflict impedes professional cooperation and functioning. When differences are viewed as necessarily adversarial and competitive or, most seriously, when factions develop and unify around the conflict itself, agreement and cooperation are impossible. The result is failure: a reduction in the overall quality of intervention and services available to children.

To avoid this result, practitioners of all types must recognize the absolute inevitability of conflict—often strong conflict—relative to specific cases or to the field of child abuse as a whole. Moreover, they must be able to accept that diversity of belief does not preclude effective services. In fact, children may well benefit from the natural advocacy that occurs when individual voices insist upon being heard from within the group. At its best, conflict means awareness and accountability.

Readings and References

Abel, G., Becker, J. V., Mittelman, M., Cunningham-Rather, J., Rouleau, S., & Murphy, W. D. (1987 March). Self-reported sex crimes of nonincarcerated paraphiliacs. *Journal of Interpersonal Violence*, 2(1), 3-25.

Aldrich, H. (1981). Centralization versus decentralization in the design of human services delivery systems: A response to Gouldner's lament. In O. Grushy & G. A. Miller (Eds.), *The sociology of organizations*, pp. 370-394. New York: Free Press.

American Humane Association. (1981). *National study on child neglect and abuse reporting*. Denver: AHA.

American Humane Association. (1984). *National study on child neglect and abuse reporting*. Denver: AHA.

Amir, M. (1971). *Patterns in forcible rape*. Chicago: University of Chicago Press.

Anderson, S. C., Bach, C. M., & Griffith, S. (1981 April). Psychosocial sequelae in intrafamilial victims of sexual assault and abuse. Paper presented at the Third International Conference on Child Abuse and Neglect, Amsterdam, The Netherlands.

Araji, S., & Finkelhor, D. (1986). Abusers: A review of the research. In D. Finkelhor & associates, *A sourcebook on child sexual abuse*, pp. 89-118. Beverly Hills, CA: Sage.

Bagley, C., & Ramsay, R. (1985). Disrupted childhood and vulnerability to sexual assault: Long-term sequels with implications for counselling. *Social Work and Human Sexuality*.

Becker, J. V. (1988 April). The shaping of adolescent male sexuality and sexual deviancy. Keynote address at the symposium on Adolescent Male Sexuality, Project IMPACT, Brooklyn Park, MN.

Becker, J. V., Cunningham-Rather, J., & Kaplan, M. S. (1986 December). Adolescent sexual offenders: Demographics, criminal and sexual histories and recommendations for reducing future offenses. *Journal of Interpersonal Violence*, 1(4), 431-444.

Bell, A., & Weinberg, M. (1978). *Homosexualities*. New York: Simon and Schuster.

Bell, A., & Weinberg, M. (1981). *Sexual preference: Its development among men and women*. Bloomington, IN: Indiana University Press.

Besharov, D. J. (1985). Right versus rights: The dilemma of child protection, *Public Welfare*, 19-27.

Blyth, D. A., & Karnes, E. L. (Comp.) (1981). *Philosophies, policies, and programs for early adolescent education: An annotated bibliography*. Westport, CT: Greenwood Press.

Briere, J. (1984 April). The long-term effects of childhood sexual abuse: Defining a post-sexual-abuse syndrome. Paper presented at the Third National Conference on Sexual Victimization of Children, Washington, DC.

Briere, J., & Runtz, M. (1985). Symptomatology associated with prior sexual abuse in a non-clinical sample. Paper presented at the annual meeting of the American Psychological Association, Los Angeles, CA.

Broberg, J. Swanson. (1988 July). Reporting: Our needs and values. Session at the symposium on Making the System Work, Project IMPACT, St. Paul, MN.

Broberg, J. Swanson. (1989 April-June). Personal correspondence.

Brown, L., & Holder, W. (1980). The nature and extent of sexual abuse in contemporary American society. In W. Holder (Ed.), *Sexual abuse of children.* Denver, CO: AHA.

Browne, A., & Finkelhor, D. (1986). Initial and long-term effects: A review of the research. In D. Finkelhor & associates, *A sourcebook on child sexual abuse,* pp. 143-179. Beverly Hills, CA: Sage.

Bulkley, J., & Davidson, H. (1981). *Child sexual abuse—Legal issues and approaches.* Washington, DC: National Resource Center for Child Advocacy and Protection/American Bar Association.

Burgess, A. W. (ed.) (1985). *Rape and sexual assault: A research handbook.* New York: Garland.

Burt, J. J., & Meeks, L. B. (1985). *Education for sexuality: Concepts and programs for teaching.* Philadelphia: Saunders College.

Chandler, S. M. (1982). Knowns and unknowns in sexual abuse of children. In J. R. Conte & D. A. Shore (Eds.), *Social work and child sexual abuse.* New York: Haworth Press.

Chein, D. P. (1981 January). *The system's response to sexual abuse of children.* St. Paul, MN: Crime Control Planning Board.

(1983 June). *Child Protective Services practice guide for the social workers and social services supervisors of Minnesota.* St. Paul, MN: Child Protection Improvement Project and the Department of Public Welfare, Division of Social Services.

Clancy, M. (1988 July). Overview of the child protection system. Session at the symposium on Making the System Work, Project IMPACT, St. Paul, MN.

Cleckley, H. (1976). *The mask of sanity* (5th ed.). St. Louis: Mosby.

Conte, J. R., & Berliner, L. (1984). *Impact of sexual abuse in children* (Report 1) (Contract No. PHS-1 RO1 M437133). Washington, DC: National Institute of Mental Health.

Courtois, C. (1979). The incest experience and its aftermath. *Victimology: An International Journal, 4,* 334-347.

De Francis, V. (1969). *Protecting the child victim of sex crimes committed by an adult.* Denver: AHA, Children's Division.

de Young, M. (1982). *The sexual victimization of children.* Jefferson, NC: McFarland.

de Young, M. (1985). *Incest: An annotated bibliography.* Jefferson, NC: McFarland.

Department of the Youth Authority. (1986 January). *Sex offender task force report.* Sacramento, CA: State of California/Youth and Adult Correctional Agency.

Diagnostic and statistical manual of mental disorders (3rd ed.—rev.). Washington, DC: American Psychiatric Press, 1987.

Emans, R. R. (1987 June). Abusing in the name of protecting children. *Phi Delta Kappan, 68*(10), 740-743.

Fine, K. K. (1985 March). *Provision of services in the child protection system: A research report.* St. Paul, MN: Research Department, Minnesota House of Representatives.

Finkelhor, D. (1979). *Sexually victimized children.* New York: Free Press.

Finkelhor, D. (1980 June). Sex among siblings: A survey on prevalence, variety and effects. *Archives of Sexual Behavior, 9*(3), 171-194.

Finkelhor, D. (1984). *Child sexual abuse: New research and theory.* New York: Free Press.

Finkelhor, D. (1986a). Abusers: Special topics. In D. Finkelhor & associates, *A sourcebook on child sexual abuse,* pp. 119-142. Beverly Hills, CA: Sage.

Finkelhor, D. (1986b). Introduction. In D. Finkelhor & associates, *A sourcebook on child sexual abuse,* pp. 10-14. Beverly Hills, CA: Sage.

Finkelhor, D. and associates (1986c). *A sourcebook on child sexual abuse.* Beverly Hills, CA: Sage.

Finkelhor, D., & Baron, R. (1986). High-risk children. In D. Finkelhor & associates, *A sourcebook on child sexual abuse*, pp. 60-88. Beverly Hills, CA: Sage.

Finkelhor, D., Gomes-Schwartz, B., & Horowitz, J. (1984). Professionals' responses. In D. Finkelhor, *Child sexual abuse: New research and theory*, pp. 200-215. New York: Free Press.

Finkelhor, D., & Hotaling, G. (1983). *Sexual abuse in the national incidence study of child abuse and neglect*. Report to National Center on Child Abuse and Neglect. (Published in 1984, *Child Abuse and Neglect*, 8, 22-32.)

Friedrich, W. N., Urquiza, A. J., & Beilke, R. (1986). Behavioral problems in sexually abused young children. *Journal of Pediatric Psychology*, 11, 47-57.

Fritz, G., Stoll, K., & Wagner, N. (1981). A comparison of males and females who were sexually molested as children. *Journal of Sex and Marital Therapy*, 7, 54-59.

Fromuth, M. E. (1983). The long term psychological impact of childhood sexual abuse. Unpublished doctoral dissertation, Auburn University.

Gebhard, P. H., Gagnon, J. H., Pomeroy, W. B., & Christenson, C. V. (1965). *Sex offenders: An analysis of types*. New York: Holt & Rinehart.

George, L. (1989 June). Personal communication.

Giaretto, H. (1982). The treatment of father-daughter incest: A psycho-social approach. In N. R. Larson, *Integrated treatment of child sexual abuse: A treatment and training manual*. Palo Alto, CA: Science and Behavior Books.

Goldman, R. L., & Wheeler, V. R. (1986). *Silent shame: The sexual abuse of children and youth*. Danville, IL: Interstate Printers and Publishers.

Goldstein, S. L. (1987). *The sexual exploitation of children: A practical guide to assessment, investigation, and intervention*. New York: Elsevier, 1987.

Goldstein, J., Freud, A., Solnit, A. J., & Goldstein, S. (1986). *In the best interests of the child*. New York: Free Press.

Goodwin, J. (1982). *Sexual abuse: Incest victims and their families*. Littleton, MA: John Wright * PSG Inc.

Goodwin, J., McCarthy, T., & DiVasto, P. (1982). Prior incest in mothers of abused children. *Child Abuse and Neglect*, 5, 87-96.

Groth, A. N. (1978). Patterns of sexual assault against children and adolescents. In A. W. Burgess, A. N. Groth, L. L. Holmstrom, & S. M. Sgroi, *Sexual assault of children and adolescents*, pp. 3-24. Lexington, MA: Lexington Books.

Groth, A. N., Longo, R. E., & McFadin, J. B. (1982). Undetected recidivism among rapists and child molesters. *Journal of Crime and Delinquency*, 28(3), 450-458.

Gruber, K., & Jones, R. (1983). Identifying determinants of risk of sexual victimization of youth. *Child Abuse and Neglect*, 7, 17-24.

Hare, R. D. (1980). A research scale for the assessment of psychopathy in criminal populations. *Personality & Individual Differences*, 1, 111-119.

Herman, J. (1981). *Father-daughter incest*. Cambridge, MA: Harvard University Press.

Howells, K. (1981). Adult sexual interest in children: Considerations relevant to theories of aetiology. In M. Cook & K. Howells (Eds.), *Adult sexual interest in children*. New York: Academic Press.

James, J., & Meyerding, J. (1977). Early sexual experiences and prostitution. *American Journal of Psychiatry*, 134, 1381-1385.

James, B., & Nasjleti, M. (1983). Treating sexually abused children and their families. Palo Alto, CA: Consulting Psychologists Press.

Jones, D., McGraw, P. H., & Melbourne, J. (1987 March). Reliable and fictitious accounts of sexual abuse to children. *Journal of Interpersonal Violence*, 2(1), 27-45.

Katchadourian, H. A., & Lunde, D. T. (1972). *Fundamentals of human sexuality*. New York: Harcourt Brace & World.

Kempe, R. S., & Kempe, C. H. (1984). *The common secret: Sexual abuse of children and adolescents*. New York: W. H. Freeman.

Kerzner, H. (1984). *Project management: A system's approach to planning, scheduling, and controlling* (2nd ed.). New York: Van Nostrand Reinhold.
Klumpp, W. (1989 March-June). Personal communication.
Landis, J. T. (1956). Experiences of 500 children with adult sexual deviation. *Psychiatric Quarterly* (supplement), *30*, 91-109.
Lawton-Speert, S., & Wachtel, A. (1982 April). *Child sexual abuse in the family: A review of trends in the literature* (Child sexual abuse project, Working paper 2). Vancouver, BC: United Way of the Lower Mainland, Social Planning and Resources.
Lyon, E., & Koulompos-Lenares, K. (1987 November/December). Clinician and state children's services worker collaboration in treating sexual abuse. *Child Welfare*, *66*(6), 517-527.
McCabe, M., Cohen, R. E., & Weiss, V. (Eds.) (Supreme Court of the State of New York and New York State Department of Social Services). (1985). *Child sexual abuse*. New York: Goldner Press.
MacFarlane, K. (1978). Sexual abuse of children. In J. R. Chapman & M. Gates (Eds.), *The victimization of women*. Beverly Hills, CA: Sage.
MacFarlane, K., & Waterman, J. (1986). *Sexual abuse of young children*. New York: Guilford Press.
Maslach, C. (1982). *Burnout: The cost of caring*. Englewood Cliffs, NJ: Prentice-Hall.
Mathews, R., & Matthews, J. (1987). Preliminary typology of adult female sexual offenders. Minneapolis, MN: Genesis II.
Mathews, R., & Raymaker, J. N. (1987). Preliminary typology of adolescent female sexual sexual offenders. Maplewood, MN: PHASE Program.
Massachusetts Treatment Center. (n.d.). MTC:CM3. Child molester classification system: Decision making criteria. Bridgewater, MA: MTC.
Mayer, A. (1985). *Sexual abuse: Causes, consequences and treatment of incestuous and pedophilic acts*. Holmes Beach, FL: Learning Publications.
Meiselman, K. C. (1978). *Incest: A psychological study of causes and effects with treatment recommendations*. San Francisco: Jossey-Bass.
Mercer, J. L., & Koester, E. H. (1978). *Public management systems: An administrator's guide*. New York: AMACOM.
Michigan Adolescent Sexual Abuser Project. (1988 January). *Sexual offenses by youth in Michigan: Data, implications, and policy recommendations*. Detroit: Safer Society Resources of Michigan.
Miller, P. (1976). Blaming the victim of child molestation: An empirical analysis. Unpublished doctoral dissertation, Northwestern University (Dissertation Abstracts International, 1976. University Microfilms No. 77-10069).
Minnesota Department of Education. (1984 April). *Minimizing abuse of the imbalance of power*. St. Paul, MN: Minnesota Department of Education.
Minnesota Department of Human Services. (1986 February). *Child maltreatment in Minnesota, 1982-84*. St. Paul, MN: DHS.
Minnesota Sentencing Guidelines Commission. (1988 August). Summary of sentencing practices for offenders convicted of certain serious person offenses at severity levels VII and VIII. St. Paul, MN: MSGC.
Minnesota statutes 260.015, 260.133, 260.185-260.191, 260.193-260.241, 609.321, 609.322, 609.342-609.3451, 609.365, 609.653, 617.241, 626.556, 626.561.
Mitnick, M. (1989 March-April). Personal communication.
Mohr, I. W., Turner, R. E., & Jerry, M. B. (1964). *Pedophilia and exhibitionism*. Toronto: University of Toronto Press.
Morehouse, D. L., & Hoaglund, M. L. (1988 October). *Project IMPACT—Training and cooperative action on child sexual abuse: Final Evaluative Report*. Menomonie, WI: QED.
Murphy, J. E. (June 1985). Untitled news release. (Available from St. Cloud State University, St. Cloud, MN 56301.)

National Center on Child Abuse and Neglect (NCCAN). (1988). *Study findings: Study of national incidence and prevalence of child abuse and neglect.* Washington, DC: Department of Health and Human Services.

O'Brien, M. (1988 April). Sibling incest: Insights from the PHASE research. Session at the symposium on Adolescent Male Sexuality, Project IMPACT, Brooklyn Park, MN.

O'Brien, M., & Bera, W. (1986 Fall). Adolescent sexual offenders: A descriptive typology. *Preventing Sexual Abuse, 1*(3), 1-4.

Olson, D. H. (1970 November). Marital and family therapy: Integrative review and critique. *Journal of Marriage and the Family,* 501-538.

Olson, D. H., & McCubbin, H. I. (1983). *Families: What makes them work.* Beverly Hills, CA: Sage.

Oppenheimer, R., Palmer, R. L., & Brandon, S. (September 1984). A clinical evaluation of early abusive experiences in adult anorexic and bulimic females: Implications for preventive work in childhood. Paper presented to the Fifth International Congress on Child Abuse and Neglect, Montreal, Quebec.

Person, E. S. (1980). Sexuality as the mainstay of identity. *Signs, 5,* 605-630.

Peters, J. J. (1976). Children who are victims of sexual assault and the psychology of offenders. *American Journal of Psychotherapy, 30*(3), 395-421.

Peters, S. D. (1984). The relationship between childhood sexual victimization and adult depression among Afro-American and white women. Unpublished doctoral dissertation, University of California at Los Angeles (University Microfilms No. 84-28,555).

Peters, S. D. (1985 August). Child sexual abuse and later psychological problems. Paper presented at the American Psychological Association, Los Angeles.

Peters, S. D., Wyatt, G. E., & Finkelhor, D. (1986). Prevalence. In D. Finkelhor & associates, *A sourcebook on child sexual abuse,* pp. 15-59. Beverly Hills, CA: Sage.

Plummer, C. (August 1984). Preventing sexual abuse: What in-school programs teach children. Paper presented at the Second National Conference for Family Violence Researchers, Durham, NH.

Porter, F. S., Blick, L. C., & Sgroi, S. M. (1982). Treatment of the sexually abused child. In S. M. Sgroi, *Handbook of clinical intervention in child sexual abuse,* pp. 109-146. Lexington, MA: Lexington Books.

Prentky, R. A., & Knight, R. A. (1986 June). Impulsivity in the lifestyle and criminal behavior of sexual offenders. *Criminal Justice and Behavior, 13*(2), 141-164.

Public Laws 93-247 and 98-457.

Revitch, E., & Weiss, R. G. (1962). The pedophiliac offender. *Diseases of the Nervous System, 23*(2), 63-78.

Rubin, M. (1987 February). *The investigation and prosecution of child sexual abuse cases.* St. Paul, MN: Minnesota Institute of Legal Education.

Rush, F. (1980). *The best kept secret: Sexual abuse of children.* New York: McGraw-Hill.

Russell, D. E. H. (1983). The incidence and prevalence of intrafamilial and extrafamilial sexual abuse of female children. *Child Abuse and Neglect, 7,* 133-146.

Russell, D. E. H. (1986). *The secret trauma: Incest in the lives of girls and women.* New York: Basic Books.

Sadler, P. (1971). Designing an organizational structure. *Management International Review, 11*(6), 19-33.

Sagarin, E. (Ed.). (1977). *Deviants: Voluntary actors in a hostile world.* New York: General Learning Press.

Santrock, J. W. (1987). *Adolescence: An introduction.* Dubuque, IA: WC Brown.

Sarafino, E. P., & Armstrong, J. W. (1980). *Child and adolescent development.* Glenview, IL: Scott, Foresman.

Saunders, E. J. (1988). A comparative study of attitudes toward child sexual abuse among social workers and judicial system professionals. *Child Abuse and Neglect, 12*(11), 83-90.

Schlesinger, B. (1982). *Sexual abuse of children: A resource guide and annotated bibliography.* Toronto: University of Toronto Press.

Schmitt, B. C., & Carroll, C. A. (1978). Human aspects of teamwork. In B. C. Schmitt (Ed.), *The child protection team handbook: A multidisciplinary approach to managing child abuse and neglect,* pp. 199-203. New York: Garland.

Seghorn, T. K., Prentky, R. A., & Boucher, R. J. (1987). Childhood sexual abuse in the lives of sexually aggressive offenders. *Journal of the American Academy of Child and Adolescent Psychiatry, 26*(2), 262-267.

Seidner, A. L., & Calhoun, K. S. (1984 August). Childhood sexual abuse: Factors related to differential adult adjustment. Paper presented at the Second National Conference for Family Violence Researchers, Durham, NH.

Sepler, F. (1988 July). Observation and documentation training for mandated reporters. Session at the symposium on Making the System Work, St. Paul, MN.

Sgroi, S. M. (1982). Family treatment. In S. M. Sgroi, *Handbook of clinical intervention in child sexual abuse,* pp. 241-267. Lexington, MA: Lexington Books.

Sgroi, S. M., Blick, L. C., & Porter, F. S. (1982). A conceptual framework for child sexual abuse. In S. M. Sgroi, *Handbook of clinical intervention in child sexual abuse,* pp. 9-38. Lexington, MA: Lexington Books.

Sgroi, S. M., Porter, F. S., & Blick, L. C. (1982). Validation of child sexual abuse. In S. M. Sgroi, *Handbook of clinical intervention in child sexual abuse,* pp. 39-79. Lexington, MA: Lexington Books.

Silbert, M. H., & Pines, A. M. (1981). Sexual child abuse as an antecedent to prostitution. *Child Abuse and Neglect, 5,* 407-411.

Swift, C. (1977). Sexual victimization of children: An urban mental health center survey. *Victimology, 2*(2), 322-326.

Symons, D. (1979). *The evolution of human sexuality.* New York: Oxford University Press.

ten Bensel, R. (1986). Child sexual abuse: Improving the system's response [Special Issue]. *Juvenile and Family Court Journal, 37*(2).

Tufts New England Medical Center, Division of Child Psychiatry. (1984). *Sexually exploited children: Service and research project* (Final report for the Office of Juvenile Justice and Delinquency Prevention). Washington, DC: U.S. Department of Justice.

Wasserman, J., & Kappel, S. (1985 September). *Adolescent sex offenders in Vermont.* Montpelier, VT: Agency of Human Services/Vermont Department of Health.

Weinberg, S. K. (1955). *Incest behavior.* New York: Citadel.

White, W. L. (1986). *Incest in the organizational family: The evolution of burnout in closed system.* Bloomington, IL: Lighthouse Training Institute.

Wyatt, G. E. (1985). The sexual abuse of Afro-American and White American women in childhood. *Child Abuse and Neglect, 9,* 507-519.

Index

Adolescent offenders, 61-80, 206-207
 academic achievement, 68
 acts committed, 12, 66, 76
 adjudication/conviction of, 71, 206-207
 age, 65, 73-79
 alcohol/drug use, 68
 coercion by, 66-67
 criminal history, 71
 demographics, 63-65
 family situation, 70-71
 female, 77-79
 intelligence, 68
 location of offense, 67-68
 myths/stereotypes, 24, 61-62
 psychological characteristics, 62-63, 68
 relationship to victim, 8, 66, 93, 94, 95-96
 research about, 61-63
 sex, 65, 77-79, 96
 sexual beliefs, 69
 sexual development, 69
 social development, 69
 treatment, 72
 typologies, 72-79
Adult offenders, 29-59, 204
 acts committed, 12, 32
 age, 12, 30-31, 44-46, 96
 alcohol/drug use, 32, 34, 37, 46
 boy victims, 93
 Child Molester Classification System, 39-40
 dichotomous classifications, 36-38
 education, 31, 34
 employment history, 31, 34, 46
 history of abuse, 35-36, 45, 46
 history of homosexual experience, 49-50
 homosexual, 44, 49-50, 127
 impulsivity, 34-35
 incest, 47-49
 intelligence, 31
 marital status, 31
 mental health, 14, 31, 33
 number of offenses, 32
 pederasts, 50
 psychological characteristics, 31, 33, 44-47, 128
 public perception of, 12
 race, 31
 relationship to victim, 8, 93, 94, 95-96
 religion, 32
 samples studied, 16-19, 29-30
 sex, 12, 30-31, 41-47, 88, 96
 sexual preference, 31
 socioeconomic status, 17-18, 31, 47
 targets, 12, 32, 33
 treatment, 32
 women, 41-47, 128
Adultocentric view, 21
Advocacy programs, 215. See also Treatment programs
Alcohol/drug use, 32, 34, 37, 46, 48, 68, 113
Anal sex, 87, 96, 144

Blockage, 51, 52
Boy victims. See Victims, boys
Burnout, 230-232

Causes of child sexual abuse. See also Theories/typologies of child sexual abuse
 adult offenders, 36
 vs. effects, 20-21
 incest offenders, 48
 women offenders, 41-47
Child Abuse Prevention and Treatment Act (P.L. 98-457), 6
Child development, 6, 100-101
Child Molester Classification System (MTC), 39-40
Child Protective Services (CPS), 193-196, 197-202
 assessment, 197-198, 214
 CHIPS petitions, 199, 201-202, 204, 206, 207
 determinations, 161-162, 198-199, 200-202
 intervention, 161-163, 198, 205
 interviewing, 198, 199-200
 liaison with law enforcement, 197-198
 liaison with parents/guardians, 200
 onsite visits, 198
 referrals, 197
 reporting to, 160-163, 175-177, 196

253

Child sexual abuse, definitions of. *See* Definitions of child sexual abuse
Child sexual abuse system. *See* System, child sexual abuse; System problem resolutions; System problems
CHIPS petitions, 199, 202-202, 204, 206, 207. *See also* Child Protective Services; Juvenile court
Circumplex Model of Families (Olson), 132-135
  adaptability, 132, 133-134
  cohesion, 132-133
  communication, 134
  family types, 135
  operation of, 134-135
Coercion, use of
  adolescent offenders, 66-67
  assurance of acceptability, 88
  bribery, 70
  enticement/reward, 74, 114, 144
  manipulation, 74
  physical force, 46, 66, 75, 94, 97, 114, 210, 211
  psychological control, 50
  seriousness of offense, 8
  use of weapons, 66, 210
  verbal threats, 66, 75, 139, 141, 144
Community organizations, 215-217
Confidentiality, 30, 160-162
Contact offenses, 4, 7, 211. *See also* Criminal sexual conduct, degrees of; Definitions of child sexual abuse; Noncontact offenses; *and specific types of offenses*
Corrections, 194, 207-213
  degrees of criminal sexual conduct, 7, 207-211
  dispositional departure, 207, 211-212, 213
  imprisonment rates, 212
  plea bargaining, 18-19, 203, 212-213
  probation, 213
  sentencing guidelines, 203, 204, 207-213
Counseling programs, 215-217. *See also* Treatment programs
County attorney. *See* Criminal court
County welfare. *See* Child Protective Services
Court proceedings. *See* Criminal court; Judicial system; Juvenile court
Criminal court, 202-204, 244. *See also* Judicial system; Juvenile court
  admissible evidence, 203-204
  county attorney's role, 203
  criminal complaints, 203
  defense attorney's role, 204
  determination to prosecute, 203
  grand juries, 203
  judge's role, 203-204
  juveniles, 206
  personal impact statements, 207
  plea bargaining, 203, 212-213
  presentence investigations, 207, 211
  probation, 213
  prosecuting attorney's role, 260
  search warrants, 203
  subpoenas, 203
  trials, 203
  victim impact statements, 207, 211
Criminal sexual conduct, degrees of (Minnesota statutes), 7, 207-211
Criminal justice system. *See* Corrections; Criminal court; Judicial system; Judicial court; Law enforcement
Cultural issues. *See* Multicultural issues

Damaged-goods syndrome, 104, 107
Definitions of child sexual abuse, 3-9, 124-127. *See also* Theories/typologies of child sexual abuse
  boy victims, 90
  clinical, 6
  federal law, 6-7
  incest, 124-127
  Minnesota statutes, 7-8
  NCCAN, 8
  psychosocial, 5-6
  research, 4-5
  sexism in, 41-42, 90
Determination, 161-162, 198-199, 200-202
Disclosure, 23, 97-98, 145, 177-179
  abandonment of responsibility, 179
  accidental, 145, 177-178
  effects on family, 97-98, 108, 178-179
  effects on offender, 178
  effects on victim, 97-98, 177
  fear of separation, 179
  guilt, 177, 178, 179
  hostility, 178, 179
  intervention, 178, 196-202, 225-226
  noncooperation, 178, 179
  purposeful, 145
  suppression/denial, 178, 179
  trauma, 23, 170, 177, 178, 196
Disinhibition, 51, 52-53, 56, 87
Documentation, 168-172, 214. *See also* Reporting
  chronologies, 170
  details, 169, 171

Index

gut feelings, 168
interviews with victims, 161, 170-171
language used, 169
multisensory observations, 169
packaging reports, 176-177
victim credibility, 172-175, 242-243
written records, 168-170
Dysfunctional families, 47, 49, 70-71, 84-88, 92-93, 123, 130-135, 145-151. *See also* Incestuous families

Educators, 214
Effects of abuse. *See also* Trauma risk factors; Victims
on family, 23
on offender, 37, 38, 45, 74, 78
on victim, 41, 86, 97, 102-113
Emotional congruence, 51, 52
Exhibitionism, 32, 45, 76, 107, 144, 203

Family dynamics, 84-88, 108, 123-153. *See also* Dysfunctional families; Incestuous families
adolescent offenders, 70-71
assessment (incest), 146-147
parental relationship, 84-88
signs of abuse, 167
theory, 130-132, 136
therapy, 131-132
Family systems. *See* Family dynamics
Female Adolescent Offender Typology (Mathews & Raymaker), 77-79
Female offenders, 41-47, 77-79, 128
Finkelhor surveys
public knowledge, 10-15, 124, 196
system professionals, 222-235
Fixated pedophiles, 37-38
Force, use of. *See* Coercion, use of
Fondling, 32, 45, 64, 66, 78, 96, 125, 144
Four-factor framework of child sexual abuse (Finkelhor), 51-57

Gender-role differences, 42-43, 137
Genesis II, 44
Genesis II Typology (Mathews & Matthews), 44-47
Government right of intervention, 241-242
Guardian ad litem, 205-206

Hand-genital contact, 125
Health care professionals, 194, 214
History of abuse, 223
adolescent offenders, 70, 74, 75, 78
child abusers, 35

homosexual offenders, 49
incest offenders, 48, 127, 128, 141, 149
rapists, 35, 36
women offenders, 45, 46
Homosexual offenders, 44, 49-50
Homosexuality, victim, 110-111

Impulsivity, 34-35, 76, 149
Incest, 32, 66, 70, 85, 86, 91, 93-94, 95, 103, 104, 108, 110, 111, 112, 123-153, 204, 211. *See also* Incest offenders; Incestuous families
by age, 129
boy victims, 93-94
defined, 124-126
extended family, 129-130
father/daughter, 126-127
father/son, 127
homosexuality, 110, 128
long-term effects, 110
mother/daughter, 128
mother/son, 128
partnerships, 126-130
phases, 144-146
prevalence, 47, 126-130
risk factors, 85-86
sibling, 128-129
theories/typologies, 130-135
treatment, 146-151
Incest offenders, 47-49. *See also* Adolescent offenders; Adult offenders
Incestuous families, 70, 76, 78, 123, 130, 136-143. *See also* Dysfunctional families; Family dynamics
alcohol/drug use, 48, 139, 140
authoritarianism/abuse of power, 136-137, 138, 147, 149, 167
blurred boundaries, 149
characteristics of, 136-138
denial, 137, 148, 149
emotional deprivation, 143, 149
family crisis, 138
fathers, 138-139
fear of authority, 148
history of abuse, 48, 127, 128, 141
homeostatic mechanisms, 151
inadequate self-control, 149
individual roles, 136, 138-143
lack of empathy, 148, 149
mothers, 139-142
multicultural issues, 150-151
overprotectiveness, 167
phases of abuse, 144-145
poor communication, 148-149
resentment, 137, 143

(continued)

Incestuous families *continued*
  rigid/symbiotic roles, 138
  role inversion, 137, 141, 149, 167
  siblings, 143
  social isolation, 137, 139, 140, 148, 149, 167
  stepfathers, 87
  stress, 138
  strict religious beliefs, 167
  treatment recommendations, 145-151
  unconscious collusion, 141, 143, 174, 175
  victims, 142-143
Incidence statistics, 15-16
Inhibition. *See* Disinhibition
Initiation (into sex) concept, 41-42
Inpatient treatment. *See* Treatment programs
Interagency Team on Child Abuse and Neglect, 236
Intercourse. *See* Penetration
Intervention, 161-162, 178, 196-202, 225-226, 241-242. *See also* Child Protective Services; Law enforcement
Interviewing
  by CPS, 198, 199-200
  by law enforcement, 199-200
  general skills, 170-172
  victim credibility, 172-175, 242-243

Judicial system, 194, 202-207. *See also* Criminal court; Juvenile court
Juvenile court, 204-207, 224
  assignment of counsel, 205
  burden of proof, 206
  CHIPS petition, 199, 201-202, 204, 206
  contact-barring order, 199
  contempt of court, 205
  county attorney's role, 204
  custody petition, 198
  custody report, 199
  delinquency petition, 206
  dependency and neglect charges, 204-205
  determination of services, 206
  guardian ad litem, 205, 206
  intervention plan, 205
  juvenile offenders, 206-207
  notification of parents/guardians, 199
  placement orders, 205
  temporary removal orders, 199
  termination of parental rights, 205
Juvenile offenders. *See* Adolescent offenders

Law enforcement, 18, 194-195, 196-198, 202-203
  criminal prosecutions, 202
  custody provision reports, 199
  determinations, 200-202
  documentation of abuse, 197
  emergency victim placements, 197
  home searches, 197
  identification of injuries, 197
  intervention by, 196-197
  interviews, 197, 199-200
  investigations, 197
  liaison with CPS, 160, 197-198, 224
  notification of parents/guardians, 199, 200
  protection of CPS workers, 198
  referrals, 196-197
  reports made to, 160-163, 175-177, 196-197
Legal system. *See* Criminal court; Judicial system; Juvenile court

Male involvement in women's offenses, 46-47
Mandated reporters/reporting, 159-160, 162, 163, 164, 168, 196, 214. *See also* Reporting
Masturbation, 69, 76, 107, 144
Minnesota statutes on abuse, 7, 198-199, 199-200, 204, 206, 228, 232, 236. *See also* Criminal sexual conduct, degrees of
Motivations for abuse
  acting out own abuse, 45, 78
  anger, 35, 36, 75
  blockage, 51, 52
  compulsion, 36, 68, 76
  emotional congruence, 51, 52
  emotional satisfaction, 48
  impulsivity in sexual offense (ISO), 34-35
  instability, 46
  intimidation, 79
  narcissistic pleasure, 74
  opportunism, 35
  peer pressure, 77
  power, 75
  sadism, 34
  self-esteem, 74
  sexual arousal, 51, 52
  sexual compensation, 34
  sexual exploration, 73
  situational problems, 37
  vampire theory, 35

Index

Motivations for incest
  compensation for stress, 138-139
  imitation of father, 129
  mental illness, 128
  provocation/seductiveness, 142
  power, 138
  unconscious collusion, 141, 143
Multicultural issues, 31, 83-84, 150-151
Mutual masturbation, 125, 144
Myths/stereotypes, 9-10, 14, 24, 41-42, 61, 62-63, 69, 81, 83, 90, 130

Noncontact offenses, 4, 64, 66, 76, 203. *See also* Criminal sexual conduct, degrees of; Definitions of child sexual abuse; *and specific offenses*
Nonmadated reporters. *See* Reporting; Voluntary reporters

Obscene phone calling, 76
Offenders. *See* Adolescent offenders; Adult offenders; Homosexual offenders; Incest offenders; Women offenders
Oral sex, 32, 45, 64, 66, 78, 96, 125, 144
Outpatient treatment. *See* Treatment programs

Paraphilia, 6, 32
Parents. *See also* Family dynamics
  reaction to disclosure, 95, 97-98, 178-179
  relationship between, 83-88, 131
  reporting by, 13
  stepfathers, 87
Pederasts, 50. *See also* Homosexual offenders
Pedophilia, 6, 36-37, 90
Penetration, 45, 64, 66, 67, 78, 87, 96, 144, 210, 211
PHASE, 62, 68, 72, 77
PHASE Typology (O'Brien & Bera), 72-77
Phases of sexual abuse (Sgroi), 144-145, 177
  disclosure, 145, 177-178
  engagement, 144
  secrecy, 144-145
  sexual interaction, 144
  suppression, 145, 178
Physical signs of abuse. *See* Signs of abuse
Plea bargaining, 18-19, 203, 212-213
P.L. 93-247, 158
P.L. 98-457, 6
Police. *See* Law enforcement
Pornography, 50

Preconditions for abuse (Finkelhor), 52-57
Preconditions for incest, 147
Preplea diversion, 243-244
Prevalence of sexual abuse, 4, 11, 16, 23
  adolescent offenders, 62
  adult offenders, 32, 93
  boy victims, 90-91
  incest, 47, 87, 124, 126-127, 128-129
  men, 41, 93
  racial breakdown, 83
  rural vs. urban, 84
  women, 44, 93
Prevention programs, 215, 217. *See also* Treatment programs
Probation, 213
Project IMPACT, 222, 236-237
Prostitution, 112-113
Pseudomaturity, 107, 145, 166
Pseudosocialization, 69
Public knowledge of child sexual abuse, 9-15

Racial issues. *See* Multicultural issues
Rape, 33, 46, 56, 112, 202. *See also* Penetration
Rapists, 35, 36
Regressed pedophiles, 37-38
Reporting, 89, 157-181, 196
  basis of, 159
  boy/girl differences, 19, 92
  boys, 19, 23-24, 90-91
  children, 12, 22-24, 89, 91, 99, 170-172
  confidentiality, 160-162, 223
  consent to investigate, 161
  credibility of children, 172-175, 242-243
  determination, 161-162, 164, 173, 200-202
  disclosure, 177-179
  documentation, 160, 168-177
  girls, 19, 78, 90
  identification signs, 164-168
  information required, 160
  interviews with victims, 161, 170-171
  liability, 162
  mandated reporters, 158-179, 196, 223-224, 225
  Minnesota statute 626.556, 158-159
  notification of parents/guardians, 161
  oral, 160
  packaging reports, 175-177
  parents/adults, 13, 22, 89, 172
  proactive characteristics, 157, 163-177
  problems, 22-24, 83, 86, 90, 99, 157
  P.L. 93-247, 158

(continued)

Reporting *continued*
  retaliation, 162
  role of school officials, 161
  record keeping, 161-162
  substantiation rates, 164, 173
  underreporting, 16, 22-24, 49, 157
  validation, 162-163
  victim credibility, 99, 172-175, 242-243
  voluntary reporters, 159, 164, 196
  to whom, 14, 160
  written, 160
Reporting of Maltreatment to Minors Act (Minnesota state 626.556), 158-159
Research methodology, 15-24, 29-30, 50-51, 57. *See also* Theories/typologies of child sexual abuse
  boys, 90-91
  confidentiality, 30
  definitional problems, 4-5, 18
  interpretation problems, 20
  interviewing problems, 16
  legal-handling problems, 18-19
  offenders, data about, 16-19, 61-63
  reporting problems, 22-24
  sampling problems, 16-22
  self-reporting problems, 17, 21
  self-selection problems, 20
  single-factor designs, 19
  subject populations, 16-18, 19
  validity problems, 15-22
  victims, data about, 19-22, 102-103
Residential facilities, 215, 216. *See also* Treatment programs
Risk factors. *See* Incest; Trauma risk factors; Victims
Ritualistic abuse, 244-245
Rule of three (signs of abuse), 168

Satanic cults, 244-245
Scott County, child sexual abuse in, 221
Sentencing guidelines, 203, 204, 207-213
Sex rings, 50
Sexist attitudes, 41-42, 90
Sexual arousal, 51, 52
Sheriff. *See* Law enforcement
Signs of abuse, 164-168
  acting out, 166
  alcohol/drug use, 113, 169
  assessing, 167-168
  behavioral, 166-167
  bullying/domination, 105, 112
  depression, 103, 106, 109, 128, 167
  eating disorders, 103, 109, 166
  family, 167
  fear of adults, 166
  fears/phobias, 103, 105, 109
  general neglect/abuse, 167
  homosexuality, 110-111
  inappropriate sexual behaviors, 166, 168
  overcompliance, 166
  physical, 89, 165
  pregnancy, 165
  promiscuity, 105, 110
  prostitution, 112-113
  pseudomaturity, 107, 145, 166
  psychosomatic conditions, 103, 105, 108, 165
  regression, 167
  rule of three, 168
  running away, 104, 107, 166
  school behaviors/problems, 104, 107, 166, 168
  social isolation, 166, 167
  suicide, 110, 167
  victimizing others, 105
Social service workers. *See* Child Protective Services
Stigmatization, 115
Substantiation. *See* Determination
Support services, 214-217. *See also* Treatment programs
System, child sexual abuse, 157-181, 193-219, 221-240, 241-246. *See also* System problem resolutions; System problems; *and specific system components*
  components, 193-194, 196-215, 236
  intervention, 196-217
  overview of, 193-196
  reporting, 157-181, 196
System problem resolutions, 189-190, 235-239
  collaboration, 235, 236, 238-239
  conflict, 245-246
  initiative, 238, 239
  local approach, 237-238
  Minnesota efforts, 236
  multidisciplinary teams, 189, 235, 236-238
  Project IMPACT, 236-237
  systems change forums, 237
System problems, 189-190, 221-235, 241-246. *See also* System problem resolutions
  burnout, 230-232
  characteristics, 227-228
  collaboration, 224-225
  interagency conflict, 245-246
  intervention, 225-226, 234, 241-242
  job overlap, 230

legal ambiguity, 232-235
overload, 234
personal involvement, 229
philosophical differences, 230, 243-244
policy issues, 228-232
professional limits, 228-232
public systems, 185, 187, 190, 222-227
reporting, 223-224, 233-234
role conflict, 229
survey of professionals, 222-227
Systems theory, 183-191
   and child protective teams, 189
   closed vs. open, 185-188, 227-228
   dynamics, 185-188
   organization, defined, 184
   organizational incest, 188
   public systems, 185, 187, 190, 227-228
   resources, 184
   structure, 184-185, 227-228
   system, defined, 183-184
   system problems, 189-190

Target charging, 244
Terminology, variations in usage, 8-9, 18
Theories/typologies of child sexual abuse.
   See also Definitions of child sexual abuse
   Child Molester Classification System, 39-40
   Circumplex Model of Families, 132-135
   Family Dynamics Model of Incest, 130-132
   Family dynamics theory, 136-143
   Female Adolescent Offender Typology, 77-79
   Four-factor framework, 51-57
   Genesis II Typology, 44-47
   PHASE Typology, 68, 69, 72-77
   Phases of child sexual abuse, 144-145
Trauma assessment. *See also* Effects of abuse; Victims
   by age, 98
   by betrayal, 114-115, 118
   by developmental stage, 98-99
   by general adjustment, 99-100
   by physical injuries, 97
   by powerlessness, 115, 118
   by stigmatization, 115-116, 118
   traumagenic dynamics, 113-120
   by traumatic sexualiation, 114, 118
Traumagenic Dynamics Model (Finkelhor & Browne), 113-120
   application of model, 116-120
   betrayal, 114-115
   four traumagenic dynamics, 113-120
   powerlessness, 115
   stigmatization, 115-116
   traumatic sexualization, 114
Trauma risk factors
   age of abuser, 96, 111
   age of victim, 95, 98, 104, 116
   assessing, 113-120
   boys vs. girls, 90, 128
   developmental stage, 98-102
   duration of abuse, 94, 96
   fear of separation from family, 105
   intervention, 196, 200, 235
   intrusiveness of abuse, 94, 96-97
   multiple abusers, 96
   parents'/others' reactions, 95, 97-98, 116
   participation in abuse, 95
   physical injuries, 97
   relationship to abuser, 94, 95, 143
   resulting marital conflict, 87
   sex of abuser, 96
   social awareness, 116
   use of force, 41, 94, 97, 114
Treatment programs, 145-151, 214-217
   assessment, 146-147
   availability, 215-216
   cost, 217
   duration, 216-217
   for families, 131, 145-151, 215, 216
   for offenders, 13, 32, 38, 72, 207, 212, 213, 214-216
   for victims, 13, 117-120, 199, 214-216
   funding, 217
   methods, 146
   multicultural issues, 150-151
   orientation, 216
   vs. punishment, 243-244
   staff experience, 223
   staff qualifications, 216
   types, 215

Underreporting. *See* Reporting
Undersocialization, 69

Vampire theory, 35, 48, 112
Victims, 81-122, 142-143
   academic achievement, 107
   acts committed against, 88-89, 93-94, 96-97
   alcohol/drug use, 113
   age, 12, 21, 32, 65, 82, 83, 91-92, 95, 98
   anger, 105-106
   boys, 33, 89-94, 105-106, 110-111
   credibility, 172-175, 242-243
   depression, 106, 109

(continued)

260 *Index*

Victims *continued*
  developmental stage, 98-102
  disclosure, 97-98
  dissociation, 110
  effects of abuse on, 41, 86, 97, 102-113
  ethnicity, 83-84
  family characteristics, 84-85, 92-93, 108
  family income, 84-85, 92-93
  fear, 105
  guilt, 106
  history of abuse, 111, 112
  homosexuality, 110-111
  hostility, 105-106
  initial/immediate effects, 102, 103-108
  long-term effects, 102, 108-113
  model of abuse, 113-120
  multiple, 93
  parental education, 87
  parental relationships, 85-88
  participation in abuse, 95
  personal relationships, 111-112
  phobias, 109
  physical effects, 103, 108-109
  prostitution, 112-113
  psychological/emotional effects, 103-107, 109-111
  public perception of, 12
  relationship to offender, 32, 45, 46, 50, 66, 77, 78, 79, 88, 93, 94
  reporting by, 12, 170-172
  resistance by, 56, 89, 95
  risk factors, 82, 94-102
  running away, 107-108
  samples studied, 19-22
  school attendance, 107
  self-destruction, 109-110
  self-esteem, 104-105, 109
  self-image, 105
  sex education, 86
  sex of, 19, 32, 33, 38, 65, 82, 89-94
  sexuality, 106-107, 110-111
  shame, 106
  social functioning, 84, 85, 107-108, 111-113
  social isolation, 84, 85, 107
  socioeconomic status, 83, 92
  testifying, 204
  traumagenic dynamics, 113-117
  trust, 106
Voluntary reporters, 159, 160, 162, 163, 164, 196. *See also* Reporting
Voyeurism, 32, 64

WCCO I-Team, 221
Window peeping, 76
Women offenders. *See* Adult offenders; Female offenders